The Foreign and
Domestic Dimensions
of Modern Warfare

The Foreign and Domestic Dimensions of Modern Warfare

VIETNAM, CENTRAL AMERICA,

AND NUCLEAR STRATEGY

Edited by Howard Jones

THE UNIVERSITY OF ALABAMA PRESS

TUSCALOOSA

The University of Alabama Press
Tuscaloosa, Alabama 35487-0380
uapress.ua.edu

Hardcover edition published 1988.
Paperback edition published 2018.
eBook edition published 2018.

Inquiries about reproducing material from this work should be addressed to the
University of Alabama Press.

Cover design: David Nees

Paperback ISBN: 978-0-8173-5937-9

eBook ISBN: 978-0-8173-9228-4

A previous edition of this book has been catalogued by the Library of Congress
as follows:

Library of Congress Cataloging-in-Publication Data

The Foreign and domestic dimensions of modern warfare.

Bibliography: p.   Includes index

1. United States—Military policy. 2. United States—Foreign
relations—1945–   3. United States—Politics and government—1945–
4. Civil—military relations—United States—History—20th century.
5. Military history. Modern—20th century. I. Jones, Howard, 1940–

UA23.F54   1988   355'.0335'73   86-19239

ISBN 0-8173-0331-6

British Library Cataloguing-in-Publication Data is available

To Martha Brown

Contents

CONTENTS

Part 4. Nuclear War and Deterrence

Acknowledgments

ALTHOUGH a book usually bears only one person's name as author or editor, the truth is that in nearly every instance numerous people contributed to the final result. In no case is this more true than with this volume.

Several people assisted in the planning and operation of the Brown Conference, which forms the basis of this work. My colleague, Tony A. Freyer, co-chaired the meeting and helped in so many ways that it would be impossible to list them. Larry Clayton and Helen Delpar offered advice on the Latin American section of the program, while Major Earl H. Tilford provided help in the early selection of topics. In addition to those participants in the conference whose papers make up this volume, there were others who helped in some related capacity: John Arthur, William D. Barnard, Dennis M. Drew, Peter M. Dunn, George Graham, Robert C. Gray, James E. Jacobson, Peter Maslowski, Allan R. Millett, Richard Millett, Richard E. Peck, Norvin W. Richards, Philip Shepherd, Paul A. Varg, John Waghelstein, and Robert L. Wells. Ruth Kibbey and Kitty Sassaman provided secretarial assistance and moral support. President Joab L. Thomas of the University of Alabama, along with his wife, Marly, took time from their busy schedules to help make the conference a success. A number of graduate students in history at the University of Alabama furnished assistance that went far beyond anything asked of them. Special appreciation goes to Mark Boazman, Bob Browning, John Dederer, Joannie Griffin, and Guy Swanson.

Others were important to the conference and to this book. Sponsors of the conference included the Department of History, College of Arts and Sciences, and Law School, all of the University of Alabama, and the Committee for the Humanities in Alabama, a state program of the National Endowment for the Humanities. I also want to express my gratitude to those associated with The University of Alabama Press: Malcolm M. MacDonald, its director, the entire staff, the anonymous readers who offered many valuable recommendations for improving the manuscript, and the copyeditor, Joanne S. Ainsworth, who read each page with the care and concern so vital to publication.

As always, my work would not be complete without a sincere thanks to loved ones—my parents; my spouse, Mary Ann; and our children, Debbie, Howie, and Shari.

ACKNOWLEDGMENTS

Finally, since this conference was held in honor of a unique individual, I dedicate this volume to Martha, the wife of General Wilburt S. Brown.

Tuscaloosa   HOWARD JONES
                                        The University of Alabama

The Foreign and
Domestic Dimensions
of Modern Warfare

Introduction

HOWARD JONES

THIS WORK grew out of a conference honoring General Wilburt S. Brown, a decorated marine veteran of World War II and the Korean War, and is intended for both the general public and the scholar. The meeting, held on The University of Alabama campus in Tuscaloosa in October 1984, focused on the theme "War in Peace: War and Society since 1945" and received support from the Committee for the Humanities in Alabama, the University of Alabama School of Law, the College of Arts and Sciences, the History Department, and the administration of The University of Alabama. The program featured some of the most eminent scholars working in American foreign and domestic policy following World War II.

At first glance, the topics covered in the conference and in this volume seem so varied that they do not appear to belong in a single volume. Their very diversity, however, is the strongest argument for their inclusion. They suggest the profound problems facing policymakers in Washington, who must make decisions not only on the basis of the unique situations themselves but also on how the issue affects (and is affected by) other foreign and domestic policy matters. The unifying theme is the complexity which confronted the United States as it tried to construct and keep a lasting peace during the atomic age. If the chapters that follow can enlighten the reader and suggest some of the areas in need of further research and examination, they will have served their purpose.

This volume examines the American experience in Vietnam, Central America, and the nuclear arms race as a way of highlighting the dangers arising from the advent of limited warfare after the development of the atomic bomb in 1945. The awareness of the certain devastation that would result from thermonuclear war, combined with the realization that international conflict will remain, has caused policymakers in Washington to emphasize the importance of limiting wars to objectives not

1

involving their opponents' homelands and to means other than nuclear weaponry. The Soviet Union likewise seemed to be grasping the same reality when it turned to what a *New York Times* correspondent in 1949 called a "new kind of war." In seeking world domination, many Americans believed, the Soviets adopted new and restricted tactics that included "shadow war," propaganda and ideological warfare, "wars of nerves," guerrilla and terrorist activities, war by "proxy," privileged sanctuaries; all were based on purposeful restraint and all were designed to undermine the morale of countries trying to combat totalitarian rule.

Partly because of the increasing difficulty in proving Soviet complicity in troubled areas of the world, the United States countered with a policy of "containment." Under this policy, economic, political, and diplomatic activities would complement military force in stopping Soviet expansionism. Initially the military strategy was "massive retaliation"—the threat of American use of atomic and nuclear weapons. Later, in 1961, military strategy was revised, and under the "flexible response" strategy, the amount of military force used would depend on whatever was necessary to defeat the antagonist's military force. Use of the atomic bomb became unthinkable because of its vast destructive powers and because the enemy was rapidly acquiring a substantial nuclear arsenal of his own. The battlefield itself became a maze of jungles, villages, swamps, and rugged terrain where the enemy was as elusive as were the new objectives of war. The United States sought to avoid direct confrontations with the Soviet Union by extending military and economic aid to governments willing to resist communism and by calling on Americans to prepare for a struggle that had no end in sight. These matters raised questions regarding how Americans could wage such local wars—often against the "people" aiding the enemy—without escalating the conflict into a general war involving the superpowers and without resorting to barbarism. Such issues struck at the heart of American democracy.

A central problem for America was that whereas the regime in Moscow was not accountable to its people or allies, the government in Washington surely was. During World War I and World War II, America's leaders were able to establish the enemy as evil and to set out territorial and ideological objectives that were based on fundamental freedoms. In short, the United States engaged in wars that were understandable to Americans and compatible with the nation's ideals. After 1945, however, this was not always the case. Wartime enemies and objectives slipped out of focus, and American policymakers had difficulty relating the country's goals to moral and legal issues. For a while it was possible to tie international problems to the Kremlin, but the so-called "Communist monolith," as some saw it, began to disintegrate when rifts developed between Yugoslavia and the Soviet Union, between Red China and the Soviet Union, and even among the Soviet-dominated countries in Eastern Europe. As America's allies today seem determined to have a greater voice in Western policymaking, so did some of the Soviets' allies appear more interested in their own affairs than in promoting the aims of the Kremlin. Without flagrant threats to the free world, the United States has faced major problems in attempting to establish democratic goals and to arouse support from both its allies and its people in foreign affairs.

In no instance were the ramifications of the new kind of war more evident than in Vietnam. That conflict caused a widespread debate over America's foreign policy by raising questions about the nation's system of morals, ethics, and values. The undeclared war in Vietnam also caused Americans to rethink many long-held assumptions about the methods and goals of warfare. In a war that largely lacked battlefronts, clearly marked enemy uniforms, territorial objectives, irrefutable vital interests, and well-defined moral and legal goals, Americans eventually became divided over what became, as one historian, George C. Herring, called it, their "longest war." By the late 1960s the United States was badly split over the issue of Vietnam, to the point that the divisions threatened to bring down the nation from within. Indeed, Americans became so disenchanted with the turn of events that many of them vented their anger on their own soldiers. Americans were bewildered that their own fighting men appeared to be guilty of inhumane behavior.

A major debate has arisen over whether the source of these foreign and domestic troubles was America's foreign policy of containment. According to critics, the theory called for too much, both materially and spiritually, from the United States. In 1945, they insist, the postwar power vacuum left the United States at the pinnacle of power and prestige, but in ensuing years the nation gradually lost its unquestioned seat of authority, primarily because of the growth of the Soviet Union's own power, the revival of America's Western allies along with that of Japan, and the rise of Third World nations—especially those commanding rich oil reserves. Though the United States still possessed superior military strength and prestige, it no longer enjoyed solitary leadership. Containment theory, these critics conclude, did not allow for this shift in power realities; it no longer made sense to define every trouble spot as Soviet-inspired and in need of American intervention. Still, given the nature of limited war, proponents of containment contended, there was no alternative. Enormous expenditures in blood and treasure became essential to America's postwar strategy. Even if the Soviet Union was using proxies in fighting its wars of conquest, the United States could not justify the use of nuclear weapons against either guerrillas or regular forces. A patient, long-range policy of containing Soviet expansionism was the only feasible approach in the atomic age.

These disagreements over containment show the complexities involved in modern warfare. Distinctions blurred between civil wars and troubles caused by outside aggression, making it increasingly difficult for America's leaders to discern the enemy, to adapt to the new type of warfare, and to arouse nationwide support for what were, at best, hazy goals. As Third World peoples strived for nationhood, the ensuing unrest sometimes led to revolutions that Americans more often than not characterized as inspired by communism rather than by nationalism. It no longer seemed possible to separate political and military objectives as the new kind of war swept the countryside to include civilians as well as those in combat. While the United States continued to espouse wartime ideals, the nonaligned, or neutralist, peoples of the Third World, sensitive to the charges of the American civil rights movement, questioned the sincerity of America's democratic professions. During the 1960s the controversial American effort in Vietnam stimulated an antiwar movement and contributed to the collapse of President Lyndon B. Johnson's Great Society program.

Containment, critics asserted, overcommitted the United States. If the nation's fighting forces could not achieve a rapid and total victory, there had to be something wrong within the nation itself. Greater numbers of people became skeptical about decisions in Washington. They wanted to know whether policymakers had carefully considered the options along with the ramifications. They wondered if leaders had defined the nation's objectives and determined whether its security was at stake in the given situation. They even wanted to know if the administration had considered the implications of withdrawal should intervention not work out as planned. These questions would convulse the nation during the late 1960s and early 1970s.

More Americans were aware that they lived in an era requiring new approaches to foreign policy. Symbolic commitments had become synonymous with national security interests, leading the United States to use shows of force to convince observers, both East and West, that it had the tenacity to hold the line against communism. To engage in these contests, Americans had to exercise the utmost patience, sacrifice, determination, and commitment. Many did not agree with the tenets of limited war; some continued to refer to General Douglas MacArthur's declaration that there was "no substitute for victory."

As the writers here suggest, misunderstandings and misperceptions

4

have played a major role in magnifying America's problems, both abroad and at home. It quickly became evident that many international issues would revolve around tests of wills as antagonists sought political objectives by convincing enemies through limited military means that they could not win. Symbols became reality as willpower and endurance became more important than firepower in achieving victory.

In the first chapter, Robert H. Ferrell contends that the study of military history is essential to understanding the history of the United States—its past from the very beginning and especially since the profound changes in military strategy ushered in by the events at Alamogordo, New Mexico, in July 1945 and in Hiroshima and Nagasaki the following month. Americans, he writes, like to believe that their country has reached its place in the world by peaceful means only. They consider their nation to have been built upon a pacifism that time and again has manifested itself in a peace movement. They especially have resisted acknowledging the existence of the nuclear age. But they must live in the world that surrounds them. They must see military history as an accompaniment of national growth since the colonization of Jamestown in 1607, and never more important than during the years since July 1945. Teachers in colleges and universities no longer can afford to ignore military history, treating it as the "stepchild" of history departments, shuttling it off to Reserve Officer Training Corps (ROTC) departments to be taught by ROTC officers to ROTC students.

Colonel Harry G. Summers, Jr., believes that the collapse of the U.S. Army's self-confidence and self-esteem following World War II was a contributing factor to the nation's failure in Vietnam. With the advent of nuclear weapons the erroneous belief developed that the entire nature of war had changed. Conventional forces were dismissed as of little value, for the foundations of American security now appeared to rest on air power and nuclear weaponry. Even though a major conventional war was fought in Korea, the outcome failed to restore the army's sense of purpose. America changed its military strategy there from the strategic offensive to the strategic defensive, and this led to a negotiated settlement which many saw as a defeat. With traditional military history apparently rendered irrelevant by nuclear weapons and conventional military theory perceived as bankrupt, the way was prepared for the dogmas of counterinsurgency and the subsequent debacle in Vietnam.

In a second essay on Vietnam, George C. Herring shows how the Eisenhower administration became committed to South Vietnam's government under Ngo Dinh Diem during the autumn of 1954. According to the White House, the government in Saigon would be the basis of an independent, non-Communist state that would prove to the rest of the world that freedom, not totalitarianism, was the wave of the future. "Nation-building" became a vital weapon of the United States in the limited tactics of the Cold War. The United States, however, had to convince its own people of the necessity of the new policy by extolling the virtues of Diem's alleged democratic regime. This raised hopes at home, thus laying the basis for the bitterness that accompanied the ultimate failure. According to Herring, the Eisenhower administration's decision to support Diem in October 1954 was perhaps the last chance the United States had to avoid intervention without causing a major impact at home and abroad. Despite the dire prospects in South Vietnam, both Eisenhower and his secretary of state, John Foster Dulles, thought the United States could succeed because of its superior resources and ingenuity. The fatal flaw in the decision to help Diem, Herring concludes, was the administration's belief that it could control events.

Captain Mark Clodfelter shows that in Vietnam the initial objective of America's 1972 bombing campaign—Linebacker I—was to undercut North Vietnam's war-making capability. While significantly reducing the north's capacity to fight, the operation did not end the war. After the failure of negotiations in December, the Americans turned to Linebacker II, which they designed to break morale in North Vietnam. The focus of both campaigns—despite their different goals—remained on military and not civilian targets. When the North Vietnamese agreed to the January 1973 cease-fire, many American civilian and military leaders believed that Linebacker II was the sole reason for settlement. Yet air power had not single-handedly broken North Vietnam's will. Hanoi's waging of conventional war, combined with President Richard M. Nixon's diplomatic isolation of North Vietnam, created the conditions that made the Linebacker campaigns one of many factors that led to the end of America's war in Vietnam.

Robert F. Burk demonstrates how racial struggles at home affected the nation's democratic image abroad, particularly in the Third World. He shows that a vital part of limited war—protecting the nation's image before the world—involved the struggle for racial justice in the United States. During the 1960s, simultaneously with the war in Southeast Asia, a battle raged over racial demonstrations, civil rights laws of the Great Society, and the development of Black Power. This struggle also became evident in America's armed forces, where at least part of the reason for ending discriminatory policy was the effort to win the propaganda battle in the Cold War. Black leaders in the United States warned that the continuation of these racial practices would drive the Asians into the Soviet camp. The United States had to defend itself against Soviet accusations of racism that could reduce the nation's stature among the emerging Third World peoples. In the twenty-five years following World War II, Burk argues, the United States made great advances in removing formal obstructions to racial fairness in the military, even though many problems remained. Washington had taken steps in the military forces that could symbolize its commitment to democracy against communism and totalitarianism. But despite these efforts, the American military never became the leader it might have been in the nation's struggle for racial equality.

Charles DeBenedetti shows how the antiwar movement in the United States aimed at ending the Cold War and then permitting the fulfillment of democratic traditions at home. He argues that during the early 1950s, the Cold War, the Korean conflict, the nuclear arms race, and McCarthyism combined to destroy the old peace movement's emphasis on global reforms led by an American-dominated United Nations. Afterward, the proponents of peace were more antiwar in relation to the Cold War than they were interested in reconstructing international affairs. Such an anti–Cold War movement was composed of varying groups who joined pacifists and traditional supporters of international reform in demanding new policies by Washington to halt the arms race and bring an end to the Cold War. They advocated increased individual responsibility for peace, which manifested itself in direct individual participation in protest actions. Their goal was not American domination of global order but American leadership in denouncing dangerous policies of military preparation and interventionism. According to their teachings, the Cold War was more dangerous to American democratic traditions than was communism. But the peace leaders lacked organization and a political base, making it difficult to counteract the widespread belief that peace rested only in strength. They provided the bases for later opposition to the Vietnam War as well as to nuclear arms competition; but they had little chance of halting the American military buildup in Southeast Asia.

James C. Schneider focuses on the Vietnam War and President Johnson's Great Society program to show how an attempt to have both guns and butter can lead to one's destroying the other. Schneider admits that American involvement in Vietnam had an adverse effect on the Great Society's reform programs, but he argues that other factors related to the program were more important in its demise. He examines congressional support for reform in 1966 and 1967 by using the Model Cities program as a case study of congressional opinion during the period of rapid American military escalation in Vietnam. He shows that the peak years of spending in Southeast Asia corresponded with declining congressional interest in the Great Society. But he concludes that in addition to the impact of the war, the Great Society was hurt by many of its own problems, as well as by a shifting balance of political power within the House of Representatives.

Growing problems in Central America have also revealed the complexities of modern warfare. By implication, the tensions in Nicaragua and Costa Rica have become inseparable from the concerns of limited war because they have meshed with the efforts made by the United States to win the Cold War.

Ralph Lee Woodward, Jr., argues that the issues in Nicaragua have their roots in matters unrelated to communism. According to Woodward, the Nicaraguan revolution has a historical base that is indigenous to the country's own problems and not attributable to communist influence. He insists that events in Nicaragua cannot be considered solely in the light of Cold War foreign policy. The Sandinistas have begun a major series of changes in society that may culminate in a Marxist-Leninist state. Many of the Sandinistas regard themselves as engaged in a struggle for a better life against the United States and the West, with the latter two defending nineteenth-century liberalism and a restoration of the old order. But more important than these historical issues, Woodward concludes, the Cold War confrontation between the United States and the Soviet Union will play a major role in determining the outcome of this revolution.

Thomas M. Leonard also shows how America's fears of communist intrusion in Central America have led the Reagan administration to exert pressure on Costa Rica (taking advantage of its economic problems) to drop its stance of neutrality in regional conflicts and side with the United States. Leonard shows how Costa Rica for years remained relatively free from the political struggles of the region. But in 1979 the country for two reasons became involved in surrounding political and military unrest. First, rising petroleum costs combined with declining export income led to economic problems in Costa Rica. Second, Anastasio Somoza's overthrow by the Sandinistas in Nicaragua put a severe strain on the country's ability to maintain neutrality from neighboring conflicts. United States policy toward Costa Rica changed as Washington put pressure on the Central American country to help ward off the communist threat to the region. The result was that from 1980 to 1984 the United States and Costa Rica often disagreed over policies. Whereas Costa Rica preferred neutrality, it has had little choice but to join the Reagan administration's anti-Sandinista policy.

On the final issue under consideration, that of nuclear strategy, Donald M. Snow discusses the debate over America's efforts to build a ballistic missile defense (BMD) that has become part of President Reagan's "star wars" program. Snow demonstrates that, historically, the pendulum has swung from strategic offense to strategic defense and suggests that this could happen with BMD. The impression has grown that instead of assured destruction, BMD offers the possibility of limited nuclear war because it would disable part of the incoming missiles. Though offensive weaponry has dominated strategic thought during the last few decades, history shows that fluctuations have occurred between offensive and defensive advantages. Strategic defense through BMD is more than a remote possibility.

Daniel S. Papp stresses that the superpowers must have accurate perceptions of each other's nuclear strength and urges each side to exchange information in an effort to promote a mutual understanding of intentions. He compares and contrasts American and Soviet perceptions of U.S. nuclear weapons programs and strategies during the early 1980s and finds the two powers in sharp disagreement on America's objectives. Such misperceptions are conducive to errors in calculation that can lead to war. Better efforts at educating each side about the other's capabilities and perceptions would help. They could also exchange viewpoints outside widely heralded summit meetings, for such meetings often degenerate into an environment suitable for propaganda.

This collection of essays shows the dimensions of modern warfare. The writers illustrate the inseparability of foreign and domestic affairs and the importance of images, symbols, and perceptions in America's effort to gain support both from allies and the Third World. More than that, they demonstrate that the formulation of foreign policy is vastly complicated, not given to easy solution or to simple explanation. And yet, they also affirm that America's central objective in the nuclear age is as simple and as clear as it was during the early days of the Republic: to safeguard the national interest.

The Importance of Studying
Military History

ROBERT H. FERRELL

MILITARY HISTORY is not in vogue today, nor has it been popular within living memory or within times more distant. Its neglect is a pity, a saddening commentary on the understanding by Americans of their past.

Several generations of historians in our country have had their chance to record and analyze the military history of the United States, and without exception, if for different reasons, they have refused their opportunity. In America the first generation of professional historians was teaching and writing in the years before World War I, and these men (and a scant few women) gave little attention to the country's military past. They did on occasion chronicle the Civil War, relating in long—and for today's readers tedious—detail the march of regiments up some hill and down another. They sometimes celebrated the defeat of one side or the other, because they came from one part of the country or the other. For the most part, however, the early historians in the United States, the generation that came to adulthood in the years before 1914–18, chose to write about the political history of the United States, narrowly (and, perhaps, absurdly narrowly) conceived. For them the signal event of American history was the Civil War, and they set out the political causes of the war, including such landmark congressional enactments as the Compromises of 1820 and 1850. For the years after the war they dealt with Reconstruction, tariffs, civil service reform, and the money question. If time remained, and it often did, they recited the quadrennial contests for the presidency beginning with the Washington administration.

A second generation of American historians constituted a group of young men born in the nineties of the last century or at the turn of the present century, young men who took part in World War I, perhaps half of whom fought in France, and whose horizons therefore were widened.

They taught not merely American political history and that epitome of political history, constitutional history, as had their predecessors, but they stretched their imaginations toward other sorts of history. They moved into the economic development of the country, so obvious to men of their generation who had seen the log cabins and sod houses disappear, the eclecticism of the Victorian era fade away, and the wealth of America at last begin to bring with it some originality. The country was coming of age, to use a phrase of the time, and they resorted to analysis of economic growth, as properly they should have. They noted other changes, such as the end of the American frontier in 1890, as announced by Frederick Jackson Turner, and frontier history began to hold a fascination for scholars that rightly has lasted to the present time. The widening outlooks of this second generation also brought to mind, and to pen, the possibility of social history, and notably the history of immigration, the latter a subject easily thought of in a country where at the time this generation was coming to manhood a third of Americans were either immigrants or sons and daughters of immigrants. Military history, however, did not obtain much attention from this second group of historians. Perhaps the reason was that they wanted to forget the war that the United States had entered in 1917, even though that war had changed their entire outlooks, making their generation much more catholic than preceding ones. For a while, too, they labored under the impression that the war of 1917–18 had made the world safe for democracy, or ought to have, and hence in a world without war there was little reason to concentrate upon its history.

In looking to the reason why American teachers and writers about history gave little attention to military history, down to the very present time, it is necessary to remark the interests of two other so-called historical generations, one of the recent past, the other of the present. The group of historians who began working with students and with historical materials in American colleges and universities after World War II—a group to which I belong—did not immediately see much attraction in military history, if only because we had just passed through the fiery furnace in Europe or in the Far East and we preferred to study something else. Some few of us admittedly gravitated back toward political history, the interest of the founding group of historians in the United States, but we stretched the meaning of politics, national and international, and sought to avoid the virtual monomania (the Civil War) of our predecessors. We looked more subtly upon politics as the art of the possible and as perhaps the primary distinction of American life—our ability to deal politically with each other, section with section, economic or social groups with similar groups across the country; the willingness not to resort to doctrinaire positions but to work things out; a desire to make politics the solvent of the country's problems. And in international relations, what some of us described proudly as diplomatic history, we sought to show how Americans likewise had been better than Europeans—we had taken the Wilsonian precepts of openness and truth and advanced them to the center of our nation's concerns, and by brandishing these two virtual weapons had sought (not always with success, of course) to change the ways of the wicked. And then those historians of my generation who did not find politics of interest turned to other subjects, not merely economic and social but, primarily, intellectual. Ideas have consequences, someone had said, and we felt that in the beginning was if not the word then surely the idea. Intellectual history already had advanced with the books of Vernon Parrington and Ralph Gabriel, but my generation sought to bring out the contributions of literary people, of philosophers, of thinkers of all sorts, who dealt with the primary stuff of life, the stuff that would advance the world from here to there, which we discerned as ideas rather than crass interests however defined.

A fourth generation of historical scholarship then appeared in the sixties and seventies. In these years, and down to the present time, college and university teachers and writers reached out for all sorts of subjects, including not merely the social history that had developed earlier and the economic history that had begun to seem important and the intellectual history that consumed my generation, but into what appeared as new realms of imagination: women's history, black history, popular history, psychohistory, quantification.

All the while, in recent years as in the past, military history has remained under a sort of cloud. Anyone, so the impression appears, can teach military history—if necessary. If the ROTC departments of the sixties desired military history it often was taught by officers of those departments. If members of regular departments of history took notice of military history it was to pass a one-semester survey course to a junior member of the department, or to someone who casually expressed interest. No one gave much attention to the outcome, either the coverage of the course or what sort of students took it or why. In the era of the Vietnam War, to be sure, military courses were downright unpopular with many students, and so were the military departments, and some institutions dropped both. Later, in the seventies, some of the departments reappeared. The military history courses crept back in. But neither the students nor the courses received much attention, and such is the arrangement nationally at the present time.

There has been a notable and fairly recent effort by the military to remedy this situation, but it has not changed matters much. It may even be a reflection of the military's tendency to spread out, to elaborate a bureaucracy. The focus is the production of official military histories, prepared by staffs of historians in the military departments in Washington that also supervise a network of service school historians, regional military historians, and a varied group of historical museums. The Center for Military History, domiciled in the Department of the Army in Washington, presided over by a brigadier general, is responsible for multivolume accounts of World War II, Korea, and Vietnam and for occasional volumes on other wars or on the organization of the army. The air force, navy, and marine corps have similar arrangements. Recently, however, it has been proposed to billet a historian with every major line unit of the armed forces; this may be taking history too far. One wonders also if the present organization for the writing of military history may be too organized—that one cannot produce histories simply by ordering them, that even trained historians will not necessarily be able to write the accounts they are supposed to bring forth, that there has to be constant infusion of new blood and stimulation from outside historians in colleges and universities. Moreover, the armed services' organization of historical research has not been able to transfer its enthusiasm to the private sector; somehow the company historians, if they may be so described, have not been able to galvanize the generality of historians, with the result that ignorance about military history continues, despite government sponsorship of a countermovement.

What a doctrinaire era we have been passing through! Quite apart from the sheer disinterest of professional historians in military history, it seems odd that the rapidly advancing military power of the United States, beginning in the thirties with the rebuilding of the U.S. Navy and continuing through World War II with the huge expansion of both the navy and the army, would not have forced a change in the thinking of scholars.

It is possible that the scholarly disinterest in military history has had three primary inspirations or reasons. One reason is that historians, like all Americans, have hesitated to admit what has often been obvious to non-Americans: that the United States of America has become a superpower because it was based, from its very beginning, on force. The Revolution of 1775–83 amounted to the imposition of the ideas of a third of Americans (to use the description of John Adams) on the contrary notions of another third and the indifference of the remainder. One thinks of the Mexican War, the Civil War, the imperial possessions of 1898 and subsequent years, including the virtual seizure of the Panama Canal Zone in 1903. And yet this heritage of force has had its embarrassment to the

14

generality of Americans, who are essentially small-d democrats. They like to believe that democracy in America has triumphed through the empire of reason, not that of force. And it is then a small movement of logic to assume, as most of us have, that it is better not to think overly much about the irrational, or at least of force, and to assume what we prefer to believe.

Another reason for the disinterest in military history has a close connection with our belief, mentioned above, that we are a peaceful and therefore a great people. Such belief rests on the forcefulness, in an ideological sense, of the American heritage of pacifism. Like other parts of our heritage, pacifism was long ago organized into what more recently came to be known as a peace movement. The extraordinary interest of Americans in world peace, with our belief that local and national groups of private citizens will influence local and national representatives and thereby the United States government in favor of world peace, has been around ever since the nineties of the last century, when the industrial revolution began to affect weaponry. In the nineties the Western world also began to notice that the diplomacy of Europe, what with the departure of Otto Von Bismarck from the German government, was turning downward—that there was talk, and thereby danger, of war. World War I was approaching, and people worried about the prospect. The result was a series of schemes, in the United States and in Europe, by which people hoped that war might be avoided. After the Great War of 1914–18 a peace movement began to grow in the United States; similar movements in European countries generated less enthusiasm. The American peace movement was very active in the twenties and thirties, only to see its hopes dashed in another world war. Since World War II the peace movement in America and elsewhere has been directed against the production and use of nuclear weapons and in favor of limitation of armaments and perhaps even the outlawing of armaments completely. The peace movement, I would say, has had something—although it is difficult to say exactly what—to do with the disinclination of Americans to examine carefully the military history of their country and that of other countries. I suspect that there is an essential obscurantism, a belief that if one does not study evil one will not be touched by evil.

A third possible cause of the scholarly disinterest in military history in the United States—the extraordinarily subtle way in which military history has impinged upon the events and circumstances of our own time—requires much more analysis and discussion than the two mentioned above. Ever since July 16, 1945, when the nuclear device suspended from a steel tower at Alamogordo, New Mexico, was detonated, the nuclear age's weapons have impinged upon our lives in ways that are often so subtle that we hardly realize what has happened. It is an unlovely period in human annals, one that most of us would like to exorcise. We would like to translate ourselves back into a time without such weapons, without the prospect of human destruction on a scale never before imagined. And so we often, therefore, like to dream that what we do not like does not really exist—that if the sun rises properly in the East each morning, our days are as yesterdays.

Military history has become central to the history of our country, and of all countries, developing as well as developed, since that early morning in July 1945. How can one ignore military history and obtain any true picture of our time? It is dismaying to see military history taught as a sort of stepchild of departments of history, as it is at present and has been for forty years, with courses given almost entirely for ROTC students and almost no history majors taking them. At Indiana University in Bloomington, where I teach, a course on Berlin and Paris in the twenties—a course, I sometimes think, in the trivia of decadence—enrolls far more history majors than does military history.

Most historians today, who comprise the past two teaching generations, and certainly the last two generations of college and university students, seem altogether unacquainted with the vast changes in military strategy since the dawn of the nuclear age. They appear to be unaware of the importance of limited war for survival of the race; of the dangerous wobbling of military policy, American and that of other countries, during the past forty years; and of how the situation has sometimes come to what one American secretary of state described as the brink, by which he meant the brink of nuclear war.

In my mind's eye I sometimes have sought to look back over the changes in military affairs since the far-off time when people of my generation heard the sirens on the tanks and beheld in nondescript Normandy fields the carcasses of cows with feet sticking straight up. The beginning of the nuclear age, in the presidency of Harry S. Truman, saw a careful measurement of the problem of new weapons and diplomacy and military policy. Truman, fortunately, was no man to push around. He kept a tight rein (the word recalls the bucolic nineteenth century) on nuclear weapons. In 1948 the U.S. Army's leaders, military and civil, asked for control of nuclear weapons, because of the imminence of a Soviet blockade of the Western Allied sectors of Berlin. Truman would have none of it, because he was commander in chief. As much as Truman admired the army, and he of course had been a reserve colonel, he refused to give up presidential control of these new weapons.[1] During the Korean War, General Douglas

MacArthur lost his head after the Chinese intervention of November-December 1950 and proposed the nuclear bombing of Red China, an astonishing and appalling suggestion. All the while the retired British statesman Winston Churchill, who came back as prime minister in 1951, was urging the president to settle the Russian problem by fixing the Russian clock. To all these importunities Truman turned a deaf ear, and kept control. But how, one might ask, can anyone study these early postwar years and understand how peace was kept, how the world proceeded in a fairly orderly way, without understanding the military history of the Truman administration?

During the Eisenhower fifties, as they were called, the Joint Chiefs of Staff of the U.S. Army were uncertain whether limited war, nonnuclear war, was possible—and here was another chapter in the history of fairly recent times that must be studied in order to understand American politics, society, and intellect at that time. Eisenhower, a military man, senior to the joint chiefs of his presidency, refused to go all-out for nuclear strategy, and like his predecessor Truman he too kept control. In retrospect it is exhilarating to read Eisenhower's diary and the commentaries to his press secretary, James C. Hagerty, to observe how Ike held the balance within the United States government in favor of limited war.[2] In July 1954, the president of South Korea, then the venerable Syngman Rhee, came to the United States for a state visit, and talked to the American president about allowing "some positive action" against North Korea. In a large meeting, with Eisenhower present, Rhee spoke in a very clear but low voice and said that a war of liberation would produce a positive result. Horrified, the president let him have it. One thing would be worse than winning any war, Eisenhower said, and that was losing it.

> There is no disposition in America at any time to belittle the Republic of Korea but when you say that we should deliberately plunge into war, let me tell you that if war comes, it will be horrible. Atomic war will destroy civilization. It will destroy our cities. There will be millions of people dead. War today is unthinkable with the weapons which we have at our command. If the Kremlin and Washington ever lock up in a war, the results are too horrible to contemplate. I can't even imagine them.[3]

In a diary entry of January 23, 1956, Eisenhower summarized a report by General Harold L. George of the U.S. Air Force, who had imagined the unimaginable. Two-thirds of the United States population needing medical care, and almost none available. Federal government wiped out. Total economic collapse for between six months and a year. And about the only way to prevent all this was to call a meeting of Congress to vote for war, and start the war before the session ended, an impossible procedure.[4]

How can one escape military history? How understand Eisenhower's concern for inflation, for balancing the budget, unless one mentions how it meant restraining the military budget? Eisenhower did define a Russian war as necessarily nuclear, yet it was certain that the Soviets were in no condition to begin a war. He did his best to ensure that American technology stayed far ahead of that of the Soviet Union. His predecessor had done the same. In 1952 the Americans tested an H-bomb, its warhead so large that, as J. Robert Oppenheimer said, it would have had to be taken to its target in an oxcart. But in 1954 American scientists managed to miniaturize the H-bomb warhead, and large-thrust missiles no longer were necessary. As a result of Truman-Eisenhower policy (whoever has heard this sort of thing in American history classes of today?) it became unnecessary to continue a large-thrust missile program. The large-thrust missile program hence was abandoned. The Russians, who did not even have a good H-bomb until 1956, and no miniaturization, continued the manufacture of oxcarts. So the next year, in what was not much more than a scientific stunt, they sent up the world's first satellite, which they named Sputnik. They announced it as a scientific triumph. Eisenhower's critics thereupon assailed him for neglecting national defense. Two of the president's chiefs of staff, Generals Matthew B. Ridgway and Maxwell D. Taylor, published highly inconvenient books in the political years 1956 and 1960 roundly criticizing their commander in chief.[5] The American educational establishment used the occasion of Sputnik to set on foot an enormous program of government support to education, the National Defense Education Act.

In their ignorance of military affairs, people during the Eisenhower fifties wove an almost unending tapestry of accusation against a president whose physical stamina was wearing thin—Eisenhower suffered a massive heart attack in 1955, an acute attack of the digestive ailment known as ileitis in 1956, a mild stroke in 1957. In his last years his stamina wore down and he allowed the critics a field day. In that bygone time I confess that I had almost no idea of the president's effort to stabilize the country's military problems, his unerring good judgment on military-diplomatic issues. Only later, when I beheld the president's diaries scattered through the files of the Dwight D. Eisenhower Library in Abilene, Kansas, and edited them into a book, did I realize how much my generation owed to this Republican president for whom I had never voted. During the time in which Eisenhower manfully was doing his duty to the nation and the world, I knew next to nothing of the close connection between American military and political policies, the essential aspect of military decisions, the need for anyone who understood American realities of the fifties to know the military realities of that time. During those years when I was an active university teacher I gave lectures each year out of a book that entranced my generation, by the columnist Marquis Childs, entitled *Eisenhower, Captive Hero.*[6] Beautifully written, apparently dispassionate, it argued that the only way the Republicans had gained power in the presidential election of 1952 and had held it throughout the rest of the fifties was to capture an ignorant military hero, just as the GOP had resorted to Ulysses S. Grant in 1868.

Military history, let us conclude, is unavoidable for anyone, student or teacher, who wishes to understand especially the recent history of the United States and the world— "recent" being defined as the years since July 1945. Almost another subject, and one that would require other explanation, is military history as an unavoidable accompaniment to American history since the faraway time when the *Susan Constant* landed the settlers at Jamestown in 1607.

Some realities remain with us, whether we admire them or not. They are simply unavoidable. It is an aspect of judgment that we accept or at least seek to understand what we cannot change.

PART 1

The War in Vietnam

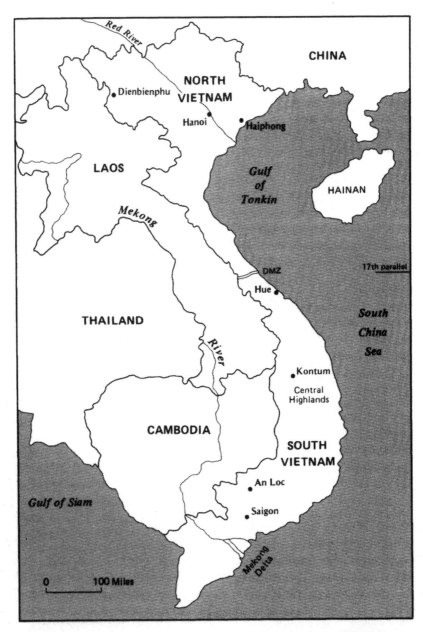

Vietnam

Prelude to Vietnam: The Erosion of the U.S. Army's Raison d'Être, 1945–1962

HARRY G. SUMMERS, JR.

To UNDERSTAND the United States Army of the Vietnam War, one must first understand its policies, strategies, and doctrines. After World War II, a paradoxical situation developed that both validated and invalidated conventional military power. The elements that gave rise to the situation were the postwar confrontation with the Soviet Union which led to the policy of containment, the fundamental shift in strategic doctrine that grew out of the war in Korea, the adoption of "massive retaliation" as the primary national strategy for the defense of the United States, the formulations of limited war theories, and the impact of "scientific management" on military strategic thinking. These factors combined to lay the basis for the debacle in Vietnam.

The Paradox of World War II

In August 1945 the American army had apparently revalidated the traditional concept that in war, land power is decisive.[1] With more than eight million soldiers under arms and some eighty-nine divisions in the field, that army represented the greatest display of military power the United States had ever produced. Confident of its capabilities, it had defeated the Nazi armies on the battlefields of North Africa, Italy, France, and Germany in bringing the European war to a close. The American army had pushed the forces of Imperial Japan back across the Pacific and now, fresh from its successes in the Philippines, was poised for a land invasion of Japan itself.

Just as the army reached this pinnacle of power, however, it ironically began to lose its place of prominence. The first instruments of this change were the detonations of atomic bombs over Hiroshima on August 6, 1945, and over Nagasaki three days later. The nuclear era had begun, for these bombings, not land power, proved decisive in Imperial Japan's surrender on August 15. Within months, America's World War II army was demobilized, leaving only skeleton divisions for disarming and occupying Germany and Japan.[2] By 1947 the army had suffered a further loss when its air corps was detached to form the newly independent Department of the Air Force.[3] With America's monopoly of nuclear weapons, the air power strategies of the Italian theorist General Giulio Douhet and the American general William "Billy" Mitchell took on new meaning: the idea developed that the air force alone could defend the United States.

Containment Policy

At the same time, another idea began to develop that had even more profound consequences for U.S. military policies and strategies. Soon after World War II, the United States faced a long-term confrontation with the Soviet Union, then seen as the fountainhead of "monolithic world communism." George F. Kennan's famous "X" article in *Foreign Affairs* in 1947 first articulated a new strategic policy to deal with these realities.[4] A distinguished diplomat and specialist on Soviet affairs, Kennan argued persuasively that U.S. policy should not be to roll back or liberate Communist-dominated territories but to "contain" Communist expansion. The first tests of this new policy came in 1948, when the United States decided to provide military aid to government forces in the Greek Civil War, and again when the North Koreans attacked South Korea in June 1950. Although the United States had earlier excluded Korea from its defense perimeter, President Harry S. Truman ordered American forces to help counter this invasion. American intervention was not for the sake of Korea alone but was part of a larger policy of containing the perceived expansion of monolithic world communism by force of arms. As evidence of this view, President Truman sent military forces into Korea and, at the same time, ordered the Seventh Fleet into the Formosa Straits to counter Chinese Communist expansion; strengthened military assistance to the Philippine government then under attack by Communist guerrillas; accelerated military aid to the forces of France and the Associated States of Indochina battling Communist insurgents in Vietnam; and later sent the first mobilized National Guard divisions to Europe to bolster American defenses. As President Truman asserted, "The attack upon Korea makes it plain beyond all doubt that communism has passed beyond the use of subversion to conquer independent nations and will now use armed invasion and war."[5]

The Korean War

The American army went into Korea filled with the hubris of World War II successes, expecting to join its United Nations allies in a quick victory against what Washington considered the tenth-rate forces of North Korea. Retribution for this overweening pride was soon coming, however, for in the Americans' first clashes, the North Korean army sent them reeling back, barely able to hold their precarious defensive positions in the Pusan perimeter.[6] Fortunes appeared to change in September 1950 with General Douglas MacArthur's brilliant envelopment at Inchon. Encouraged by this military success, the United States abandoned its new policy of containment in favor of liberation and rollback and ordered the military to defeat the North Korean army and reunite Korea under South Korean control.[7] By October the North Korean capital of Pyongyang had fallen and the Seventeenth Infantry Regiment reached the Chinese border in November. It appeared that the war was won.

This victory was not to be, however, for on November 26 the Chinese intervened in the Korean War. United Nations (UN) forces had to withdraw from North Korea, the South Korean capital of Seoul fell to enemy forces, and the army found itself back on the defensive. By January 1951, under the leadership of its new battlefield commander, General Matthew B. Ridgway, the UN army once again regained its confidence and went on the tactical offensive to push the Chinese north of the thirty-eighth parallel. Still, while the army seized the tactical initiative again, the Chinese intervention precipitated a change at the strategic level which had a profound effect not only on the war in Korea but also on the subsequent war in Vietnam. Intending to limit the war, President Truman returned to the policy of containment and rejected MacArthur's requests to carry the war to the Chinese homeland.[8] In adopting this policy the United States also unwittingly changed its fundamental military strategies from the strategic offensive, which had undergirded its victories in World War II, to the strategic defensive. The immediate effect was to cause an imbalance on the battlefield. In warfare the traditional object of both sides is to destroy the opposing armed forces so as to break the adversary's will to resist; but because of the prohibition against carrying the war to Chinese territory, the objective of the UN forces was no longer to destroy the enemy's armed forces and his will to resist but was instead to "resist aggression." Testifying on this point before the Senate in 1951, General MacArthur commented:

> It seems to me the worst possible concept, militarily, that we would simply stay there, resisting aggression, so-called. . . . [I]t seems to me that [the way to "resist aggression" is to] destroy the potentialities of the aggressor to continually hit you. . . . When you say, merely, "we are going to continue to fight aggression," that is not what the enemy is fighting for. The enemy is fighting for a very definite purpose—to destroy our forces.[9]

MacArthur's resistance to this change in military strategy led to his relief in April 1951. By July, cease-fire talks began which were to culminate in an armistice two years later. With this armistice, the United States achieved its political objective—restoration of the status quo antebellum—and rational judgment should have indicated that it had also achieved victory in Korea. Because America's experiences in World War I and World War II had led it to define victory as total defeat of the enemy's armed forces, however, the Korean War armistice became to many a defeat; instead of upholding the army's confidence, the results of the Korean War further undermined the army's sense of self-worth.[10] Part of this despair resulted from failure to understand fundamental military theory, for the outcome of the change in military policy from the strategic offensive to the strategic defensive should have been predictable. In the late nineteenth century the distinguished military strategist Colmar, the Baron von der Goltz, warned that the best result of a strategic defensive was stalemate on the battlefield.[11] In such instances military force could blunt an adversary's military power. Since it was not to destroy that power, that approach alone could not be decisive, yet it could provide the basis for the decisive use of political (i.e., diplomatic) power. This situation was precisely what occurred during the Korean War. Americans, however, regarded the experience in Korea not only as a defeat but as an aberration in the nuclear age, and neither the nation nor the army learned lessons from it which could have proved valuable in the subsequent war in Vietnam.[12]

With the election in 1952 of a former general, Dwight D. Eisenhower, to the presidency, one might assume that the army would grow in prestige and authority. Indeed, the opposite was the case. President Truman's earlier decision to reverse the traditional army mission of carrying the war to the enemy and breaking his will to resist by destroying his armed forces on the battlefield was revalidated by President Eisenhower's decision to end the Korean War in 1953 on the basis of the status quo antebellum.

Eisenhower reinforced this decision three years later by forgoing liberation or rollback during the Hungarian uprising.

Massive Retaliation

During the 1950s massive retaliation became the official military strategy of the United States as its leaders downgraded and ignored conventional forces. The effects of this national policy on military strategy remained hidden, however, by the decision of the Eisenhower administration to rely almost exclusively on strategic nuclear weapons as the basis for America's defenses.[13] Army Chiefs of Staff General Matthew B. Ridgway and General Maxwell D. Taylor bitterly resisted this policy. But because nuclear weapons appeared to provide "maximum deterrence at a minimum cost," their efforts were ultimately unsuccessful.[14] The army's budget was cut to the point where ammunition and gasoline for training were almost non-existent, and the army was made to feel as if it had no part to play in America's security. To show its adaptability to the nuclear battlefield, the army reorganized: it eliminated the regimental system which had proved successful in World War II and Korea in favor of "pentomic" battle group organizations, and it began to integrate tactical nuclear weapons into its basic formations. These weak attempts at "relevance," however, did little to restore the army's confidence. As the historian Russell F. Weigley has written: "A national military policy and strategy relying upon massive nuclear retaliation for nearly all the uses of force left the Army uncertain of its place in the policy and strategy, uncertain that civilians recognized a need even for the Army's existence and uncertain therefore of the service's whole future."[15]

Limited-War Theories

This rapid shift in less than a decade from the heights of glory to the depths of despair had a stultifying effect on the army's strategic thinking. Under the leadership of Chief of Staff General Ridgway, the army had successfully resisted efforts to involve it in French operations in Indochina in 1954,[16] but after his retirement it began to opt out of strategic thinking. More and more civilian academic theorists filled this vacuum.[17] One of their prime concerns was the impact of nuclear weapons on the battlefield. Many believed that such weapons had changed the nature of war to the point where military history and battlefield experience had no meaning. They began to rewrite the rules, and one of the first changes was the definition of limited war. Whereas after the Korean War General Ridgway had properly defined war as a political act constrained and limited by political objectives, by 1962 the army rejected this definition and regarded war as limited not by political ends but by military means. Limited war became a conflict in which neither side used nuclear weapons. The army's Field Service Regulations reflected this new thinking by laying out a spectrum of war which ranged from cold war ("a power struggle between contending nations") through limited war to general nuclear war. The regulations ignored the furor that had arisen during the Korean War when the administration labeled it a "police action," and they eliminated the threshold between war and peace that had proved so important to the American people. As the army's own manual said, "The dividing line between cold war and limited war is neither distinct nor absolute."[18] This doctrine helped to promote America's gradual slide into the Vietnam morass where no one clarified the break between war and peace.

Limited-war theorists deliberately excluded the American people from their strategic calculations because they feared that stirring public emotions in a nuclear age would lead to unconstrained escalation. The distinguished theorist Robert Osgood concluded that "even though the American people will be hostile, because of their national traditions and ideology, to the kind of strategy he proposes, that strategy must still be adopted."[19] One unfortunate result of such theories was the failure of the White House to mobilize the national will for fighting the war in Vietnam.[20]

Yet another of the fallacious theories was that in the nuclear age military forces were not for fighting but for "signaling." As the military analyst Stephen Peter Rosen has pointed out, during the Vietnam War, "when an increase in the stakes was considered, the question the leaders in Washington asked themselves was not 'How will this affect the resolution of combat?' but 'What signal are we sending the enemy?' "[21]

Because of the abdication of the military professionals and the declining emphasis on military science, political scientists as well as social scientists began to formulate military doctrine. With the former came theories of limited war; with the latter came theories of counterinsurgency. The foundations for disaster began to take shape.

Scientific Management

The army's loss of confidence in its battlefield abilities not only created a vacuum in military strategic thought; it caused the officer corps to shift its orientation from operational to managerial considerations. Army officers themselves argued that the army did not make strategy, and that strategy was budget driven and therefore a function of resource allocation. These views came into full bloom during the John F. Kennedy administration when Secretary of Defense Robert S. McNamara introduced the systems analysis approach to military strategy. As two of the leading "whiz kids" of the McNamara era, Alain Enthoven and K. Wayne Smith, put it, "What is commonly called 'military science' is not scientific in the same sense as law or medicine or engineering. . . . Modern day strategy and force planning has become largely an analytical process . . . [and] civilians are often better trained in modern analytical techniques."[22] Unfortunately, in Vietnam the United States opposed an adversary who, in the words of Corelli Barnett of Cambridge University, "was terribly old-fashioned" in fighting a war where (as America's own earlier definitions had emphasized) moral factors were more decisive than physical factors.[23]

Counterinsurgency Dogma

As has been argued elsewhere, when President Kennedy took office in 1961, his policy of "flexible response" at first made it seem that the army had come into its own and that there was again a place for conventional strategy.[24] No sooner had the army begun to adapt its doctrine to these new policies, however, than America's adversaries—the U.S.S.R. and China—changed the rules of the game. Suddenly the threat was not so much nuclear war or conventional war but "a whole new kind of warfare"—wars of national liberation and people's war. Today it is difficult to envision the force with which the concept of counterinsurgency struck the army. Its impact was particularly powerful, both because of the partial doctrinal vacuum that still existed as a result of the massive retaliation era and because President Kennedy himself "took the lead in formulating the programs, pushing both his own staff and the government establishment to give the matter priority attention."[25] The president appointed former army chief of staff General Maxwell D. Taylor as his special military representative and assigned him the duties of monitoring counterinsurgency efforts. Kennedy himself sent a letter to the army indicating the need for new doctrine and tactics.

Some appreciation of the effect became apparent from such publications as the March 1962 issue of *Army*, the influential publication of the Association of the U.S. Army, which was devoted to (in its own words) "spreading the gospel" of counterinsurgency. To today's reader it sounds more like the description of a new liturgy than a discussion of strategic doctrine. Not all observers became converts. The article reports that Army Chief of Staff General George H. Decker "stoutly stood up to the President with the assurance that 'any good soldier can handle guerrillas.'" The president's response was "a brisk and spirited homily to the effect that guerrilla fighting was a special art." Six months later Decker was replaced by General Earle G. Wheeler. Army leadership got the message, especially since, according to contemporaries, "[President] Kennedy dropped a broad hint that future promotions of high ranking officers would depend upon their demonstration of experience in the counterguerrilla or sublimited war field."[26] Counterinsurgency became not so much the army's doctrine as the army's dogma.

Conclusion

During the early 1800s the German military theorist Karl von Clausewitz warned that "The first, the supreme, the most far-reaching act of judgment that the statesman and commander have to make is to establish . . . the kind of war on which they are embarking; neither mistaking it for, nor trying to turn it into, something that is alien to its nature. This is the first of all strategic questions and the most comprehensive."[27]

As America began its slide into the Vietnam morass, that question was never asked, let alone answered. The army bears primary responsibility for that failure, for land warfare is the very reason for its existence. In past wars the army took the lead in formulating strategies, plans, and policies for the conduct of military operations, but in the Vietnam War that was not to be.

By the early 1960s the army's self-confidence and sense of mission had so eroded that the army allowed the nature of the war to be defined by the various counterinsurgency "experts." The result was that there was never a strategy worthy of the name during the entire course of the Vietnam War. As military history could have foretold, no battlefield successes, no amount of American heroism or bloodshed, could make up for that fatal deficiency.

"In the Lands of the Blind":
Eisenhower's Commitment to
South Vietnam, 1954

GEORGE C. HERRING

FOR NEARLY twenty years, the study of Vietnam decisionmaking has been a cottage industry. Americans have naturally been eager to determine where they went wrong in Vietnam and to learn the appropriate "lessons," and historians, journalists, and political scientists have subjected numerous important decisions to the closest scrutiny. Articles and books have been devoted to topics ranging from Franklin D. Roosevelt's nondecisions regarding disposition of the French empire in Indochina, to Dwight D. Eisenhower's decision not to intervene militarily in Vietnam during the 1954 Dienbienphu crisis, to Lyndon B. Johnson's decision to commit ground troops to Vietnam in July 1965. These studies and others have provoked sometimes lively debate on the doctrinal fallacies or systemic flaws that led to America's involvement and ultimate failure in Vietnam.[1]

Curiously, one major Vietnam decision has escaped serious study: Eisenhower's commitment to Ngo Dinh Diem and South Vietnam in October 1954. This may indeed have been one of the most crucial Vietnam decisions. Or, put another way, this may have been the last opportunity for the United States to refrain from involvement in Vietnam without major political repercussions at home and abroad. The decision is especially intriguing because all objective criteria suggested that the chances of success were slim to nonexistent. Analysis of this decision thus offers clues to the thinking of U.S. policymakers in the mid-1950s. It provides important insights into the larger debate on Vietnam policymaking and on the making of foreign-policy decisions in general.

The commitment to South Vietnam in the fall of 1954 stemmed log-
ically from America's involvement in the First Indochina War. Although
reluctant to underwrite a war for French colonialism in Indochina, the
United States committed itself in 1950 to recognizing the French-con-
trolled government of Emperor Bao Dai and to furnishing military and
economic aid to the French in their war against the Communist-led Vietminh insurgency. As early as 1946 the United States government had concluded that Ho Chi Minh's Vietminh was an instrument of the Soviet
drive for world domination. In the aftermath of the Communist victory in
China in 1949, U.S. policymakers had concluded that the loss of any
further Asian territory to communism could tip the precarious global balance of power against the United States and fuel political turmoil at
home. In this context, Vietnam, terra incognita to Americans before
1941, suddenly became a vital interest. When the Korean conflict turned
the Cold War in Asia into a hot war, the importance of Indochina increased. By 1954 the United States was paying nearly 80 percent of the
cost of the French war.[2]

The likelihood of French defeat in 1954 posed a grave dilemma for the
United States. Even more than its predecessor, the Eisenhower administration feared the international and domestic consequences of the loss of
Asian real estate to communism. It was, therefore, most reluctant to stand
by and watch while Indochina went down the drain. Yet, having just ex-
tricated the United States from the bloody, indecisive war in Korea, the
administration was not eager to commit American troops to another war
on the Asian mainland. Unwilling to send its own forces, the administration did not want the French to pull out of Indochina. At the same time,
because of perceived French military incompetence and France's reaction-
ary colonial goals, it despaired of success as long as the French remained.
Faced with these quandaries, Eisenhower and his secretary of state, John
Foster Dulles, equivocated and eventually did nothing. Though they seriously considered various forms of military intervention in the spring and
summer of 1954, they ultimately held back, primarily because Congress
required British backing and French concessions, neither of which Dulles
was able to obtain during a period of frantic globetrotting diplomacy. The
two men thus prepared to wash their hands of a Geneva Conference settlement they expected to be unacceptable and to acquiesce in the loss of
all of Vietnam to communism.[3]

The Geneva agreements actually turned out much better than they had
dared to hope. Eager to end the war for their own reasons, the Soviets and
Chinese compelled the Vietminh to accept much less than they felt entitled to receive. Vietnam was partitioned at the seventeenth parallel pre-

liminary to elections to be held in two years to unify the country. From the outset, the terms were interpreted differently. Some of the participants assumed that they simply provided a cover behind which the communization of Vietnam would take place by peaceful means. To Eisenhower and Dulles, however, partition and the long delay before elections provided an unexpected opportunity to save the southern part of Vietnam from communism. If the United States could lure some non-Communist Vietnamese from north of the seventeenth parallel and help the Vietnamese build a stable government in South Vietnam, perhaps within two years the Communists could be defeated in elections. Or, fearing defeat, they might refuse to participate. That failing, the United States might still be able to preserve an independent, non-Communist South Vietnam as a bulwark against further Communist expansion in Asia.[4]

Despite these optimistic scenarios, the reality in Vietnam after Geneva was anything but promising. Of the total 25 million Vietnamese, an estimated 14 million were left north of the seventeenth parallel as a result of the partition settlement, and most observers agreed that the northerners were more vigorous and industrious than their southern counterparts. Ho Chi Minh's Vietminh had won the war against France and enjoyed great prestige throughout the country. Their control even in the north remained somewhat tenuous, but they had a tightly organized government and a powerful army. Between 10,000 and 15,000 Vietminh remained in the south to promote by legal and extralegal means the unification of Vietnam.[5]

In the south, by contrast, chaos reigned. Non-Communist Vietnamese were dispirited by the Geneva settlement and uncertain to what extent they could count on the United States and France. Political fragmentation was *the* fact of life below the seventeenth parallel. The Vietminh retained pockets of control, even at the doorstep of Saigon. The so-called sects, politico-religious groups accustomed to autonomy and maintaining their own private armies, ruled much of the Mekong Delta and the major Saigon suburbs. The influx after Geneva of huge numbers of northern Catholics into predominantly Buddhist South Vietnam added new ethnic and religious tensions to an already volatile mixture.[6] Created only belatedly and out of a sense of desperation by the French, the army was accurately characterized by General Henri Navarre as a "rabble." The government whose responsibility it was to bring order out of the chaos was singularly ill-equipped to do so. Its officials were in many ways more European than Vietnamese and were tainted by association with French colonialism. Navarre dismissed them contemptuously as a "band of marionettes."[7] Much of their energy was devoted to saving their own political skins and building their private fortunes. Presiding over all this, usually from afar, was Emperor Bao Dai, whose reputation for gambling, womanizing, and living the good life on the Riviera was well earned—a "plump and sleepy-looking man," the *New York Times* correspondent C. L. Sulzberger snarled. "I wouldn't die for anything he sponsored."[8] Dulles conceded that turning loose Bao Dai's government would be like "putting a baby in a cage of hungry lions."[9]

The emergence of Ngo Dinh Diem as prime minister of South Vietnam did little to alter these pessimistic appraisals. Indeed, what is striking in retrospect is the extent to which initial estimates of Diem by the United States pointed toward the tragic denouement of November 1, 1963. The staunchly anti-Communist and anti-French Catholic leader first approached the United States in 1950, expressing hope "somewhat wistfully" that America would send troops to Vietnam. The Truman administration quietly rebuffed the overtures of a man it stamped as too rigid and too "monkish" to be an effective leader.[10] Whether the Eisenhower administration helped to promote the rise of Diem or merely acceded to it is unclear, but in either case top U.S. officials had little confidence in him. Walter Bedell Smith did express hope that he would turn out to be a "modern political Joan of Arc" who could rally his country behind him.[11] In Paris, however, Ambassador Douglas Dillon conceded that this "Yogi-like mystic" was "too unworldly and unsophisticated" to lead South Vietnam. Inasmuch as Diem appeared to offer promise, he said, it was only because the "standard set by his predecessors is so low."[12] Chargé d'Affaires Robert McClintock in Saigon characterized him as a "messiah without a message," complained of his "narrowness of view," and commented scornfully that his "only formulated policy is to ask immediate American assistance in every form."[13] Even Diem's staunch supporters admitted his liabilities. That he was a northern Catholic in Buddhist South Vietnam, Leo Cherne of the International Rescue Committee noted, was a handicap comparable in American political terms to that faced by a "rigid, devout Roman Catholic anti-segregationist Yankee opposing Herman Talmadge in Georgia."[14] In the aftermath of Geneva, therefore, official and unofficial estimates of the chances of South Vietnam's survival were universally pessimistic, even despairing. On one occasion Dulles estimated the chances as no better than one in three; in his more pessimistic moods, the numbers fell to one in ten.[15]

By late September 1954, the Eisenhower administration approached a crossroad in Vietnam. For months the United States had been deeply involved behind the scenes. Army officers helped to organize the South Vietnamese army, while operatives of the Central Intelligence Agency (CIA) like Edward Lansdale advised Diem on how to deal with his multiple problems and even launched clandestine operations in North Vietnam. Despite U.S. backing, Diem lurched from crisis to crisis, threatened by his old enemies the French and by dissident groups within South Vietnam apparently backed by the French. To bolster the stature of the Diem government and perhaps thereby to save South Vietnam, the State Department proposed that the United States formally and openly commit itself to Diem by providing economic aid directly to him instead of through the French and by assuming full responsibility for training the South Vietnamese army.[16]

The most vocal opposition to the commitment came from the Defense Department. The Joint Chiefs of Staff expressed grave doubt that anyone could build an effective army when political stability did not exist. They were skeptical of French intentions and despaired of making any progress with the South Vietnamese as long as the French remained.[17] Secretary of Defense Charles E. Wilson was especially outspoken against the commitment. Describing the situation in South Vietnam as "utterly hopeless," he claimed that the "only sensible course" was for the United States to get out of the area "completely and as soon as possible," leaving the Vietnamese and French to "stew in their own juice." In words that would take on the ring of prophecy in little more than a decade, Wilson indicated that he could "see nothing but grief in store for us if we remained in that area."[18]

Eisenhower and Dulles conceded the Defense Department's premises but rejected its conclusions. The secretary of state agreed that the chances of success were slim and feared committing U.S. prestige in an area "where we had little control and where the situation was by no means promising." He too wanted the French out of Indochina, but he warned that for them to leave right away would be "militarily disastrous." Admitting that he was indulging in the "familiar hen and egg argument," he advised the joint chiefs that building an army in South Vietnam might help promote the political stability that was then so conspicuously missing.[19] To abandon Southeast Asia without a struggle would be unthinkable, Eisenhower added, and continued retreat in that area could result in a "grave" threat to American security. At a National Security Council (NSC) meeting on October 22, 1954, the president affirmed "with great conviction" that "in the lands of the blind, one-eyed men are kings," by which he apparently meant that despite the bleak outlook, the United States had the resources and ingenuity to succeed.[20] Thus, in late October, Eisenhower made the initial commitment to South Vietnam.

Why did the administration buck such overwhelming odds and make a commitment which seemed to promise so little? Eisenhower and Dulles seem to have feared, first, that to do nothing risked the loss of all of Vietnam and possibly Indochina to communism. South Vietnam might collapse of its own weight and the Communists take over by default. Or, more likely, the Diem government might fall and be replaced by a government under French influence. In both Europe and Asia the French seemed to the administration to be pursuing a policy of "peaceful coexistence" that was playing into the hands of the Communists. The State Department especially feared that the French might work out some kind of deal with North Vietnam to preserve their own influence at the expense of South Vietnam. At best, the government of Pierre Mendès-France seemed willing to provide only token assistance to South Vietnam while keeping all options open. Its approach to the upcoming elections, to the horror of Americans, seemed to be to "let the best man win."[21] Thus if the United States was to preserve South Vietnam as a "free world bastion," it must assume the burden of leadership and firmly commit itself to Diem.

From the administration's standpoint, the possible consequences of the loss of Vietnam were sufficiently grave to merit taking risks. Vietnam was not deemed important in and of itself; it was significant because of the impact its fall might have elsewhere. Indeed, U.S. policymakers agreed as early as March 1953 that Indochina had "probably the top priority in foreign policy, in some ways even more important than Korea, because the consequences of its loss could not be localized."[22] The fall of Indochina might cause the loss of all of Southeast Asia, leaving the Communists enormous stocks of rice and vital raw materials. The lack of food sources, raw materials, and markets would be especially hard on Japan. "The situation of the Japanese is hard enough with China being Commie," Dulles warned. If Southeast Asia were also lost, "the Japs would be thinking on how to get on the other side."[23] Nothing happened during the next year to modify this assessment. On the contrary, the crisis atmosphere generated by Dienbienphu and Geneva seemed to heighten the importance of Indochina.

The administration appears also to have been influenced by the "lessons" of the First Indochina War, the most important of which was that defeat had been mainly the result of French ineptitude. In American eyes, the French military effort had been victimized by poor leadership, bad tactics and strategy, and a defensive posture that reflected chronic defeatism. U.S. military leaders had tried desperately, in General J. Lawton Collins's words, "to put the squeeze on the French to get them off their fannies," but they had accomplished little.[24] To Americans, French political failures had been even more important. The French had used "weasel words in promising [the Vietnamese] independence," Eisenhower complained to a friend, "and through this reason as much as anything have suffered reverses that have been inexcusable."[25]

Implied in this criticism and sometimes stated openly was the conviction that because of its superior skills and the purity of its motives the United States could do better. Few if any top U.S. military leaders wanted to fight in Vietnam, and in the spring of 1954 Army Chief of Staff General Matthew B. Ridgway had vigorously opposed U.S. intervention in the First Indochina War. If the nation were forced into the war, however, at least some Americans were convinced that it could succeed where France had failed. "Two good American divisions with the normal aggressive American spirit could clean up the situation in the Tonkin Delta in ten months," a marine colonel, deeply frustrated with the French, had observed in 1953.[26] Some Americans were also certain that given the opportunity they could create a viable nation in South Vietnam. Departing to some degree from his colleagues, the chairman of the joint chiefs, Admiral Arthur Radford, affirmed that the United States "could do just as much with the Vietnamese as the Vietminh had done with their own people."[27] American success in training the South Korean army seemed to show what skilled leadership and methods could accomplish with Asian people. U.S. mass production achieved results, Undersecretary of State Walter Bedell Smith boasted, "whether in producing automobiles or training troops."[28]

Eisenhower shrewdly perceived the difficulties facing an outside nation trying to galvanize people of an alien culture. He recognized the importance of native leadership. During the Dienbienphu crisis, he pondered the use of religion to inject into the non-Communist Vietnamese cause the "dynamism" that was so sorely missing. He raised the possibility of finding some "good Buddhist leader to whip up some fervor." When reminded, amid the laughter of his colleagues on the NSC, that Buddha had been a pacifist, he expressed hope of mobilizing the Catholics with a Joan of Arc.[29] The administration remained uncertain precisely how to mobilize the Vietnamese, but it was certain that the United States must try. "We must work with these people, and then they themselves will soon find out that we are their friends and that they can't live without us," he affirmed toward the end of the Geneva Conference.[30]

Lurking beneath the pessimistic appraisals of success in Vietnam was an inner confidence that, given a lucky break here or there, the United States could succeed. Such confidence reflected what the English scholar D. W. Brogan once called "the illusion of American omnipotence," the conviction based on the nation's spectacular record of success that it could accomplish the difficult tomorrow but that the impossible might take a while. In the case of Eisenhower and Dulles, the confidence was probably reinforced by a remarkable record in their first two years in office of manipulating foreign governments at low cost and with minimal risk. In August 1953 the United States had toppled a popularly elected government in Iran, and in June 1954, while the Geneva Conference had been in its most critical stage, the CIA had mounted a coup which had overthrown the leftist government of Jacobo Arbenz in Guatemala.[31] Having succeeded in these cases with little effort, Eisenhower could understandably conclude that "in the lands of the blind, one-eyed men are kings."

To minimize the consequences of failure, the administration carefully qualified the commitment to Diem. Dulles and Eisenhower scaled down the proposed aid package of $500 million to $100 million on the ground that South Vietnam needed an army large enough only to combat internal subversion. A direct North Vietnamese attack across the seventeenth parallel would trigger the Southeast Asia Treaty Organization (SEATO) agreement. Aware that too close a connection with Diem might be a liability for him and would dangerously commit U.S. prestige to a risky cause, Eisenhower made the commitment conditional on Diem's performance.[32] "We do not wish it [to] appear that Ngo Dinh Diem [is] our protégé or that we are irrevocably committed to him," Dulles emphasized.[33] In the event that "Diem's intrinsic faults" created a situation making his replacement necessary, in Ambassador Donald Heath's words, the United States initiated a quiet talent search for what Heath called a "relief pitcher" and was ready at any time to get that person "warming up in the bullpen" if not indeed to send him into the game.[34]

What does this particular decision tell us that is relevant to the larger debate on Vietnam decisionmaking? If this case is any indication, it appears, first, that the praise given the Eisenhower administration by people like the political scientist Alexander George has been misplaced or at best overstated. George has argued that the open political process created by Eisenhower ensured a large degree of "multiple advocacy," thus resulting in good decisions. In this instance, opposing points of view did emerge and they were stated with some force, at least by Secretary of Defense Wilson. The open process George describes seems not to have existed, however, and the opposing point of view was irrelevant or merely for the record. Inasmuch as there was discussion and debate, it seems to have been pro forma. Eisenhower appears to have decided to commit the United States to Diem before the Joint Chiefs of Staff stated their opposition. As the historian Ronald H. Spector has pointed out, moreover, the objections, such as they were, were qualified and in the final analysis innocuous, the joint chiefs indicating that they would go along with the commitment if the administration decided that "political considerations were overriding." The joint chiefs seem to have considered this a relatively minor issue and were content to cover their collective posteriors without doing anything drastic to head off something about which they were skeptical.[35]

This episode does not seem to confirm any of the major explanations of where U.S. decisionmaking on Vietnam went wrong. It certainly does not validate the so-called quagmire theory, the notion that overoptimistic advisers led unsuspecting presidents step by step into the quicksand of Vietnam. In this case, at least some of the advisers were quite pessimistic, and Eisenhower and Dulles themselves conceded that the chances of success were slim. At the same time, this decision does not seem to confirm Leslie Gelb's argument that "the system worked," that administrations from Harry S. Truman's to Richard M. Nixon's, unwilling to lose Vietnam but also unwilling to commit the United States to all-out war, did just enough to keep South Vietnam afloat until the next election.[36] It is conceivable, of course, that Eisenhower and Dulles were thinking in these terms. It seems more likely, however, that, despite the odds, they felt they could succeed, or, at least, if things went wrong, they could quietly extricate themselves from an untenable commitment. The fatal flaw in the administration's thinking may therefore have been its belief that it could control events.

In the most curious and roundabout way, this belief turned out to be misplaced. To the shock of many observers, Diem converted the near disaster of 1954 into one of the world's great success stories of 1955, emerging out of the chaos to secure firm control over South Vietnam. Ironically, however, his near-miraculous success of 1955 contained within it the seeds of the disaster that some Americans had foreseen from the outset. The more successful he was, the closer the United States became identified with him and the more the freedom of action of Eisenhower and his successors became circumscribed. At the same time, Diem's refusal to go along with the elections called for in Geneva and his repression of dissent provoked an internal revolution which in time drew support from North Vietnam and, by the early 1960s, had produced a major crisis in South Vietnam. This crisis exposed the flaws in Diem's leadership and the weaknesses in South Vietnamese society which had been viewed as major roadblocks to success in 1954. Eisenhower's successors found it increasingly difficult to back away from the commitments he had made. By the mid-1960s, Wilson's prophecy of grief for the United States was well on the way to fulfillment. Perhaps as the historian Gordon Wood has recently observed, "History does not teach lots of little lessons. It teaches one big one: that nothing ever works out quite the way its managers intended."[37]

4

Applying Air Power in Vietnam: The 1972 Linebacker Bombing Campaigns

MARK CLODFELTER

"WAR," Karl von Clausewitz proclaimed, "is not a mere act of policy but a true political instrument, a continuation of political activity by other means." Whereas the Prussian staff officer believed that a commander should require the designs of policy to be consistent with the means of waging war, he also asserted that war could do no more than modify political aims. "The political object is the goal," Clausewitz concluded. "War is the means of reaching it, and means can never be considered in isolation from their purpose."[1]

The introduction of the airplane in 1903 added a new dimension to the "political instrument" of war, although by 1918 the idea of aerial bombardment for "strategic" purposes remained little more than theory. Following World War I, men such as Giulio Douhet, Hugh Trenchard, and William "Billy" Mitchell espoused the belief that strategic bombing could not only destroy the capability of an enemy to wage war, but could also destroy the enemy's will to fight. In the United States, proponents of strategic bombing stressed these concepts at Maxwell Field's Air Corps Tactical School (ACTS), which trained many of the army air force commanders of World War II. Although ACTS officers emphasized air power as a means to demolish an enemy's war-making potential, they did not disregard the belief that bombing could destroy an enemy's national will.

World War II gave American air strategists a chance to vindicate their faith in air power, as they directed huge armadas against Germany and Japan in pursuit of "unconditional surrender." In Korea, however, air force commanders employed air resources that supported limited political objectives vacillating between the aim of South Korean independence and the elimination of communism from the Korean peninsula. American policy restricted the struggle to the peninsula to prevent the conflict from expanding into another world war. American air leaders used bombing to support the goal of a viable, non-Communist government in South Vietnam during the presidency of Lyndon B. Johnson, and, as in Korea, fears of a broadening conflict limited the application of air power. In each of these campaigns, American air commanders initially either employed or advocated the employment of air power against an enemy's capability rather than against his will. Only after attacks against an enemy's war-making potential had proven unsuccessful, or had been denied, did American air chiefs attack an opponent's morale—and even then, the raids came against military-related targets. The American strategic bombing campaigns during World War II, Korea, and the first half of the Vietnam War achieved varying degrees of success in securing national political goals. The perceived effectiveness of these campaigns to further war aims caused American civil and military leaders to direct the Linebacker I bombing offensive against North Vietnam's war-making capability and to aim Linebacker II against the country's morale.

The conduct of American bombing campaigns during the Korean War and during the Vietnam War while Johnson was president revealed that strategic bombing was ill-suited to the furtherance of American war aims in a limited conflict. Bombing had complemented the objective of unconditional surrender during World War II, largely through the destruction of the economic fabric of Germany and Japan. Both nations were highly industrialized states whose economies were susceptible to bombing, but this was not the case in either Korea or Vietnam. Both North Korea and North Vietnam relied on external sources for the bulk of their war materials, and the American political leadership did not consider attacks against these sources appropriate in light of the limited war aims of the United States.

Those commanders who advocated a lessening of constraints during "Rolling Thunder," President Johnson's air campaign against North Vietnam, likely never accepted the limited nature of the American objective. Despite their desire for the traditional American goal of victory, few if any advocated indiscriminate attacks against North Vietnamese population centers. In Korea, where the Far East Air Forces (FEAF) commander had considerably more flexibility in target selection than the commander of Pacific Command in Vietnam, the FEAF commander refused to strike targets that did not yield a direct military benefit. General Carl Spaatz's campaign against Germany also targeted military objectives and even though General Curtis LeMay's B-29s raided Japanese cities, the cities contained factories dispersed throughout their residential districts.

According to the United States Strategic Bombing Survey (USSBS), the strategies employed by the Combined Bomber Offensive in Europe and LeMay's XXI Bomber Command could possibly have produced victory even without the final assault against Germany or the use of the atomic bomb against Japan.[2] Yet the USSBS also concluded that the air offensives could not have produced victory without the complementary efforts of Allied ground and naval forces. In the larger sense, the bombing campaigns complemented the primary American goal of unconditional surrender, accomplishing this by a preponderance of effort rather than through surgical precision. The army air forces *hammered* both Germany and Japan, but use of the bludgeon rather than the sword meshed with the purpose of obliterating the political, as well as the military, foundations of the Axis nations. The USSBS determined that the magnitude of the bombings did not stiffen either German or Japanese morale, although it also revealed that the two populations could withstand the assaults.[3] Perhaps the USSBS's most significant determination for the future application of American air power appeared in the summation regarding the effectiveness of strategic bombing against the Japanese:

> The experience of the Pacific War supports the findings of the Survey in Europe that heavy, sustained and accurate attack against carefully selected targets is required to produce decisive results when attacking an enemy's sustaining resources. It further supports the finds in Germany that no nation can long survive the free exploitation of air weapons over its homeland. For the future it is important fully to grasp the fact that enemy planes enjoying control of the sky over one's head can be as disastrous to one's country as its occupation by physical invasion.[4]

In Korea and Vietnam, air commanders sought to apply the lessons of the USSBS. The FEAF launched a campaign of "air pressure" against Chinese and North Korean forces during the last year of the Korean War. The ability of this campaign to force a Communist settlement proved doubtful, although many commanders left Korea with the notion that air power, operating independently, had compelled the Communists to come to terms. In similar fashion, many military leaders in Vietnam believed that had Johnson removed the restrictions on Rolling Thunder and mined North Vietnamese harbors, the air effort against North Vietnam could have proven decisive.

The 1968 Tet offensive altered the character of the Vietnam War in two important respects. First, while the North Vietnamese goal of toppling the southern government remained, the decimation of the Vietcong forced the North Vietnamese to accomplish this goal by conventional military means. Second, the offensive turned American public opinion against the war, and in so doing forced the eventual withdrawal of American ground forces and shifted the primary objective of the United States from preserving a South Vietnam capable of standing alone against communism to "peace with honor."

President Richard M. Nixon initially relied on negotiations to extricate the United States from direct involvement in the war. After ten months of no progress in the public talks begun in Paris by the Johnson administration, Nixon dispatched Henry A. Kissinger, his assistant for National Security Affairs, to meet secretly with North Vietnamese representatives in Paris in August 1969. Kissinger met with Hanoi delegates Le Duc Tho and Xuan Thuy twelve times during the next twenty-six months, achieving no more than the deadlocked public negotiations paralleling his unannounced sessions. In October 1971 the president of South Vietnam, Nguyen Van Thieu, agreed to a new American proposal. This offer provided for the withdrawal of all American forces from South Vietnam within six months, a prisoner exchange by both sides, and a cease-fire throughout Indochina. Thieu also agreed to an internationally supervised election in South Vietnam, before which he and his vice president, Nguyen Cao Ky, would resign to ensure that all candidates received equal opportunity for selection.

To Nixon, Thieu's agreement to this latest American proposal was essential prior to submitting it to Hanoi. Although Kissinger's negotiations had not involved the South Vietnamese, Nixon equated the concept of "peace with honor" with an American withdrawal that did not abandon South Vietnam to imminent Communist takeover. The president shunned any settlement that threatened the survival of South Vietnam as an independent, non-Communist state, and he trusted Vietnamization to preserve the country's status following American departure. The continued existence of South Vietnam would, Nixon believed, demonstrate the resolve of the United States to support its allies. Equally important, an independent Saigon would remove much of the tarnish that American prestige had garnered after seven years of war.[5]

Relying on world opinion to compel Hanoi to negotiate, Nixon broadcast his October proposal in a television address on January 25, 1972. Concurrently, he publicized Kissinger's secret negotiating record. The president emphasized that the United States would conclude either an agreement on both military and political issues or one that would "settle only the military issues and leave the political issues to the Vietnamese alone." Nixon reiterated his pledge not to abandon South Vietnam, asserting that "if the enemy wants peace, it will have to recognize the important difference between settlement and surrender." The president's call for a return to negotiations ended with a warning. "If the enemy's answer to our peace offer is to step up their military attacks," Nixon declared, "I shall fully meet my responsibility as Commander in Chief of our Armed Forces to protect our remaining troops."[6]

Nixon's concern over North Vietnam's projected invasion led him to pursue combined policies of diplomatic and military pressure to forestall a Communist attack. Although Nixon continued to seek an accord with Hanoi, he had little faith that the North Vietnamese would respond positively to future bargaining efforts. As a result, Nixon concentrated on severing ties between North Vietnam and its main benefactors, China and the Soviet Union. On the one hand, should diplomatic dealings with Peking and Moscow prove successful, Nixon would have free rein to deal militarily with a North Vietnamese assault. If, on the other hand, this attempt failed, Nixon would have to risk increased air and naval power to convince Hanoi that military victory was impossible.

The North Vietnamese war minister, Vo Nguyen Giap, finally unleashed his attack on March 30, the Thursday before Easter. Despite knowledge of the coming invasion, American civil and military officials had underestimated its magnitude. Giap sent three divisions, backed by two hundred tanks and heavy artillery, streaming across the demilitarized zone into South Vietnam's Military Region I. This assault was the first of a three-pronged offensive, and it signaled the movement of nine other divisions to staging areas in Laos and Cambodia. Early in April three divisions struck Military Region III from Cambodia. These units surrounded An Loc, located on the highway leading south to Saigon, on April 13. The remainder of the North Vietnamese troops settled west of Kontum, causing American and ARVN (Army of the Republic of Vietnam) commanders to brace for an assault against South Vietnam's Central Highlands.

Giap's Easter offensive strengthened Nixon's resolve to preserve South Vietnam as an independent political entity. The president viewed the attack as a desperate move by the North Vietnamese to forestall Vietnamization. Nixon believed that defeating the invasion, along with a massive counterblow against the enemy homeland, would compel Hanoi to seek an accord. Kissinger concurred with the president's assessment, telling Nixon on April 3, 1972, that the United States "would get no awards for losing with moderation."[7] The national security adviser felt that the timing of the attack revealed much about North Vietnamese intentions.

Striking seven months prior to the presidential election, Hanoi aimed at battlefield victory while political pressures prevented Nixon from interfering decisively. Still, the unprovoked nature of the Communist assault provided Nixon with the public toleration necessary to retaliate.[8] The president directed his retaliatory response, named Operation Linebacker I, against North Vietnam's war-making capability rather than its national will.

Jointly conducted by air force and navy fighter aircraft, Linebacker I was a massive interdiction campaign against North Vietnam. From May 10, 1972, until its October cessation, 155,000 tons of bombs pummeled North Vietnamese roads, bridges, railroads, and power facilities, although Nixon prohibited any attacks threatening to cause civilian casualties.[9] Simultaneously, the president ordered the mining of North Vietnamese harbors to restrict seaborne imports, and pursued détente with the Communist Chinese and Russians to sever North Vietnam from its two greatest supply sources. Nixon was perhaps the first American president to exploit the rift existing between the two Communist superpowers. He used his trip to China in February 1972 and the Moscow summit in May to heighten the mutual suspicions of the Chinese and Russians, and to convince them that a lessening of tension with the United States over Vietnam would best serve their individual interests.

Nixon's massive application of air and sea power shocked the North Vietnamese Politburo. Moreover, Linebacker I and the corresponding air campaign in South Vietnam combined with stiffening South Vietnamese resistance to negate any chance the Easter offensive had to produce victory. American intelligence experts estimated that air power alone had decimated the twelve attacking North Vietnamese divisions by August.[10] As a result of Nixon's shrewd diplomacy, his decision to bomb and mine stood unopposed by both Moscow and Peking. Furthermore, the Moscow summit and its Strategic Arms Limitation Talks agreement gained Nixon the public support the Politburo sought to undermine with its assault, virtually assuring his reelection. The disastrous Easter offensive and the prospect of Nixon's reelection caused the Politburo to reconsider its emphasis on a military takeover. While the goal of unifying the two Vietnams remained, by mid-September North Vietnamese leaders had made the decision to seek a negotiated settlement.[11]

As Hanoi shifted toward negotiations, Nixon did not diminish military pressure but instead increased it. He answered Hanoi's concessions made during the July and August round of talks with added bombing in August.[12] The intensification of the air war, along with mining, prevented replenishment of the north's dwindling supplies. While Hanoi continued to seek an accord prior to November, the military situation dictated that it secure a cessation of hostilities as soon as possible. The British guerrilla warfare authority Sir Robert Thompson asserted, "For the first time in the Indochina wars the communist side was being compelled to negotiate in order to forestall the possibility of defeat."[13]

Hanoi had four objectives at the bargaining table. Its first priority was to remove the American air force and navy from the war, which would both prevent defeat and allow the North Vietnamese army to rebuild for later operations. Second, Hanoi aimed at restricting future military activity in South Vietnam by the United States. Third, the Politburo wanted to retain North Vietnamese units in the south; in this regard Nixon's proposal of May 8, 1972, stressing a cease-fire, offered North Vietnam a chance for some military gain from the Easter offensive. Finally, Hanoi desired the removal of the South Vietnamese president and the establishment of a coalition government in the South. Speaking for the Politburo, Le Duc Tho stated that President Thieu was the overriding obstruction to a unified nation, and the chief North Vietnamese negotiator believed that the Thieu government would collapse once the Americans withdrew support.[14] Hanoi sought to obtain these objectives with minimum concessions, although a rapid curtailment of American military pressure was paramount. Ideally, the Communists hoped, election stresses would force Nixon to sign an imprecise agreement dealing with general principles and ending American involvement in South Vietnam.[15]

During the September and October negotiations, with Nixon still refusing to reduce the bombing significantly, Le Duc Tho displayed a sense of urgency to end the war.[16] Le Duc Tho produced a schedule on September 26 geared to achieving a settlement within one month, and yet he continued to demand Thieu's removal before signing an agreement. At the decisive October 8 session, Le Duc Tho immediately suggested that the United States and North Vietnam sign an accord resolving strictly military issues. Accepting Nixon's proposal for a cease-fire, Le Duc Tho dropped the requirements for a coalition government and for Thieu's resignation. By October 12 only two substantive issues remained—prisoner release and continued American military assistance to Saigon. Kissinger departed from Paris to brief Thieu on October 18, sending Hanoi a proposal for the disputed points and stating that an additional negotiating session with Le Duc Tho probably would be required. The next day, in Saigon, Kissinger received a message from Hanoi accepting verbatim the text he had submitted.

Of all the concessions made by Hanoi, surrendering the demand for a political settlement proved the most difficult. In refusing to call for the demise of the Thieu government, North Vietnam accorded it a measure of legitimacy that ran counter to the aim of unification. When asked by a member of the French Communist party in May 1972 if the North Vietnamese could deal with Thieu, Le Duc Tho replied:

> Impossible; he is responsible for Vietnamization. Without him, it [the government of South Vietnam] will fall apart immediately. He has become—necessarily—our number one enemy: his departure is imperative. In addition this [struggle at the negotiating table] is a test for us against the Americans. Through our demands, we come to know how much longer Nixon will support him; as soon as he drops him, we will have won. We can, therefore, go slowly . . . without letting up.[17]

The Communist party leaders understood the importance that Nixon placed on the Thieu government's survival. Le Duc Tho's offer to accept a military solution did not sacrifice North Vietnam's war aim, although it did sacrifice a major principle of Hanoi's policy. In accepting the cease-fire, Le Duc Tho managed a degree of face-saving by refusing to acknowledge the presence of "foreign" North Vietnamese soldiers in South Vietnam. However, Hanoi's decision to seek a military accord resulted in only negligible decreases in bombing on October 13 and 16.

To obtain a substantial bombing reduction, on October 19 the Politburo accepted Kissinger's proposals resolving the issues of prisoner exchange and material support for South Vietnam. Kissinger had informed Hanoi that he would travel to the North Vietnamese capital to initial an agreement, and his message of October 18 stated: "With the text of the agreement completed . . . [the United States] would stop bombing the North altogether twenty-four hours before my arrival in Hanoi."[18] The Politburo's latest concessions were additional violations of principle, and they revealed its desperation to curtail American involvement. Hanoi shunned its Vietcong ally by accepting release of all prisoners except captured Vietcong cadres in South Vietnamese jails. More important, the Communists agreed to let the United States resupply South Vietnam following American withdrawal. In consenting to a strictly military accord, the Politburo had ensured the retention of the Thieu government; by permitting that government to receive military aid, the Communists helped to ensure its survival. Nixon notified the North Vietnamese prime minister, Pham Van Dong, "that the agreement could now be considered complete," although the president called for a one-day delay in Le Duc Tho's September 26 schedule to resolve unilateral declarations concerning Laos and Cambodia.[19] Hanoi accepted the American position on the declarations on October 21, and two days later Nixon suspended bombing above the twentieth parallel, ending Linebacker I.

Linebacker I did not, however, achieve the "honorable peace" espoused by Nixon. Paradoxically, while the bombing contributed to Hanoi's willingness to settle on Nixon's terms, it also persuaded the South Vietnamese president to oppose an agreement in the belief that he could gain total victory. In neither case was Linebacker the sole cause of the response, yet—as bombing was the most noticeable aspect of American military and diplomatic activities—many attributed the October attitudes of Hanoi and Saigon to air power. Nixon encouraged this belief by making bombing the "carrot" to force a settlement, although his bombing carrot differed greatly from that of his predecessor's. Johnson curtailed bombing in hopes of gaining negotiations; Nixon reduced the raids only after achieving concessions.

Linebacker's effectiveness in wringing concessions from Hanoi stemmed from a number of factors that included Nixon's diplomatic isolation of North Vietnam, the war's conventional nature, and the relative freedom of air commanders to conduct operations as they desired. Moscow and Peking's priority on détente, strengthened by Nixon's diplomatic initiatives, convinced Hanoi of its isolation and allowed Nixon to increase attacks in August without fear of reprisal from the Communist superpowers. The success of the Moscow summit further provided Nixon with sufficient American public support to conduct an extensive air offensive.

Still, isolating North Vietnam did not alone guarantee Linebacker's success. Another important factor was the conventional nature of the war in 1972. Rolling Thunder caused little damage to the southern insurgency, as Vietcong operations required few resources. The Vietcong's demise during Tet had compelled Hanoi to commit its army. Relying heavily on logistical backing, the Easter offensive was a large-scale conventional attack supported by tanks and heavy artillery. These forces demanded resupply, and mining negated Hanoi's primary source of matériel. With no possibility of provisioning by sea, the Communists turned to stockpiled goods and overland transportation. Both sources were vulnerable to air power, the latter especially because of technological improvements in ordnance. Laser and electro-optically guided "smart" bombs destroyed the rail lines to China, forcing the North Vietnamese to rely on an insufficient number of trucks. Linebacker I, together with mining, tactical air support, and stiffening South Vietnamese resistance, wrecked North Vietnam's capacity to conduct offensive warfare. Moreover, the bombing and mining restricted *all* imports destined for North Vietnam, and the Politburo found its populace in danger of starving.[20]

Nixon's removal of many bombing restrictions that had hampered Rolling Thunder was another reason for Linebacker's effectiveness. The president granted the commander of the Seventh Air Force, General John W. Vogt, considerable authority to direct the campaign, and the general used his flexibility to conduct systematic assaults on North Vietnam's resources. True, the North Vietnamese did not feel the full effects of bombing until after depleting their stockpiles, but once supplies dwindled, Linebacker rapidly proved decisive.

Most American military chiefs believed that Linebacker was significant in forcing Hanoi to make negotiating concessions, and operational reports reflected this perception. An air force study completed in 1975 observed that "interdiction operations were a primary factor in the decision of NVN [North Vietnamese] leaders to abandon their hope for an outright military victory and to step up their diplomatic efforts in order to achieve their goals through political means."[21] Admiral U.S. Grant Sharp compared Linebacker to Rolling Thunder and concluded that reduced political restrictions made Linebacker effective. General William C. Westmoreland attributed the campaign's success to its intensity. He commented, "When President Nixon decided to use our available military power in a manner that truly hurt North Vietnam, negotiations began to move in a substantive way."[22] Perhaps the military's most representative assertion concerning Linebacker's impact came from the man responsible for its implementation. Speaking in 1978, General Vogt acknowledged that "after Linebacker I, the enemy was suing for peace. They were hurt real bad. Most of the major targets had been obliterated in the North . . . and they were ready to conclude an agreement."[23]

Thieu's refusal to accept the agreement revealed not only his desire to vanquish the Communists through Linebacker's assistance but also to demonstrate that he was no American lackey incapable of independent action. He argued with Kissinger for additional provisions in the agreement, but these proposals, Kissinger noted later, were a façade. He wrote, "We failed early enough to grasp that Thieu's real objection was not to terms but to the fact of *any* compromise. Conflict between us and Thieu was built into the termination of the war on any terms less than Hanoi's total surrender" (emphasis in original).[24] Viewing the concessions Linebacker helped to extract from Hanoi, Thieu reasoned that continued strikes could produce victory. The North Vietnamese army neared collapse with the ARVN poised to deliver a knockout blow. Additional bombing would only further weaken Hanoi's capacity to fight. Agreeing to the settlement, however, might lead to defeat. American withdrawal matched by a cease-fire committed Thieu to a political struggle against the disciplined organization of the Communists, and Thieu was unwilling to risk his demise either politically or militarily. Hanoi grasped the objective of Thieu's opposition. The Politburo understood—as did Thieu— that Nixon's commitment to "honor" prevented the president from considering a unilateral settlement. Having obtained a curtailment of bombing that would allow the receipt of overland supplies, Hanoi had no intention of granting Thieu added stature. Accordingly, Le Duc Tho rejected Kissinger's attempt to incorporate Thieu's proposals when negotiations reconvened in November.

Although Linebacker I did not result in an agreement, it did increase South Vietnam's chances for survival. The campaign helped wreck North Vietnam's military capability, ensuring that Hanoi could not soon launch another offensive. Linebacker also contributed heavily to wringing the concessions from Hanoi that Nixon considered essential to an "honorable peace." Still, the bombing did not end the war. After the December collapse of further negotiations in Paris, Nixon geared the next round of Linebacker toward compelling both his ally and the enemy to accomplish that goal.

Linebacker II, beginning in late 1972 and lasting less than two weeks, stressed maximum effort in minimum time against "the most lucrative and valuable targets in North Vietnam."[25] Whereas many of these targets matched ones raided in Linebacker I, Linebacker II relied almost exclusively on B-52s and was no interdiction campaign. While seeking to avoid civilian casualties, Nixon aimed Linebacker II at destroying North Vietnam's will. The president sought maximum psychological impact on the enemy to demonstrate that the United States would not stand for indefinite delay in the negotiations. The B-52, with its massive conventional bomb load and all-weather capability, provided the best tool that air power offered to disrupt an enemy psychologically. Attacking at altitudes of over 30,000 feet, the bomber could neither be seen nor heard by those on the ground. Admiral Thomas H. Moorer, chairman of the Joint Chiefs of Staff, directed General John C. Meyer, commander of the Strategic Air Command (SAC), "I want the people of Hanoi to hear the bombs, but minimize damage to the civilian populace."[26] B-52s would attack rail yards, storage areas, power plants, communication centers, and airfields located primarily on Hanoi's periphery. Using smart bombs, Seventh Air Force fighter-bombers would strike objectives in populated areas. Most targets were within ten nautical miles of Hanoi, forcing its inhabitants to respond to each attack. B-52s would strike throughout the night to prevent the populace from sleeping. These night raids would also reduce the Communist fighter threat, although the air force did not devise Linebacker II to achieve air superiority. The time constraints stemming from Congress's threat to curtail war funding in January dictated an immediate assault, and continual pressure was necessary to achieve results. SAC planners estimated that they would lose 3 percent of attacking B-52s to enemy defenses.[27] Nixon agreed that the bomber force would not emerge unscathed, confiding in his diary that "we simply have to take losses if we are going to accomplish our objectives."[28]

General Meyer's tactical deployment revealed his concern for Nixon's order to avoid civilian casualties. The president felt that indiscriminate raids might disrupt détente and persuade the Soviets and Chinese to increase support to Hanoi. As no SAC pilot had flown over Hanoi prior to December 18, Meyer demanded routes and formations for the first days to minimize chances of collateral damage. Major George Thompson, director of targets for Eighth Air Force Intelligence, observed that "we were not allowed to bomb many targets much more lucrative because of civilian casualties."[29] Using smart bombs during a rare period of good weather, Seventh Air Force F-4s attacked Thompson's choice for the most lucrative target in the country, the Hanoi Rail Yard. F-4s also destroyed Hanoi's surface-to-air missile assembly plant. The joint chiefs prohibited Meyer from striking the complex, claiming that B-52s would kill 24,000 civilians from the misses.[30] Eighth Air Force briefers instructed radar navigators to bring the bombs back if they were not 100 percent sure of their aiming point. All B-52 target maps contained the locations of schools, hospitals, and prisoner-of-war (POW) camps, and briefers cautioned crews when bomb runs neared such facilities.[31]

Despite efforts to restrict civilian casualties, Nixon realized that massive B-52 employment signaled an escalation in the war that would not go unnoticed by the public. Kissinger's declaration that "peace is at hand," followed by the resumption of talks, led many Americans to speculate that the war would end by Christmas. Instead, as the holiday season neared, Kissinger announced little progress in Paris, and Nixon, without explanation, unleashed the war's greatest aerial assault. "How did we get in a few short weeks from a prospect for peace that 'you can bank on,'" asked a *Washington Post* editorial on December 28, "to the most savage and senseless act of war ever visited, over a scant ten days, by one sovereign people upon another?"[32] Tom Wicker of the *New York Times* labeled the raids "Shame on Earth."[33] Much of the world press concurred with these viewpoints. The *Times* of London noted that Nixon's action was "not the conduct of a man who wants peace very badly," while Hamburg's *Die Zeit* concluded that "even allies must call this a crime against humanity."[34]

The surge of domestic criticism dismayed both American military and civilian leaders. "I cannot understand why it is that people in this country are so quick to accuse their own country of taking these kinds of actions [obliteration bombing] when they simply are not true," Admiral Moorer proclaimed in January 1973.[35] Nixon perceived the uproar as the media's first opportunity to strike out against his reelection. Both men, however, refused to answer the charges during the Linebacker campaign. Moorer feared that if he announced that most B-52 targets lay on Hanoi's periphery, this would allow the Communists to mass surface-to-air missiles for maximum effect. Nixon believed that any hint of the purpose of the attacks would appear as an ultimatum, and the North Vietnamese would delay their response to "save face."[36]

Democrats in Congress echoed the public outcry over Linebacker II, convincing Nixon that the campaign was his last chance to end the war "honorably." Senator Edward Kennedy stated that the raids "should outrage the conscience of all Americans." Senator William Saxbe contended that Nixon "had taken leave of his senses." Vowing to force an end to the war, Senate Majority Leader Michael Mansfield termed the bombing "a Stone Age tactic." Democratic representatives expressed similar sentiments.[37]

Fifteen B-52s were lost during the eleven-day span of Operation Linebacker II, but the 20,000 tons of bombs dropped helped to achieve Nixon's goals. The "Eleven Day War," from December 18 to December 30, 1972, was not the only reason for the 1973 peace accord, but it was the primary one. Nixon's promise of a future Linebacker campaign should Hanoi violate the agreement and refuse a settlement, combined with the congressional furor stemming from the raids, finally gained Thieu's support and forced the Politburo to accept terms.

Nixon did not easily gain Thieu's backing. The South Vietnamese leader rejected Nixon's mid-December ultimatum to back the American proposal or settle separately, asserting that he could not accept the continued presence of North Vietnamese troops in the South. Nixon believed a break with Thieu justifiable, yet the president hesitated to take such a step. "I was still reluctant to allow our annoyance with him to lead us to do anything that might bring about Communist domination of South Vietnam," Nixon explained.[38] On January 5 Nixon again wrote Thieu, emphasizing that Hanoi's acceptance of the agreement's November text with one or two changes would result in a settlement. The president warned that many congressmen, angered by Linebacker II, would vote to stop Saigon's funding if Thieu spurned an accord. Nixon ended by reiterating his November pledge: "Should you decide, as I trust you will, to go with us, you have my assurance of continued assistance in the post-settlement period and that we will respond with full force should the settlement be violated by North Vietnam."[39] Thieu's January 7 reply was noncommittal.

After Kissinger and Le Duc Tho decided on the text of the agreement in Paris, Nixon sent General Alexander Haig to Saigon on January 14 in a final attempt to gain Thieu's approval. The general delivered a letter from Nixon that stated:

> I have . . . irrevocably decided to proceed to initial the Agreement on January 23, 1973 and to sign it on January 27, 1973 in Paris. I will do so, if necessary, alone. In that case I shall have to explain publicly that your Government obstructs peace. The result will be an inevitable and immediate termination of U.S. economic and military assistance which cannot be forestalled by a change of personnel in your government.[40]

Arguing for Thieu's consent, the president again promised to react strongly if the North Vietnamese violated the agreement. On January 17 Thieu requested an additional negotiating session. Nixon replied that further changes were impossible, demanding a final response from Thieu by the morning of January 20. On that date the South Vietnamese president dispatched Foreign Minister Tram Van Lam to Paris to participate in the negotiations. Kissinger deemed this measure "a face-saving formula" for Thieu to indicate consent for the agreement.[41]

Thieu's stalling resulted more from a desire to salvage prestige than from opposition to an accord. The South Vietnamese president had told his military chiefs in November to prepare for a cease-fire by Christmas. Haig departed from Saigon in that month, convinced that Thieu knew that total intransigence would lead to a cutoff in aid. Thieu realized that Nixon would not seek an agreement significantly improved over the October draft, although Thieu also understood that Nixon's commitment to "honor" prevented the president from forsaking Saigon until the last possible moment. Similarly, Thieu's desire to demonstrate independence precluded an early acceptance of Nixon's terms. Linebacker II gave credibility to both the promise of continued American support and Nixon's willingness to use air power to uphold an agreement. The campaign further sparked a congressional demand to end the war. Congress threatened to terminate support for Saigon should Thieu reject a negotiated settlement. The South Vietnamese president could not risk losing the American support that he considered essential for survival. Thus, Thieu acquiesced to the accord, but not before Nixon's deadline.[42]

Fear of renewal of Linebacker II persuaded Hanoi to conclude a settlement. Continued détente prevented North Vietnam from receiving additional Soviet assistance, and Hanoi had not fully recovered from Linebacker I. Linebacker II destroyed the supplies stockpiled during the preceding two months and, combined with mining, isolated Hanoi and Haiphong. Although impressed by the damage inflicted by Linebacker II, the North Vietnamese were more impressed by its magnitude. In eleven days aircraft dropped 13 percent of the tonnage deposited during the five months of Linebacker I. Unlike the earlier campaign, Linebacker II continued night after night regardless of weather. Defenses failed to deter the strikes. Only when Hanoi promised to negotiate did the raids stop, and "the threat of renewed and effective bombing," an American negotiator in Paris recalled, "was implied in all that we signed with Hanoi."[43] The Politburo could not afford to ignore that threat. Continued bombing would not only further disrupt an already disoriented populace but also endanger its survival. The North Vietnamese had not built sufficient food reserves to endure a sustained air campaign, and by December 29 they had exhausted their supply of surface-to-air missiles, making defense impossible.[44] At the Paris meetings in January, Kissinger noted that Le Duc Tho's "mood and businesslike approach was as close to October as we have seen since October." "What has brought us to this point," the national security adviser continued, "is the President's firmness and the North Vietnamese belief that he will not be affected by either congressional or public pressures. Le Duc Tho has repeatedly made these points to me."[45]

Compared with the damage inflicted, Linebacker II caused few civilian casualties even though the bombing unsettled North Vietnam's populace. Hanoi's mayor claimed 1,318 civilians killed and 1,216 wounded, and Haiphong reported 305 dead.[46] The low toll resulted both from B-52 targeting and evacuations. Acknowledging the accuracy of the raids, the journalist Tammy Arbuckle observed during a trip to Hanoi in March 1973, "Pictures and some press reports had given a visitor the impression Hanoi had suffered badly in the war—but in fact the city is hardly touched."[47] Evacuations from the capital occurred throughout Linebacker II. The writer Michael Allen, in Hanoi with Telford Taylor on Christmas Day, observed numerous buses evacuating people to the countryside. Those remaining in Hanoi received only an hour or two of sleep per night, their nerves strained by the continual assaults. Foreigners in the

Gia Lam airport discovered workers wandering around completely disoriented following a strike.[48] American POWs witnessed a more graphic consequence of Linebacker II. The former commander James B. Stockdale, a POW for over seven years, recalled,

> when the ground shook, and the plaster fell from the ceiling. . . .
> [T]he guards cowered in the lee of the walls, cheeks so ashen you
> could detect it even from the light from the fiery sky. . . . [B]y day,
> interrogators and guards would inquire about our needs solicitously.
> The center of Hanoi was dead—even though like our prisons, thou-
> sands of yards from the drop zone. We knew the bombers knew
> where we were, and felt not only ecstatically happy, but confident.
> The North Vietnamese didn't. . . . They knew they lived through last
> night, but they also knew that if our forces moved their bomb line
> over a few thousand yards they wouldn't live through tonight.[49]

The havoc created by Linebacker II deterred Hanoi from its goal of an eleventh-hour victory over the United States. After Linebacker I, the North Vietnamese repaired the rail lines leading to China, resulting in a massive influx of Soviet supplies. Guaranteed a short-term logistical base, the Politburo then strove to delay an agreement. Hanoi perceived that Saigon's dissatisfaction with the October accord, combined with the imminent return of Congress, provided a chance to achieve the triumph denied Giap's army. Realizing that Nixon would attempt to modify the settlement, the Politburo sought to prolong negotiations until Congress terminated U.S. involvement. American withdrawal would allow Hanoi to renew military operations unhampered logistically, whereas a curtailment of support for the south would soon deplete its supply of American-made weaponry. Politburo members believed that Thieu's government could not survive if abandoned by the United States, and they did not think Nixon would willingly shun Saigon. Surmising that Nixon might resume Linebacker I to spur the talks, the Politburo ordered the evacuation of old folks, women, and children from Hanoi on December 4. In the midst of the northeast monsoon season and with sufficient matériel, the North Vietnamese felt secure against the resumption of fighter-bomber raids north of the twentieth parallel.[50]

The Politburo did not expect Linebacker II, and its magnitude tempered the North Vietnamese response. On the eve of the assault, Radio Hanoi reiterated Le Duc Tho's pleas that "the U.S. side adhere to the context of the agreement mutually agreed to on 20 October and sign that agreement without further delay."[51] Vice Foreign Minister Nguyen Co Thatch, North Vietnam's representative to the technical discussions accompanying the sessions between Kissinger and Le Duc Tho, provided Hanoi's first reaction to the bombing. Kissinger termed Thatch's adjournment of talks from December 20 to December 23 "a minimum gesture under the circumstances." The denunciation of the raids by the northern negotiator Nguyen Minh Vy at the public discussion on December 21 also included a promise to renew talks on December 28. Arriving in Washington on December 26, Kissinger was prompted by Hanoi's call for a resumption of the Kissinger–Le Duc Tho sessions to comment, "We had not heard such a polite tone from the North Vietnamese since the middle of October." Nixon responded to Nguyen Minh Vy on December 27 with his "conditions" for a return to negotiations: discussions between Kissinger and Le Duc Tho's technical experts must begin on January 2; formal negotiations would begin on the eighth, with a time limit attached; and the North Vietnamese would not reinitiate deliberations on matters covered by the basic agreement. Acceptance of these procedures would result in an end to bombing north of the twentieth parallel within thirty-six hours. The Politburo's approval arrived in Washington in less than twenty-four hours—"an amazing feat," Kissinger noted, "considering the time needed for transmission to and from Paris and the time differences."[52]

In deciding to settle, Hanoi abandoned its attempt to score a belated success over the United States, but the north did not surrender its goal of unifying Vietnam. The Politburo gambled that Nixon's commitment to "honor" prevented him from discarding many of Thieu's demands and that the president's fear of public and congressional denunciation forestalled a massive military response. The bid failed. Nixon answered Le Duc Tho's stalling with Linebacker II on December 18. Soon afterward, Hanoi learned of Nixon's ultimatum to Thieu.[53] By the tenth day of Linebacker, North Vietnam's defenseless nature compelled negotiation, the only alternative Nixon offered to continued attack. Threatening to renew Linebacker if the Communists again proved intransigent, the president increased bombing below the twentieth parallel. Bomber efforts against Giap's army in January jumped from thirty-five strikes a day to fifty.[54] Hanoi could ill-afford destruction of those forces which provided a base for future activity in the south. And yet, concluding an agreement presented the Politburo with three advantages. First and most important, a negotiated settlement would end American involvement. Battered by Linebacker, the north could follow without interruption the reconsolidation policy of Truong Chinh, the chairman of the National Assembly. Meanwhile, Congress might curtail funding to South Vietnam. Second, an accord would "legally" permit the north to maintain its army in the south. Finally, an agreement would involve minimal "loss of face." Knowing that

Nixon planned to settle regardless of Thieu's temperament, the Politburo felt that it would concede nothing to Saigon by signing an accord. Hanoi's major concessions remained those surrendered to Kissinger in October, and the Politburo perceived that Thieu's influence on the January terms was minimal.

At his news conference on January 24, Kissinger voiced approval of the agreement. "It is clear," he commented, "there is no legal way by which North Vietnam can use military force against South Vietnam." He then added, "now, whether that is due to the fact there are two zones temporarily divided by a provisional demarcation line or because North Vietnam is a foreign country with relation to South Vietnam—that is an issue which we have avoided making explicit in the agreement, and in which ambiguity has its merits."[55] In all likelihood the Politburo concurred.

American civilian and military leaders believed that Linebacker was the major reason that the Communists agreed to a settlement. "The bombing had done its job," Nixon later reflected.[56] Kissinger asserted that Linebacker II "speeded the end of the war," adding, "even in retrospect I can think of no other measure that would have."[57] Admiral Moorer and the air force chiefs thought that the campaign vindicated strategic bombing. Moorer remarked, "Airpower, given its day in court after almost a decade of frustration, confirmed its effectiveness as an instrument of national power—in just nine and a half flying days."[58] Generals Meyer and Vogt shared Moorer's opinion.[59]

The conviction that air power played a decisive role in gaining an agreement permeated the air force. Commanders cited participation in Linebacker II on officer efficiency reports. Major Clyde E. Bodenheimer, who viewed the assault from Eighth Air Force Headquarters at Guam, asserted that Linebacker II "was the single, most important action in the Vietnam campaign which convinced the North Vietnamese that they should negotiate."[60] Major Robert D. Clark felt that the operation in which he flew three missions "was something that had been long overdue, because in an eleven day period we brought their [North Vietnam's] civilization . . . to a grinding, screeching halt." Clark, however, did not believe that Linebacker II gained "peace with honor." "There was no way we could do that," Clark contended. "The fact we retreated nullifies the words."[61]

Nixon disagreed with Clark's assessment. The settlement ended direct U.S. involvement in the war—a goal since Johnson curtailed bombing on March 31, 1968—and gained the return of American prisoners. Both Nixon and his predecessor had fought for limited political ends. Despite Sir Robert Thompson's charge that after Linebacker II the North Vietnamese "would have taken any terms,"[62] Nixon's goals during the January negotiations remained the ones espoused almost a year earlier. To the president, the Linebacker-facilitated agreement achieved those objectives. South Vietnam remained an independent, non-Communist state with a chance for survival. That survival rested on American support and, if necessary, the reapplication of air power. Kissinger commented,

> We had no illusions about Hanoi's long term goals. Nor did we go through the agony of four years of war and searing negotiations simply to achieve a "decent interval" for our withdrawal. We were determined to do our utmost to enable Saigon to grow in security and prosperity so that it could prevail in any political struggle. We sought not an interval before collapse, but lasting peace with honor.[63]

The Linebacker campaigns ensured that Hanoi would not soon attempt major military operations, permitting Vietnamization to continue unhindered. Nixon thought that Linebacker boosted American prestige by demonstrating U.S. resolve to defend an ally.

Nixon's willingness to defend South Vietnam after Linebacker ended was never tested. When the North Vietnamese army rolled across the seventeenth parallel in March 1975, Nixon was no longer president, and Congress precluded a military response. The peace gained by Linebacker proved only an interval.

The Linebacker campaign complemented the traditional American employment of air power and played a significant role in securing Nixon's war aims, but the bombing alone could not have achieved those aims. The decisive results in Vietnam in 1972–73 resulted from the diplomatic isolation of an enemy highly dependent upon foreign aid and waging conventional warfare, the careful cultivation of public support, a shrewd mating of means to carefully delineated ends, and the relative military freedom to utilize the means to best advantage. Whether Linebacker-type operations in 1965 would have achieved success, as some military and civilian critics maintain, is problematical, since conditions were fundamentally different. Still, the Linebacker campaigns do demonstrate that under certain circumstances, air power can be a useful tool in conducting diplomacy "by other means."

PART 2

The Home Front

Cold War, Limited War, and Limited Equality: Blacks in the U.S. Armed Forces, 1945–1970

ROBERT F. BURK

THE POSTWAR YEARS in America have been marked by the global super-power confrontation with the Soviet Union and the search for racial justice at home. During the 1960s in particular, the escalation of the war in Southeast Asia ran parallel to the rise of direct-action racial protest, new civil rights legislation of the Great Society, and the emergence of Black Power ideology. Still, students of the postwar period have placed relatively little emphasis on the relationship between these two preeminent issues, even within an institution deeply affected by both of them—America's armed forces. For it was during this unprecedented era of nuclear escalation, limited wars, and Cold War ushered in at the end of World War II that American political leaders slowly took steps toward removing long-standing practices of racial segregation and discrimination in the military. Fearing racial violence, desiring Cold War domestic unity, and wishing to counter Soviet charges of American colonialism and racism in the Third World, presidential administrations sought visible, symbolic progress in race relations within the military. The formal barriers were largely removed over the course of twenty-five years, but other, less easily countered forms of racial inequality continued to perplex military commanders and their civilian leaders.[1]

In the postwar period the armed forces of the United States offered a logical starting point for action by presidents concerned about the nation's racial image, for they were among the most visible of American official representatives around the globe. Racial progress in the military might rally black citizens to support foreign and defense policies, and it could contribute to winning the propaganda battle of the Cold War. Desegregated black troops in Third World settings could help to reassure foreign peoples of America's repudiation of colonialism. As an issue in domestic politics, racial desegregation and nondiscrimination in the military also carried less risk of white southern fallout on states'-rights grounds, for the armed forces were clearly under federal jurisdiction. In short, a "color-blind" American military would symbolize a nation united in support of democratic principles and determined to halt Communist expansion and totalitarianism.

Still, deep-seated reservations came from those directly involved in implementing presidential antidiscrimination initiatives. Commanders asked whether the attempt to revamp the military's racial arrangements would lessen the combat effectiveness of American forces and thereby hamper the nation's ability to conduct limited conventional war. Would the armed forces become a "sociological laboratory" at the cost of ceasing to be an efficient fighting machine? With such doubts in mind, how thoroughly should administrations pursue the goal of military racial reform? Was a clean image sufficient, or was the actualization of racial equality required? Throughout the Cold War, from training bases in the American South to Korea to Vietnam, the tug-of-war between readiness and racial equality continued to vex presidents and military commanders alike. For the black soldier, sailor, and airman fighting in America's limited wars against communism, nondiscrimination produced a paradoxical, limited equality and a sharply restricted opportunity.

By the end of World War II, a number of forces had converged to provide a new impetus for racial reform in official America. Intensified partisan competition and close elections encouraged both major political parties to vie for a growing number of black voters in northern urban districts. Although in later years the Democratic party came to rely upon the almost complete loyalty of the black vote, such assumptions of partisan fealty were far riskier in the 1940s. Northeastern Republicans controlled their party's presidential nomination process throughout the 1940s and 1950s, and they were more receptive to minority interests than was the Republican party as a whole. A number of prominent national Republicans, such as presidential candidates Wendell Willkie and Thomas E. Dewey, Senators Henry Cabot Lodge of Massachusetts and Irving Ives of New York, and Congressmen (later senators) Jacob Javits of New York and Hugh Scott of Pennsylvania, were public supporters of civil rights measures, including racial reform in the armed forces.[2]

The less predictable level of black support for the Democrats, part of a general erosion of Democratic electoral strength in the 1940s, coincided with renewed migrations of blacks to northern cities in the decade and with dramatic increases in the size, financial resources, and visibility of civil rights organizations. The National Association for the Advancement of Colored People (NAACP), for example, grew from approximately 50,000 members in 1940 to seven times that number by 1945. Other organizations experienced similarly dramatic increases. Such growth strengthened the hands of civil rights leaders in their dealings with politicians and government officials of both parties. On the basis of increased political clout, they could and did press for a "two-front" war during and after World War II against both foreign totalitarianism and American racism. In his book *A Rising Wind,* the secretary of the NAACP, Walter White, predicted wholesale postwar abandonment of the peoples of Asia into the Soviet orbit if America, including its representatives in the military services, failed to measure up to the promise of racial equality.[3]

Not all American officials, to be sure, were as troubled as civil rights leaders at the moral gap between national democratic ideals and actual racial practices. Nevertheless, they could not ignore the risks either of domestic racial violence and disunity or of the damage to U.S. prestige abroad created by official bigotry. By the end of World War II, a growing number of politicians at the national level, whether conservative or liberal on other issues, shared the belief that official American racial practices required modification. The hypocrisy of a Jim Crow America fighting to defeat Nazi racist totalitarianism had already helped trigger violent racial outbreaks in the military and a major race riot in Detroit in 1943. With the Cold War already looming on the horizon, American officials could not afford to expose the country's foreign or domestic policies to Soviet charges of deliberate racism.[4]

Federal government actions were necessary to demonstrate the official American commitment to racial justice at home and abroad, but the wisdom of such steps had to be measured against the relatively low level of support for them among the white public and in Congress. By the late 1940s most white Americans were either unaware or unconcerned with racial segregation in the armed forces, and white support for any changes in racial matters became clear only in the drives for antilynching and anti–poll-tax legislation. Alterations in official racial practices which required legislative action also faced southern congressional opposition— an especially formidable barrier because of southern control of key committees. Political realities, therefore, encouraged executive-branch officials concerned about America's postwar racial image to rule out legislative remedies initially and to focus upon executive initiatives that would neither raise federal-state jurisdictional issues nor generate racial confrontations at home.[5]

The armed forces seemed to offer such an area in which to accomplish visible, yet relatively noncontroversial, racial progress. Accordingly, the first halting steps toward formal desegregation and nondiscrimination followed the wartime disputes over segregation and the growing pressure from civil rights leaders. During World War II itself, most military leaders had interpreted the Selective Service and Training Act as endorsing "separate but equal" facilities. Although Walter White and A. Philip Randolph, civil rights leader and head of the Brotherhood of Sleeping Car Porters, had urged President Franklin D. Roosevelt to order integration, military commanders had rejected the notion as "destructive to morale." During the crisis days of the Battle of the Bulge in the winter of 1944–45, the Supreme Commander of Europe, Dwight D. Eisenhower, temporarily released blacks from the supply services for duty as riflemen in integrated units, but he quickly countermanded his order on the advice of his chief of staff, Walter Bedell Smith. A belated reevaluation of service racial policies did occur, however, largely due to manpower needs, wartime pressures from black servicemen and leaders, the documented bravery of black personnel, and the moral requirements of the war against the Nazis. In 1945 a three-man military board, headed by Lieutenant General A. C. Gillem, recommended the gradual abolition of all-black divisions.[6]

Despite the Gillem report, government action was not swift. It was not until the following year that, in response to fears of racial violence expressed by civil rights leaders, President Harry S. Truman pledged to create a committee to study racial problems in America. To Truman's credit, he did not pack the committee with obstructionists, and the report of the Committee on Civil Rights in 1947 contained among its recommendations the end of segregation and official discrimination in the military services and in other federal agencies. On the basis of that body's findings, and needing political support from liberals and blacks for his reelection bid, Truman submitted a sweeping civil rights message to Congress on February 2, 1948. Still, his proposals did not specifically indicate that he would immediately use his powers as commander in chief to end segregation in the military. According to the recollection of a Truman aide, the strategy was "to start with a bold measure and then temporize to pick up the right-wing forces."[7]

Truman eventually issued an executive order proclaiming a policy of equal opportunity and desegregation in the armed forces, but only after additional political developments in the summer of 1948 forced his hand.

Besides his fear of losing southern Democratic support, Truman's hesitancy had stemmed from the skepticism expressed toward racial integration by military commanders, who anticipated declines in morale and readiness. He finally moved after Dixiecrats walked out of the Democratic convention and A. Philip Randolph threatened to lead a black boycott against the military draft. With the southerners' pullout, the president had little more to lose politically by issuing an antidiscrimination order to the armed forces. Moreover, he had black support to regain and civil unrest to head off by doing so. In addition to the order requiring formal military nondiscrimination, a second Truman directive created a seven-member advisory committee, headed by the former solicitor general Charles Fahy, to supervise a program for ending military segregation.[8]

Few could question the military's need for such guidance. By the middle of 1949, no blacks served as officers in the navy or marines, and the highest percentage of black officers in any service branch was the army's 1.8 percent. Nearly four hundred all-black units still existed in the armed forces at the beginning of the Korean War. Widespread discrimination remained in assignments, transfers, promotions, housing, and education. For its part, the Fahy Committee's report of 1950 spurred the armed services' desegregation effort by establishing a target date of summer 1954 for the abolition of all-black units. Goaded by the report, by Soviet propaganda attacks on American racism, and by the need for additional troops to fulfill the Truman administration's new defense buildup and the requirements of the "police action" in Korea, the military made impressive gains in desegregation. The air force and marines, owing to their small numbers of black enlistees, finished desegregating their units by late 1952. Although the army's progress was slower, by August 1953 only eighty-eight all-black units remained.[9]

Despite the relatively rapid progress in implementing formal desegregation, the armed forces continued to worry about the impact of integration on efficiency and morale, given the American military's expanded role as global frontline of the Free World in the Cold War. For its part, the army commissioned tests to determine the attitudes of servicemen toward the changes and provide warning of impending problems. One such study, "Project Clear," indicated encouraging changes in the attitudes of white soldiers. Most GIs surveyed judged that the performances of integrated units were equal to those of segregated ones, and that white soldiers' estimation of integrated units appeared to increase with actual experience in them. Seventy-three percent of more than 4,000 northern whites questioned and 65 percent of more than 500 southern whites claimed black friends, although only 19 percent said they spent off-duty time with them.

A large majority of interviewees in Korea approved sharing post exchanges with black soldiers, and a smaller majority also favored sharing rest areas.[10]

Despite the early progress in integrating units, a wide range of less overt forms of discrimination persisted. Blacks faced continuing obstacles in gaining promotions or transfers; service designations still contained racial labels; housing, whether due to local custom or seniority systems based on prior discrimination, remained segregated and unequal; and educational facilities for black servicemen and dependents remained subject to Jim Crow practices of local communities. Overseas the picture was strikingly similar, with most nations' own concepts of race and caste adding new obstacles for the black serviceman to overcome. Private policies of segregation and discrimination also carried over to the treatment of black civilian workers employed on federal military property. An internal navy memorandum of January 1952 endorsed such policies by sanctioning segregated accommodations for civilians when consistent with "local custom."[11]

A new president well versed in the problem of military integration, Dwight D. Eisenhower, assumed the responsibility for completing the nondiscrimination program of his predecessor in January 1953. But owing to his own training and socialization in the segregated U.S. Army, Eisenhower was not eager to advance race relations in the military beyond carrying out the previous administration's symbolically important integration plan. Indeed, while army chief of staff in 1948, he had testified before Congress against integrating military units below the platoon level, citing the harm it would cause black promotion chances and insisting that "if we attempt merely by passing a lot of laws to force someone to like someone else, we are just going to get into trouble." Notwithstanding his campaign claims in 1952 that implementation of nondiscrimination in the armed forces would proceed more rapidly and smoothly with a military man in the White House, Eisenhower intended to follow the preferences of field commanders for an unobtrusive, gradual introduction of formal desegregation.[12]

Unfortunately for the new president, black correspondents, activists, and politicians were determined to increase pressure for full implementation of nondiscrimination orders. Only two months into his term, Eisenhower was confronted by an Associated Negro Press correspondent, Alice Dunnegan, inquiring about the continued existence of segregated schools in southern army bases. In a presidential statement on March 25, 1953, Eisenhower announced the banning, by autumn, of segregation in post schools completely operated by the federal government (a decree affecting only one post school), but two days later the Department of Health, Education and Welfare (HEW) identified twenty-one segregated schools on military bases unaffected by Eisenhower's order. Further fuel for the controversy came from Congressman Adam Clayton Powell, Jr., whose public telegram to the White House charging the administration with ignoring its own desegregation directives hit the Washington, D.C. front pages on June 3.[13]

Despite repeated assurances from the Defense Department and HEW, it was not until the fall of 1955, after the Brown integration decisions, that the administration began final integration of base schools. Even then, two schools with long-term leases received extended exemptions from desegregation, and, over NAACP protests, the navy leased on-base buildings in New Orleans for a new, all-white school. Making matters worse, none of the government's actions altered the segregation of military dependents attending outside schools or the segregation of college facilities in the South for servicemen themselves. Black servicemen in the South, depending upon the educational policies of different states, were either denied on-post opportunities altogether or had to attend an all-black school with inferior resources. The air force, in attempting to get around the segregationist practices of southern states without directly challenging them, gave black airmen the option of attending all-black facilities or going to desegregated schools in other states. Black servicemen, like blacks in general, waited until well into the 1960s for the opportunity to attend integrated southern colleges in significant numbers.[14]

For servicemen and civilians alike, formal integration of military units also failed to provide comprehensive desegregation of base accommodations and housing. Following the charges by Powell in June 1953, Secretary of the Navy Robert Anderson ordered desegregation of facilities on navy bases and shipyards in August, and by the end of November only one of sixty bases remained unconverted. The army, however, with more facilities and more black personnel to integrate, proved slower to respond, and even then it only "encouraged" rather than ordered the elimination of Jim Crow practices on its property. Even after the eventual elimination of regulations requiring segregated base housing, assignments based on rank or seniority, combined with shortages in military housing, forced black personnel to seek off-base dwellings and heightened their likelihood of exposure to civilian racism in transportation, dining, and other accommodations. Similar patterns of discrimination pervaded the military health-care system, with many Veterans' Administration (VA) hospitals in the South continuing segregation by wards and dining areas and providing inferior care to blacks. Despite documented cases of discrimination,

HEW continued to provide federal money to offending VA facilities until well into the 1960s.[15]

One of the most blatant areas of segregation in the military establishment, and one especially damaging to the national image, remained virtually untouched throughout the 1950s—the National Guard and Reserves. The propaganda damage from this failure was particularly harmful because of the guard's symbolism as the modern-day equivalent of the Revolutionary-era "citizen-soldier." In 1954 the army issued a directive ordering the removal of racial designations from the reassignment orders of Reserve unit members. The administration, however, helped to defeat repeated attempts by Congressman Powell in the House of Representatives to legislate the desegregation of the guard and Reserves. By 1960 the National Guard and Air National Guard remained segregated in sixteen states and the District of Columbia. As late as the end of 1961, ten states still excluded blacks from guard and Reserve units. Civil Defense and Civil Air Patrol programs also remained virtually all white, and southern cities even maintained segregated fallout shelters.[16]

Given the symbolic value of a "color-blind" American military in the emerging Third World battleground of the Cold War, blacks might have expected better treatment in overseas postings. Such was not the case. Black servicemen abroad found themselves caught in a crossfire between military officials who continued to blame integration of units for insufficient readiness and the continued mistrust and discrimination of white enlistees and host peoples. In 1960, prompted by an air force reprint of Hanson W. Baldwin's Reader's Digest article, "Our Fighting Men Have Gone Soft," Representative Charles Diggs of Michigan launched his own fact-finding excursion in air force bases in the Pacific. Baldwin had blamed integration in part for lowering the quality of American troops stationed abroad, but Diggs's report placed greater fault with the half-hearted implementation of antidiscrimination decrees and the resultant low troop morale. Black airmen complained that they and their dependents received unequal treatment in housing and other accommodations and that symbols of white racism continued unchecked, including cross-burnings and the display of Confederate flags.[17]

Black hopes for remedial action to end military discrimination were raised anew in 1960 by the election of John F. Kennedy to the presidency. Although the Massachusetts Democrat provided few specifics during the fall campaign, antidiscrimination advocates interpreted his October intercession on behalf of jailed civil rights leader Martin Luther King, Jr., as a positive indicator. Like his predecessors, however, Kennedy hesitated to take other than symbolic steps in military nondiscrimination unless politically forced to do so. At his inaugural, Kennedy did notice the absence of blacks in the coast guard's contingent, and his inquiry led to the uncovering and reversal of a "whites only" policy at the Coast Guard Academy. Kennedy also prodded Defense Secretary Robert McNamara into providing more black servicemen for honor guard units. Still, for nearly a year and a half, the president refused to respond to the continuing segregation problems on southern military facilities, overseas bases, and in guard and Reserve units. Although Assistant Secretary of Defense Carlisle P. Runge announced in 1961 that gradual progress in Reserve units could be accomplished by assigning blacks to already activated units, Assistant Secretary of the Army Ralph Horton warned against additional steps because of the opposition of the powerful Senate Armed Services Committee chairman, Richard Russell of Georgia.[18]

Kennedy himself did not respond until the early summer of 1962, after having been put under pressure by civil rights leaders and challenged to act by the October 1961 report of the U.S. Commission on Civil Rights. In April the Defense Department finally ordered the integration of six remaining all-black Reserve units, and within a year formal integration was accomplished. More important, in June the president appointed a special committee on equal opportunity in the military, headed by a Washington, D.C., lawyer, Gerhard A. Gesell, and including such luminaries as the attorney Abe Fortas and the executive director of the National Urban League, Whitney M. Young, Jr. Before announcing the creation of the Gesell Committee, Kennedy had been informed through the civil rights adviser Lee White that the Pentagon would not object to a fact-finding committee if its focus was narrowed to domestic installations and it did not assume any enforcement function. Accordingly, Kennedy charged the committee to study "problems of equal opportunity affecting Negro military personnel on and off base within the United States," while solutions would be left in the hands of "responsible citizens of all races in those communities."[19]

After the publication of the Gesell Committee's first report in June 1963, only five months before Kennedy's assassination in Dallas, Defense Secretary McNamara issued a formal directive threatening sanctions against those who discriminated against black servicemen in off-base accommodations. Unfortunately the action, part of the administration's civil rights offensive following the March on Washington and the demonstrations in Birmingham, carried little bite behind the rhetoric. Kennedy did authorize the Gesell Committee to launch a second investigation into the treatment of servicemen abroad and into continued segregation in the National Guard and Reserves, but the findings were not released until

November 30, 1964, months after the passage of the Civil Rights Act of 1964 in July and several weeks after Lyndon B. Johnson's landslide election victory over Barry Goldwater. Despite McNamara's call for an "affirmative commitment" to nondiscrimination by the Defense Department, follow-up in the Johnson administration remained sluggish. Within the Defense Department itself, structural changes created a better chain of accountability, and President Johnson appointed the first black deputy secretary of defense, James Davenport. Still, with the administration increasingly preoccupied with the war in Vietnam, a minimal amount of actual desegregation occurred that affected the guard, Reserves, and overseas bases. As late as 1967, the Kerner Commission reported that blacks made up barely 1 percent of Army National Guardsmen and 0.6 percent of the Air National Guard.[20]

During the racial turbulence of the 1950s and 1960s, the focus of military officials in the Eisenhower, Kennedy, and Johnson administrations remained on implementing formal desegregation and nondiscrimination in the armed forces without provoking additional racial conflict through haste or "excessive" thoroughness in detail. As a consequence, although black servicemen in general found their opportunities less restricted than before, individual cases of discrimination and racism continued to mar the military's record. Despite this imperfect record, black hopes of advancement in the military ranks proved less frequently thwarted in the 1960s by the traditional forms of segregation and discrimination than by newer and more elusive patterns of unequal opportunity. As early as 1959, the racial adviser to the Defense Department, James C. Evans, hinted at the emerging dilemma when he noted that "segregation" and "overt discrimination" were yielding as his chief concerns to the problem of the "refinement" of equality in the rank and distribution of black personnel. The American military would increasingly find that formal segregation was no longer the main problem. Instead, officials would uncover an increasing and disquieting concentration of black servicemen in lower echelons and a corresponding dearth of black officers. In short, they would discover an emerging black "underclass" in the armed forces.[21]

Even in the formally segregated U.S. military, black concentration in menial service categories had been a persistent if overlooked problem. For critics of military racial policies in the early 1950s, the most glaring example had been the Stewards' Branch of the U.S. Navy, which had employed half of the service's blacks on mess duty. Adam Clayton Powell had denounced the Stewards' Branch as a "modernized, 20th century form of slavery" and had added, "No one is interested in today's world in fighting communism with a frying pan or shoe polish." The navy had recognized its image problem, for a research committee headed by Commander Durward Gilmore advised paying "particular attention" to the Stewards' Branch. "The segregation in that branch is a sore spot with the Negroes," Gilmore noted, "and it is our weakest position from the standpoint of public relations." In rectifying the situation, however, the navy faced a continuing obstacle that would frustrate other services also developing their own black "underclasses"—large-scale black voluntary enlistment, owing to the lack of civilian opportunities, and reenlistment rates of over 80 percent. The navy phased out its separate recruitment of black stewards, but with whites not reassigned to stewards' duty and black enlistments remaining high, the problem persisted. By the late 1950s a slight improvement had occurred in the percentages of blacks in categories other than the Stewards' Branch, but a closer examination of the statistics revealed that the small percentage gains were attributable to declines in white enlistments in the 1950s, or "white flight," rather than to an actual increase in the number of black seamen in other branches.[22]

The navy was by no means alone in its problem. Throughout the services, white flight from lower ranks, an increase in minority enlistments (often from those of low income and educational training), and the growing bureaucratic and technical demands of military service all contributed to the growth and concentration of the black military "underclass" from the 1950s into the 1960s. Hopes disappeared in the U.S. Army–European Theater (USAEUR), for example, of a 10 percent maximum black quota for all units. At many stations, even revised limits of 12 percent for combat units and 18 percent for service units were soon exceeded. Other commanders, still skeptical of their black soldiers' ability to perform in combat, adhered to the prior limits, sometimes using disciplinary actions as an excuse. USAEUR admitted to withholding reenlistment from soldiers "whose conduct has been prejudicial to the integration program in a disciplinary sense or who had discredited the U.S. Army in the eyes of the European public." It conceded that a "large proportion" of those dismissed were blacks.[23]

One possible solution to the insufficient number of black officers was to institute greater efforts at recruiting better-educated enlistees. Service promotional literature traditionally had failed to highlight career possibilities for young blacks with requisite skills. Once in the military, structural obstacles to promotion also limited black upward mobility. Promotion boards, manned by officers above the rank of colonel in the army and captain in the navy, both reflected and perpetuated white dominance of the officer ranks, and personnel folders of applicants for promotion still included photographs and other racial identification materials in the

1950s. Not surprisingly, the navy, for its part, contained only about one hundred commissioned black officers by 1955, and well into the 1960s attempts by all of the service branches to increase the black officer pool were frustrated by southern legal obstacles to black admission to colleges offering ROTC training. Even at the three largest service academies, blacks in 1957 numbered only twenty-one out of approximately seven thousand cadets.[24]

Although the armed forces began to modify their recruitment policies in the 1950s by attempting to increase the number of better-educated minority servicemen, the efforts remained inadequate because of the reliance upon subjective mental aptitude measurements which disproportionately screened out black recruits for higher responsibilities. Beginning in 1952, at the very time that formal desegregation was being phased in, Defense Department concerns with force efficiency and readiness led it to mandate a recruitment quota system based upon intelligence tests. Of the four different "mental group" categories drawn up, the Defense Department had aimed for reductions in the number of enlistees in the lower category, or "Group IV." As the services attempted to meet the guidelines, they soon discovered that full compliance with the intelligence quota system cost them minority recruits. In 1959 the navy and air force requested an abeyance of "qualitative recruiting" after experiencing manpower problems, and the navy's figures showed that nearly 70 percent of its black recruits in the previous five years had been in Group IV and 90 percent in either groups III or IV. The navy report pointed out the dilemma that whereas continuation of qualitative recruiting would lead to reduced minority enlistments and charges of discrimination, its suspension would create a situation in which "the only alternative which would permit maintaining present Caucasian/Negro ratios would be to actively recruit Negroes in the higher mental groups. This solution would not be without pitfalls, as quotas would have to be established which might result in more accusations of discrimination."[25]

The dramatic increases in conventional military spending, the "flight" of white enlistees into technical and "white collar" military job categories, the revival of counterinsurgency doctrine, and the subsequent escalation of the Vietnam conflict largely determined which course the armed forces would take in the 1960s. Already by 1962, while the percentage of America's military manpower in frontline combat arms had shrunk from 44.5 percent in 1945 to 26 percent, the percentage of black soldiers in combat units had risen from slightly over 12 percent at the end of World War II to better than 33.3 percent. The increasing demand for troops in the middle to late 1960s to fight the Vietnam War, necessitating a big increase in draft calls, now brought in a disproportionately large number of black enlistees and conscripts as frontline soldiers without a comparable increase in black officers. The Defense Department was neither prepared nor willing to engage in the kind of unprecedented, massive "affirmative action" program which would have been required to balance minority officer and foot soldier percentages in Vietnam or elsewhere, and the immediate task of "winning" the war required frontline manpower, whatever its color.[26]

As the American role in the Vietnam War dramatically escalated during the mid-1960s, so too did the black role in the fighting, if not the command. As of 1965, black Americans, approximately 11 percent of the national population, made up over 14 percent of army, 13 percent of air force, and 8 percent of marine enlistments, compared with 8, 9, and under 6 percent for the same services four years earlier. By December 1965 more than 20,000 blacks were in service in Vietnam. By the end of the war, approximately 320,000 blacks would see duty in Southeast Asia, or 12.5 percent of all American forces in the conflict. In the first eleven months of 1966, nearly 22.5 percent of all U.S. Army troops killed in the war were black GIs. That figure in itself no longer shocked Pentagon officials, for the quota of black battle deaths for the preceding five years had been nearly as high. By 1967, blacks still constituted only 5 percent of the officers in Vietnam but 14.5 percent of army units and 11 percent of enlisted personnel. Such figures reflected a socioeconomic as well as a racial imbalance, but blacks took little comfort from that fact.[27]

High black casualties, growing controversy over the war at home, and the violent decline of the civil rights movement and rise of Black Power all left indelible imprints upon the attitudes and grievances of black troops in the late 1960s and upon their relations with commanders and white comrades. An obvious and growing informal racial segregation of black and white soldiers away from the battle front led to new concerns among commanders about unit morale and efficiency. Reports of racial gangs roaming and attacking each other in rear guard areas alarmed officials, as did reports of racially motivated "fragging" incidents. Black soldiers bitterly observed the greater ease of whites in receiving draft deferments and preferred assignments, and black leaders at home noted that as of 1967 an average of only 3 percent of those on draft boards were black. In Alabama, Arkansas, Louisiana, and Mississippi, not a single black manned a local draft board. Black GIs displayed Black Power flags and salutes and forced confrontations between their expressions of racial pride and conventional military standards of deportment and discipline. Minority servicemen still complained that racial discrimination persisted in basic matters of promotion, awards, and, perhaps most important to the battle-weary GI, coveted rear-area assignments. In turn, field commanders complained that attempts to respond to criticism by adjusting combat assignments by race only hampered unit efficiency and exposed everyone to greater risks.[28]

Because of his special perception of the way in which the American commitment in Vietnam had served to drain national resources from the fight for racial justice at home, the black soldier in Vietnam found himself in the unusual position of serving in the vanguard of a military cause he often did not support. As early as August 1966, national polls indicated that well over half of American blacks believed the draft unfair, and 35 percent openly opposed the war. By September 1969 a *Time* reporter, Wallace Terry, found in his own informal poll of some four hundred blacks in Vietnam that three-fifths of them did not think they should be fighting in Southeast Asia as long as racial discrimination remained at home. Less than a quarter felt that their combat role should be as great as that of whites. The Vietcong and North Vietnamese tried, without notable success, to direct propaganda at the disgruntled black GI. Still, the greatest irony was that despite the growing unpopularity of the war, the lack of comparable economic opportunities at home, and the slow nature of racial progress in the military, black soldiers consistently reenlisted at far higher rates than whites and performed with notable heroism. Over the course of the war to 1968, three times as many blacks reenlisted as whites, and even in 1969, blacks stayed at a rate of 45 percent, whereas the rate was only 17 percent for whites.[29]

The Vietnam experience of black military personnel illustrated the paradoxical journey that blacks had traveled in their pursuit of equal opportunity in the armed forces. Blacks had proven their mettle as fighting men, but their leadership and strategic capabilities had not been similarly tested because of a lack of opportunities. Formal unit segregation had been lifted, and both black soldiers and the national image had benefited from the action, but the social customs of racial segregation and cultural exclusion had proven more difficult to dislodge for the sake of military efficiency. Opportunities to serve one's country and to derive the basic material benefits of that service had been obtained by a growing number of black Americans in the armed forces, but those opportunities remained limited by private prejudice, inequalities of education and economic opportunity in civilian society, and the rapidly changing technical skills required of the military profession. Blacks had become a sizable underclass in the military, and in the post-Vietnam volunteer force, rapid redressing of the imbalances appeared unlikely. Much had changed for the better in twenty-five years for blacks, both in the armed forces and in the society they served, but in its racial profile and policies, the American military remained after a quarter of a century still more a mirror of the nation's racial struggles than a triumphant symbol of racial democracy in action.

6

The Antiwar Movement in America, 1955–1965

CHARLES DeBENEDETTI

AMERICAN PEACE SEEKERS have oscillated throughout the twentieth century between two poles of activism. On the one side, they have worked to move the United States into taking the lead in building a new world order capable of sustaining multilateral processes of peace and security. On the other, they have protested against Washington's involvement in foreign wars. At the turn of the century, peace seekers in the Progressive period tried to fashion a new international system based on American-style federal and juridical practices. The outbreak of World War I, however, wrecked their efforts and precipitated the rise of a brief but transforming new antiwar movement.[1] After 1919, peace activists resumed their struggle for a reformed world order by demanding U.S. participation in the League of Nations. This ended when the world crisis of the 1930s moved many of them to oppose American involvement in great power entanglements and the encroaching world war.

During the 1940s, peace seekers returned to the fight for a new world order by supporting the United Nations and plans for a federal world government. After 1950, however, the combined shocks of the Cold War, the Korean War, the nuclear arms competition, and McCarthyism broke the back of this latest drive for American-led global reform. In its place, there emerged a new antiwar movement that was more opposed to the immediate threat of the Cold War than committed to the reconstruction of the international system. Joined more by common concerns than by any organized cadres, this new movement claimed only a small audience and slight political strength. Yet it established itself between 1955 and 1965 as the most vocal source of domestic dissent from Washington's Cold War policies; and it formed the framework for building internal opposition to America's deepening military involvement in Vietnam.

A new type of antiwar movement came forward in America after 1955 as kinetic new groups of independent liberals, social radicals, women, students, intellectuals, and Roman Catholics joined pacifists and traditional internationalists in demanding national policies designed to reverse the arms race and end the Cold War. Beyond this critical new commitment, this antiwar Cold War movement differed from earlier peace movements in two main ways. Tactically, its advocates shared an ethic of personal responsibility for peace and a corollary commitment to direct individual involvement and action. Strategically, they aimed less to establish America at the head of a new world order than to change America's Cold War emphasis on unilateral military preparations and armed interventionism. Convinced that their country was on a collision course with disaster, a new constellation of antiwar activists came forward after 1955, determined to advance the kind of policy criticisms and alternatives that America's established political parties failed to provide. This antiwar movement insisted that the Cold War, not communism, was the major threat to American democracy and international security. This same group formed the core of the broader domestic opposition that arose early in the 1960s against Washington's armed intervention in Vietnam and that expanded so incredibly when that intervention turned into full-scale war after 1965.

The anti–Cold War movement began in the mid-1950s among various world-minded citizens who decided, because of changing conditions at home and abroad, to press Washington to end the Cold War. Internationally, the possibility of positive change appeared more promising because of the convergence, paradoxically enough, of easing tensions and new threats. On the one side, the end of hot wars in Korea and Indochina, the emergence of summit diplomacy and the talk of disarmament between the great powers, the rise of Third World neutralist nations, and the de-Stalinization drive within the Soviet Union and accompanying calls for "peaceful co-existence" cumulatively effected a thaw in the Cold War. On the other side, the deployment of hydrogen bombs, continued atmospheric testing, the appearance of missile-borne weaponry, and accelerating conventional arms competition all pointed toward new dangers. Perversely, even as the Cold War thawed, the arms race heated up, deepening fears that the world might never pass beyond the Soviet-American confrontation.[2]

At the same time, changing domestic conditions within America bred hopes for policy change. The decline of McCarthyism after 1954 helped quiet ranker attacks on policy dissidents. The bus boycott in Montgomery, Alabama, and the spread of the civil rights movement (largely inspired by pacifists) provided proponents of social and policy change with a working model of success and an incentive for further action. Most important, several thousand people (estimates ranged from 85,000 to 500,000) from the "issue-oriented, educated, middle-class" decided to protest publicly against the Cold War crisis.[3] Some were moved by ethical or moral impulses, others by immediate fear. Some felt prompted to act by what they termed "an anguish of mind." Others were driven by what contemporary analysts termed a "crucial episode," such as the Sputnik space shot, that shattered their sense of security.[4] What counted for the gathering opposition, however, was that they decided to act.

These dedicated but diverse anti–Cold War activists included a wide variety of notable and articulate people, such as the internationalist Norman Cousins, the pacifist Clarence Pickett, the reformer Norman Thomas, the writer Lewis Mumford, the atomic scientist Leo Szilard, the social scientist David Riesman, the comedian Steve Allen, and ordinary citizens like the Washington housewife Folly Fodor. Together, they looked to no common leadership nor to any single directing organization. Rather, they joined in the common conviction that the Soviet-American rivalry and its related arms race were subverting America's democracy and pointing the way toward global extinction. They would have neither. Convinced that Cold War tensions were breeding the irresponsible concentration of executive-bureaucratic power and a frightful "moral insensibility" within America, these antiwar dissidents took it upon themselves to shake their country out of its torpor and demand alternatives to the Cold War and arms race.[5] Informed and realistic, they realized that they possessed no major political constituencies and no social support groups, nor did they have reliable means of affecting national policy. Yet they came together in the late 1950s to advance their cause through a combination of arguments, actions, and new-style organizations.

At first, dissidents enunciated the arguments that communicated their two axial convictions: that expansion in number and quality of destructive weapons threatened the survival of the species and that passive acquiescence to this development was madness. In July 1955, several leading American and international scientists, headed by Albert Einstein and Britain's Bertrand Russell, issued a public letter demanding that nations face the "stark and dreadful and inescapable" question: "Shall we put an end to the human race; or shall mankind renounce war?"[6] Shortly afterward, the prominent psychologist Erich Fromm wondered in a widely read book if Cold War America could yet "be converted to sanity—or will it use the greatest discoveries of human reason for its own purposes of unreason and insanity?"[7] The pacifist American Friends Service Committee (AFSC) carried Quakers beyond their traditional opposition to individual involvement in war into the position that *"an armed world in this age is itself madness"* (emphasis in original).[8] Similarly, liberal and left-wing journals and critics attacked the "crackpot realism" of the "military metaphysics" dominant in both Russia and America and warned that modern peoples were "at a curious juncture in the history of human insanity: in the name of realism, men are quite mad."[9]

In addition to their words, antiwar dissidents acted both in protest against headlong preparations for suicidal war and in search of alternative ways toward peace and security. In June 1955, radical pacifists led by the Catholic Worker activists Dorothy Day and Ammon Hennacy refused to take shelter in New York City during a state-mandated civil defense drill and ignited the first of several anti–civil defense protests that continued until the program was dismantled seven years later. In 1957, other radical pacifists were arrested as they tried to enter U.S. nuclear installations in Nevada and Omaha; and in 1958, two additional groups were jailed after trying to sail two small ships into Pacific waters set aside for U.S. H-bomb testing. Other operations were launched to institutionalize the more self-conscious peace activism. In the San Francisco Bay area the AFSC leader Robert Pickus organized Acts for Peace, which aimed to involve local community groups, from Chambers of Commerce to Parents-Teachers Associations, in networks that familiarized ordinary citizens with everyday peace work. Also, in 1957, several social scientists long interested in questions of war and peace began *The Journal of Conflict Resolution* at the University of Michigan to relate their theoretical work to "the greatest problem of our time—the prevention of war."[10]

These words and actions converged early in 1957 with the issue of nuclear testing and atmospheric fallout to yield two new organizations— the Committee for Nonviolent Action (CNVA) and the National Committee for a Sane Nuclear Policy (SANE)—that encompassed in complementary ways the first concerns of the new antiwar movement. Inspired by such radical pacifists as A. J. Muste and Lawrence Scott, the CNVA originated as an action agency for several hundred disobedients who refused to concede legitimacy to the warmaking state and who attacked "the policies of military deterrence and massive retaliation" by non-violently invading missile sites and bomber bases.[11] Although supportive of SANE and other peace workers, CNVA activists identified themselves primarily as nonviolent revolutionaries. They were decided neutralists in the Soviet-American Cold War and insistent that peace required the radical redistribution of global wealth and power and the adoption of the revolutionary principles of nonviolence.

SANE meanwhile emerged as a vehicle for a broader collection of religious pacifists, social radicals, and, especially, political liberals who shared a common opposition to atmospheric nuclear testing and a common hope that an end to testing might open the way toward real disarmament. Developed by the Quaker leaders Robert Gilmore and Lawrence Scott, SANE started when a group of prominent liberals, including Eleanor Roosevelt and Walter Reuther, sponsored a newspaper advertisement in October 1957 that called for an end to nuclear testing and its attendant health hazards. Unexpectedly, their advertisement generated such a wave of grass-roots enthusiasm and financial support that the national organizers felt moved to establish a national membership organization and a popular "campaign to regain sanity" amid Cold War tensions.[12]

Rallying more than 20,000 members within six months, SANE brought to the surface at least three factors that gave new tone to the antiwar movement. First, it demonstrated that many Americans believed their government was not doing enough to bring about nuclear disarmament and an end to the Cold War. Second, its very name reflected broader fears about the escalation of a maniacal arms race and the hope that reason might yet prevail. Finally, its focus on the fallout danger, which brought insidious and indiscriminate suffering to unknowing innocents, provided a short-hand expression of the basic belief among antiwar activists that the Cold War more than communism was America's enemy. According to antiwar activists, the Cold War meant chronic insecurity, the declension of democracy, and the likelihood of annihilation. The first responsibility of U.S. policymakers was to overcome these threats through negotiations, accommodation, and multilateral cooperation in a world that had to be shared with revolutionary Marxists.

The rise of SANE as an organized body of liberal and left-wing peace activists failed, however, to win critical support from the great majority of American liberals. In the course of that failure, American liberalism itself began to crack and come apart. More concerned with communism than with modern war, the great body of American liberals proceeded during the 1950s to fall away from their traditional concern with advancing world order and, instead, threw themselves behind demands for more aggressive U.S. interventionist and armaments policies. Liberal support for U.S. leadership in the UN remained steady but stagnant. The United World Federalist crusade for a genuine world government faltered in the face of lagging liberal support. Moreover, when the longtime internationalist leaders Grenville Clark and Louis Sohn produced a highly acclaimed new blueprint in their book *World Peace through World Law,* their work failed to rally the kind of broad liberal backing that had been crucial to the earlier struggles for the League of Nations and the UN. Instead (and especially after the Soviet Sputnik spaceshot in fall 1957), security-minded liberals like Democratic Senator Henry Jackson of Washington demanded that the Eisenhower administration accelerate a U.S. arms buildup and confront the Kremlin more aggressively. Peace liberals and other anti–Cold War activists meanwhile raced in another direction. They insisted on attacking what they considered to be the two main impediments to a negotiated settlement of the Cold War: the superpowers' mutual strategies of deterrence and their corollary global interest in military interventionism.

Deterrence claimed first priority. When deterrence was first enunciated during the mid-1950s as explicit U.S. strategy, antiwar critics complained that this "massive nonsense" would fuel a worsening arms race, generate ever-higher levels of tension, and complicate the Soviet-American political differences that were at the root of the Cold War.[13] Deterrence was not an answer to international tensions, critics insisted. It contained "no provisions for its own resolution," nor any way of considering "the seldom asked question—when and how does it end?"[14] It simply anticipated endless Cold War. Furthermore, antiwar leaders attacked deterrence for abetting the domestic politics of unreason and wrecking the need for rational democratic discourse. Deterrence crazily held out the promise of defense through heavier armaments in an age when there was no defense. It offered hope of security through improved killing technology at a time when there was no security. Deterrence was a logical extension of the notion of maintaining the national security through superior armed strength. Yet it demanded the kind of public debate over defense through mass death that struck critics as mad if not genocidal. Lewis Mumford condemned the strategic debates over "protective extermination," while economist Kenneth Boulding felt that national defense planning smacked of "sheer lunacy."[15] Inevitably, declared the critics, the national commitment to massive armaments in the name of deterrence was corroding those liberal, humane values that made for America's historic uniqueness. Indeed, it made for "a moral climate that is plainly corrupting."[16] The policy of deterrence "will not ensure peace," insisted Erich Fromm. "It will most likely destroy civilization, and it will certainly destroy democracy even if it preserves peace."[17]

In line with their opposition to deterrence, antiwar activists came together during the late 1950s in common opposition to the associated doctrine of arms control. Encouraged by elite groups such as the Council on Foreign Relations, a number of geopolitical strategists proceeded in the mid-1950s to replace the prevailing notion of "massive retaliation" with more flexible strategies of deterrence that featured military alternatives ranging from counterinsurgency to limited nuclear war. Strung out between Herman Kahn and the RAND corporation and "Charles River Boys" like Harvard's Henry A. Kissinger, these architects of a more flexible deterrence strategy were especially eager to develop a system of stabilized deterrence through reciprocal restraint. One of their inventions in this effort was the notion of arms control. This doctrine turned on two key assumptions: first, that attempts at controlling arms competition hinged upon stabilizing the superpowers' mutual deterrence capabilities; and, second, that the prospects of genuine disarmament were slim. Arms control was purposed "to enhance stability," wrote Kissinger. It was a means, agreed two of his top associates, "of supplementing unilateral military strategy" in the understanding that the "aims of arms control and the aims of a national military strategy should be substantially the same."[18]

Peace critics were outraged. Various dissidents blasted deterrence strategists for merchandising "super-rationality" as "hard-headed realism" and attacked arms control as a nuclear-era "attempt at alchemy—to turn the very means of violence, death, and destruction into the foundation of safety and lasting peace."[19] Dismissing arms control as "a theory of armament, not disarmament," antiwar activists condemned it as a sophisticated way of deflecting domestic demands for disarmament and persisting in the endless pursuit of military containment and deterrence.[20] Arms control, they complained, promised "a permanent, regulated international military-deterrence system" which precluded "the great essential idea of disarmament."[21] Even more, it purported to realize "the hope of mutual 'invulnerable' deterrence" in the name of a national security that depended on "militant and authoritarian social organizations" which contradicted America's democratic traditions.[22] With deterrence, arms control served to sanction the spread of irresponsible national security agencies that would defend America at the cost of its very moral principles.

Determined to break free of deterrence, most antiwar critics argued late in the 1950s for various unilateral initiatives toward disengagement and disarmament that might encourage a new international spirit of trust and accommodation. Some urged a unilateral U.S. cessation of atmospheric testing. Others wanted Washington to repudiate its first-strike nuclear option. Whatever their preferences, advocates of unilateral initiatives wanted policymakers to open "a deliberate 'peace offensive'" that would induce the Soviets to reciprocate and assist both powers in "breaking through the thought barrier" of Cold War tensions toward some mutual, graduated reduction in their differences.[23] They realized that their policy prescriptions entailed real risks, but they felt sure that these risks were far less threatening than deterrence and "the dangerous circle of seeking peace by means of threat and counter-threat."[24]

Going beyond the call for unilateral initiatives, a tiny but vocal band of radical pacifists demanded immediate and total U.S. withdrawal from the arms race and war system. Given voice by Muste and the philosopher Mulford Sibley, these unilateral disarmers believed that nothing short of revolutionary action could save America and the world from the dangers incumbent in the atomic age. As Muste put it, "the drastic choice is: Disarm or Perish, i.e., break with war unconditionally or perish."[25] Dedicated to a global revolution from war to peace values, these radical pacifists believed that conscientious individuals must take the immediate lead in the everyday peace struggle and that America must lead the nations through the example of its own unilateral disarmament. America had a special responsibility to renounce war because of its superpower status and because of its singular position as the only nation that had used nuclear weapons. After all, reasoned the writer Paul Goodman, "the bomb was our baby and we first made it mighty." Now America must be first among "the refusers."[26]

Antiwar dissidents understood that any attempt to move America and the world beyond the Cold War required domestic changes within America. One change that attracted their early support involved the need to move the country through planned conversion from a war to a peace economy. Economists Emile Benoit and Kenneth Boulding surveyed the problems and possibilities that disarmament would bring to the U.S. economy. The Columbia University management expert Seymour Melman detailed plans for the stabilization of a growing U.S. economy that required fewer arms expenditures, while Democratic Senator George McGovern of South Dakota submitted legislation calling for the formation of a National Economic Conversion Commission. Pacifists and social radicals meanwhile carried the ideas to target communities. In 1960 the CNVA conducted its Polaris project in New London, Connecticut, trying to attract workers from the construction of nuclear submarines to peace-related jobs. Members of the Students for a Democratic Society worked in the same way during 1962–64 in New York and Boston to win workers from the arms race and to what Melman had already identified as "the peace race."[27]

The new-style antiwar movement furthermore distinguished itself through the formation of new organizations expressive of the unique concerns of various constituent groups. Early in 1959 a combination of Chicago-area Quakers and social radicals organized the Student Peace Union to engage students in study and action against the arms race and for alternatives to war. One year later, a high-powered group of intellectuals, including Lewis Coser and S. I. Hayakawa, formed the Committees of Correspondence to stimulate hard thinking about the "fundamental changes" necessary to help America "slow down and end the arms race."[28] During the Berlin crisis in late summer of 1961, Norman Thomas inspired Turn Toward Peace as a national clearinghouse of voluntary organizations and a springboard for a national campaign to build support for alternatives to war "as the central thrust of American policy."[29] Also, in the fall of 1961, Leo Szilard launched the Council for a Livable World as a Washington-based "Peace Lobby"; a group of Boston-area physicians formed the Physicians for Social Responsibility to warn people of the horrific health hazards inherent in nuclear war; and Washington-area housewives organized Women Strike for Peace (WSP) to rally women more directly against nuclear testing and the larger arms race.[30] Using networks already established by SANE and the Women's International League for Peace and Freedom, WSP activists engineered on November 1 a nationwide protest against testing that drew an estimated twenty thousand people in demonstrations in over twenty cities. Four months later, more than four thousand students descended upon Washington to protest the lack of public debate regarding deterrence and the arms race and to demand unilateral U.S. initiatives toward disarmament. With the other people in motion, the students invested their bodies in the new "spirit of the times: a desire to 'do something' to insure peace."[31]

In Washington, the rise of citizen peace activism prompted inquisitorial congressmen to search for dangerous subversives. In May 1960, a Senate Internal Security subcommittee headed by the Connecticut Democrat (and former world federalist) Thomas Dodd announced that it was launching an investigation of Communist involvement in SANE and the antitesting movement. Dodd's attack turned up no Communists; but it provoked a fearsome internal debate within SANE and among antiwar activists over the questions of collaborating with Communists and cooperating in congressional witchhunts. In the same way, the House Un-American Activities Committee tried two years later to discredit the Women Strike for Peace with similar charges of Communist infiltration. But the attack worked less well. WSP leaders refused to discuss the political predilections of their fellow activists and used the hearings as a platform for propounding their peace preferences. Still, their listening audience was limited. Public opinion pollsters estimated that 37 percent of the American people believed it "impossible" for the United States to negotiate a political settlement with the Soviet Union.[32] Furthermore, no major political faction existed that might introduce their concerns into the national political dialogue, let alone help change official policy.

Yet they persisted. In the middle of 1962, antiwar critics channeled their energies behind several congressional campaigns that peace-oriented candidates ran from Massachusetts to California. Predictably "as diverse and unorganized as the peace movement itself," these various campaigns evolved largely in response to local conditions and realities. Yet the candidates were joined in the common demand that "the arms race be ended and war abolished."[33] Whatever momentum these candidates enjoyed, however, was abruptly halted—along with the larger antiwar movement—during the Cuban missile crisis of October 1962. While Moscow and Washington approached the brink of war, antiwar critics gathered in scattered rallies to demand negotiations and UN intervention. Yet they could hardly conceal their failure to affect superpower diplomacy or even domestic public opinion in a moment of incomparable danger.

Of the many aftershocks of the Cuban missile crisis, the most ironic involved the way in which it drove Russian leaders into a new determination to match U.S. strategic power and, in so doing, set off a new round in the arms race while the antiwar movement fell back in size, strength, and self-confidence. In fact, the movement's retreat turned into a rout during 1963, when Kennedy appropriated the language of the "peace race" and outflanked his antiwar critics. In June, at the American University, the president called for détente with the Soviet Union, and planning soon began for a special Washington-Moscow "hotline." In August the two powers concluded a partial test-ban treaty against nuclear explosions in the atmosphere. Antiwar liberals rallied elatedly to Kennedy's side. With the superpowers improving their relations in ways opposed only by China abroad and the Barry Goldwater Right at home, large chunks from the liberal side of the antiwar movement turned to support an administration that was acting out its highest wishes. Government officials were "eloquently speaking the language one heard earlier only from fringe groups like SANE," I. F. Stone rhapsodized in fall 1963. "Peace has broken out, and hopes leap up again."[34]

Yet, as if in counterpoint, the decline of liberal antiwar activism was offset during 1963 by the rise of a reinvigorated Left that aimed to assemble student radicals, civil rights militants, radical pacifists, community organizers, philosophical anarchists, and various Marxist splinter groups into an aggressive "politics of insurgent protest" for change at home and peace abroad.[35] Committed first to domestic reform, this "New Left" intended to mobilize "a popular left opposition" that would effect radical reforms in race relations, poverty, and unemployment, at the same time that it argued for disarmament, improved Soviet-American relations, and an end to U.S. counterrevolutionary interventionism in the Third World.[36] As one SDS leader put it, this New Left "opposition would be a 'peace movement,' even if the advocacy of foreign policy alternatives were not a major feature of its program," because the drive for radical domestic change required "a fundamental reordering of priorities for our society" and an end to military adventurism abroad.[37]

The spread of the civil rights movement early in the 1960s only strengthened the cause of the Left as it heightened the priority of domestic reform efforts and reinforced anti-interventionist sentiment among antiwar activists. Convinced that America's greatest problems were at home and not abroad, the antiwar liberals and radicals threw their support to the black protest movement, confident in the rightness of the cause and pleased with the "new prestige" and impetus that it lent the cause of nonviolent change. "When there is movement and dynamism on one basic issue," explained Muste, "it tends to predispose people to be critical and seek ways to act in other fields also."[38] Antiwar dissidents nevertheless argued over how the civil rights movement was related to the struggle against the Cold War. Radical pacifists, for instance, valued the confrontational politics of the civil rights movement and praised it as a working example of liberating nonviolence. Others, however, were not so sure. Antiwar liberals did not believe that the model of the "more intensely emotional" civil rights struggle could be used in the fight against the Cold War and deterrence; and they wondered to what extent the politics of nonviolence was relevant to Cold War hotspots like Berlin and Cuba.[39]

Actually, the debate over the civil rights movement as a model for peace action was only a minor matter among the many divisions that cleaved the antiwar movement after 1963 and set it on a new course. Essentially, these divisions crystallized around differences between antiwar liberals, who conceived of peace as expanding global order, and antiwar radicals, who saw it in the wholesale liberation of oppressed peoples. But their differences only ramified from there. Where liberals saw the world's first problem in the Soviet-American Cold War and arms race, radicals saw it in the widespread poverty and maldevelopment that followed upon America's aggressive maintenance of the international capitalist system. Whereas liberals favored policy change through lobbying and electoral action, radicals favored such irregular tactics as nonviolent direct action and massive civil disobedience. Whereas liberals respected the anti-Communist canons of American politics, radicals dismissed them as Cold War shibboleths. Whereas liberals emphasized the importance of policy change within a reformed international order, radicals demanded policy change through the revolutionary transformation of American society. Most important, whereas liberal antiwar activists saw themselves as a political force bent upon foreign policy change, radical critics never decided whether they were a political force bent upon revolutionary change or a self-generated mystique devoted to fashioning new forms of personal consciousness and liberating social values. Unsure of its identity, the radical New Left never figured out whether it constituted a movement geared for the radical redistribution of wealth and power, or an existential experience that allowed disaffected people to play out their individual anxieties regardless of political consequences. Radical New Leftists knew one thing, however: they aimed to act.

Despite these many differences, liberal and radical antiwar activists found themselves forced together early in the 1960s in opposing Washington's deepening involvement in Vietnam. As the United States progressively pumped money, matériel, and troops into South Vietnam during 1961–65 in an effort to maintain an anti-Communist regime, opposition to intervention grew among those anti–Cold War activists who saw different dangers in the common problem of Vietnam. Antiwar liberals feared that the escalating conflict in Vietnam would produce a new and more threatening great power confrontation. Antiwar radicals shared that concern, but they complained more angrily that U.S. policy only extended a pattern of counterrevolutionary American interventionism against Third World struggles for revolutionary self-determination. In large measure, of course, these varying but convergent criticisms were conditioned by the views held by antiwar activists toward the ongoing Cuban crisis, where liberals wanted an international settlement and radicals demanded a hands-off approach and, sometimes, support for Fidel Castro's revolution. Yet, no matter what the immediate context, the fact was that anti-Cold War critics took an early and antagonistic interest in Washington's growing intervention in Vietnam and protested U.S. policy on the grounds that Vietnam was at least irrelevant to U.S. security interests and at most a source of worsening Cold War tensions. From the start, anti-interventionist critics insisted that America had no substantive interests in Vietnam. On the contrary, they argued, Vietnam was nothing more than a test case for the perceived requirements of America's greater deterrence strategy. In the context of global deterrence, wrote leaders of the Student Peace Union (SPU), Vietnam was merely "a proving ground" in which the United States aimed to administer "the same lesson the peoples of Eastern Europe learned from Hungary: that rebellion against the status quo is futile." It was "the Cold War itself in a frightening microcosm," with America fighting to keep the Vietnamese from quitting "its war camp" no matter what the cost to Vietnam.[40]

The rise in the 1960s of domestic opposition to U.S. policy in Vietnam proved notable in three main ways. First, it originated above and beyond the country's bipartisan political system. Second, it was characterized by an incredible heterogeneity that brought together U.S. senators and local community organizers, traditional liberals and revolutionary leftists, principled pacifists and worried realpolitickers. Finally, it subsisted on a few basic arguments which gave the opposition a political and moral dimension that overrode the tremendous ideological diversity of its advocates.

Calling for military de-escalation and negotiations, antiwar critics basically maintained that it was politically fatuous and morally wrong for the United States to fight to the last Vietnamese in order to preserve a non-Communist regime in Saigon against a Communist-led revolution on the fringes of China. Remembering Korea and the French failures in Indochina and Algeria, antiwar activists called for an internationally negotiated settlement and warned that a continuing conflict would escalate into a vicious, counterrevolutionary race war ("America's Algeria"), a Sino-American confrontation ("another Korea"), and possibly World War III.[41] Antiwar dissidents felt unsure about many things in Asia, but they agreed on one point: an expanding war in Indochina would neither improve the lives and fortunes of the Vietnamese people nor enhance chances for a larger breakthrough to peace. Persuaded that war only bred more war, they resolved to stand against the drive toward violence and to demand instead a military cease-fire, an internal Vietnamese settlement, negotiations among all parties (including the Vietcong and China), restoration of the Geneva agreements of 1954, and international neutralization of all Indochina, under, it was hoped, UN supervision. "The only remaining possibility," warned one group of academic dissidents, "is an increasingly oppressive police state in the South, accompanied by increasing unrest among the confined peasants, and the final liberation (and this will be a literally applicable term by the time it comes about) of South Vietnam by the North."[42]

In 1963, the regime of Ngo Dinh Diem suffered a series of military and political reversals; and the U.S. government reacted by expanding its military involvement in Vietnam. In response, there came forward an overt antiwar opposition, metamorphosizing mainly from those anti–Cold

War forces in movement since 1955. Without central direction and yet with a common purpose, small but notable collections of women, intellectuals, clergymen, students, pacifists, social radicals, and U.S. senators decided for different reasons in 1963 to protest against continued American support for Diem and to call for a multilateral political settlement. In the process, they set down the main salient points for a more dynamic domestic opposition. In early March, fifty-five American notables, including the Harvard sociologist Pitirim Sorokin and the Nobel scientific and peace prize laureate (and early SANE member) Linus Pauling, issued an open letter urging the Kennedy administration to call an international conference under UN auspices and to disengage from the war. Shortly afterward a score of socialists connected with the thirty-year-old Youth against War and Fascism protested in New York City against the "mutual slaughter of Vietnamese and Americans," and warned against "another Korea or Algeria."[43] Two months later, after a bitter internal argument over whether they should concentrate on nuclear issues or the whole of U.S. foreign policy, members of Women Strike for Peace announced that they had "a special responsibility" to alert the American public of "the dangers and horrors" of the war in Vietnam, since "Vietnam is the only place in which our own armed forces are actually engaged."[44] In July a second collection of national notables, including the pacifist scholar Roland Bainton and the Marxist theoretician Paul Baran, published an open letter protesting that America had become involved "in a conflict that it cannot win despite its tremendous military power." They urged Kennedy to disengage.[45]

One month later, the clergymen Harry Emerson Fosdick and Donald S. Harrington issued a public statement in the name of the Vietnam Ministers Committee and its fifteen thousand supporters, calling for an end to U.S. aid to Diem's Roman Catholic-dominated minority government because of its persecution of Buddhists and other religious minorities. Acting with the same concern, Democratic Senator Frank Church of Idaho and thirty-two cosponsors introduced a resolution in the Senate on September 10, asserting that U.S. aid to a South Vietnamese government "which persists in religious persecution offends the conscience of the American people and should not be continued."[46] Early the next month, a coalition of young radicals from SDS and SPU, who cared more about America's counterrevolutionary activism than Diem's religious persecutions, conducted a number of public demonstrations against the visit to the United States of Diem's sister-in-law, Madame Ngo Dinh Nhu. Clearly, the first sources of explicit opposition to U.S. policy in Vietnam were as diverse as were the concerns of the war's opponents. Yet these concerns converged on the need to halt American military escalation and to effect a political arrangement between the great powers that would stop the war from dragging on, "poisoning the air of freedom at home, imposing misery on the bewildered people of South Vietnam and risking a wider conflagration."[47]

In November 1963 the assassinations of Diem and John F. Kennedy brought a period of political instability in Saigon which the new Lyndon B. Johnson administration tried to overcome by expanded U.S. military support. In America the antiwar opposition grew more vocal. With Washington committed to military success and Republican opposition leaders such as Barry Goldwater and Richard M. Nixon arguing openly for a larger war, antiwar dissidents reached out to sympathetic supporters and solidified the principal arguments that sustained antiwar activism for the next decade. Contending that there was no military solution to this fundamentally political conflict, antiwar critics condemned further U.S. escalation and called for a negotiated settlement. They insisted that the war was a civil conflict that could best be contained—it could not be "won"—by means of a political arrangement among the great powers, including China, which would facilitate Vietnam's emergence as an "Asian Yugoslavia."[48] With equal force, they dismissed Washington's proclaimed defense of freedom in South Vietnam as pure cant; and they denounced as murderously fatuous the idea of fighting on for national honor. "I have heard of 'throwing out the baby with the bath water,' " said Senator Wayne Morse, "but never before have I heard it suggested that we should blow off heads to save face."[49]

Convinced that protracted U.S. involvement in an Asian land war would kill both domestic reform plans and possibilities for an international détente, antiwar activists urged their countrymen to recognize the irrelevance of Vietnam to America's larger interests. The "real tragedy and the real dilemma" for the American people in Vietnam, said antiwar critics, were that they were there "to win the war. But they cannot win the war. They can succeed only in doing what the French did, prolong the agony till the final withdrawal must come."[50]

The antiwar opposition took on a more pronounced leftist coloration during 1964, despite the essentially moderate proclivities of most of its members. In part, this deepening radical cast resulted from the eversharper language that the critics used in condemning U.S. war policy. Partly, too, the opposition took on a radical cast because of its apartness on the American political landscape, which was so dominated by conservative forces that the only significant partisan debate on Vietnam during the 1964 election year occurred between supporters of the Johnson administration who called for limited war and their right-wing Republican critics who wanted to go farther. Serious talk of negotiations scarcely penetrated the nation's everyday political debate. The thought of withdrawal never did. In addition, the opposition assumed a more leftist coloration as antiwar liberals continued either to lend support to the Johnson administration or to drift about in uncertainty, and radical pacifists started in the spring of 1964 to demand Washington's immediate withdrawal from Vietnam in the name of Vietnam's self-determination. Nearly instantaneously, the call for immediate withdrawal aggravated longstanding divisions within the antiwar opposition. Religious pacifists in the Fellowship of Reconciliation opposed the ideas for fear of exposing anti-Communist Vietnamese to a guerrilla victory and "a blood bath," while antiwar liberals attacked it as both dishonorable and contrary to America's interest in countering Chinese expansion in Asia.[51] Yet the demand for immediate withdrawal would not subside; and it added to the radical coloration of an antiwar opposition whose largest aim through 1965 centered on an end to the war's escalation and a negotiated settlement.

The war in the meantime grew larger, even as politics at home and abroad grew more complex. In August 1964 the United States launched a series of air attacks on North Vietnam following a clash in the Gulf of Tonkin between U.S. destroyers and North Vietnamese patrol boats. Having shown his mettle, President Johnson promised to proceed carefully and won a runaway victory in November over Republican challenger Goldwater. Yet, within weeks of Johnson's inauguration in January 1965, the United States opened a sustained air war against North Vietnam; and the antiwar opposition catapulted into an outright protest movement. While religious figures condemned the air attacks and called for negotiations, pacifists took to the streets in demonstrations intended to emphasize their determination to stand "in peaceable conflict" against Washington's war in Asia.[52] Dissident intellectuals stepped up the distribution of a "Declaration of Conscience" in which they avowed their "conscientious refusal to cooperate" in the U.S. war effort and to encourage acts of civil disobedience that would "stop the flow of American soldiers and munitions to Vietnam."[53] Quakers and women peace leaders organized emergency lobbying campaigns on Capitol Hill. Liberal leaders of SANE and Americans for Democratic Action called for a bombing halt and negotiations, and faculties and students on a few campuses long accustomed to Cold War criticism mobilized to raise questions and suspicions that sprang from a nagging belief that Washington was politically, "legally and morally in the wrong."[54]

A polyglot antiwar movement gained public attention during the spring of 1965 as large numbers of people acted on their doubts regarding Washington's Asian policies—and there were doubts because, for the preceding decade, clusters of antiwar critics had framed a number of political, intellectual, and moral challenges to the premises of American Cold War policy that were absorbed by networks of social dissidents as ardently as they were avoided by official Washington. Between 1965 and 1975, the anti–Vietnam War movement underwent many changes in tenor, temperament, complexion, and purpose in line with changing conditions at home and the changing nature of the war in Indochina. In its origins, however, the antiwar movement was less the product of change than of continuity, an extension of an ongoing domestic conflict over the Cold War and America's role in the world.[55]

More precisely, organized opposition to the U.S.–Vietnamese War emanated from an antiwar movement that had mobilized after 1955 to crack America's Cold War foreign policy consensus with a battery of fresh political values; namely, negotiation was preferable to confrontation; security was compatible with disarmament; strength was achievable without competitive armament; credibility was realizable without interventionism; and citizens should share with experts in shaping national policies. After 1955, an antiwar movement came forward in an attempt to change the dimensions of the debate over Washington's Cold War policies and to challenge some of the most cherished beliefs of Cold War American political culture. It was attempting, as one observer put it, "the most awesome task of reforming popular attitudes ever attempted by a minority in the history of American politics."[56] It was attempting to show that America could have strength in peace.

What the antiwar movement possessed in ambition, however, it lacked in power. Congenitally undisciplined, the movement was incapable of resolving its own contradiction as a protest culture whose very distinctiveness precluded it from gaining the political power needed to revamp the country's governing international values and policies. As a protest culture, the antiwar movement was rich in ideas, tactics, style, thinkers, and proposed alternatives. As a political force, it was humiliatingly weak. Despite efforts at everything from electoral contests to economic conversion, the movement failed to "find an entirely new way to break through the constraints of American politics" and build "meaningful political support for a concrete alternative" to the Cold War.[57] It failed partly because of internal factionalism and limited resources. It failed, too, because of official suspicion, media treatment that ranged from condescension to calumny, and popular reaction that varied from indifference to anger; primarily, however, it failed because of the sheer intractability of the country's prevailing political wisdom. Advancing basic policy criticisms and untried alternatives, the antiwar movement as a protest culture ran head-on into the political orthodoxies of anti-Communist America, starting with the belief that peace subsisted in the deterrent power of superior armed strength. Washington insisted that it sought peace through strength; antiwar activists urged the country to seek strength through the kind of negotiations and accommodations that defined the very processes of peace. Few others, however, were prepared to risk this route in defense of the national interest. Instead, the United States rolled deeper into Southeast Asia, and farther from any serious hope of ending the greater Cold War.

Guns versus Butter: Vietnam's Effect on Congressional Support for the Great Society

JAMES C. SCHNEIDER

THAT AMERICAN involvement in the Vietnam War undercut support for President Lyndon B. Johnson's Great Society programs is obvious, yet much about the relationship between war and domestic reform in the 1960s has remained obscure or incompletely understood. To view it merely as competition over spending, which the military won almost by default, is to reduce complex historical reality to an oversimplified and distorted account. Such a one-dimensional view isolates both the war and the reform program from their historical contexts, thus implicitly denying that other factors could have influenced the relationship, and ignores the evolving nature of the reform program itself and the reactions it engendered among various segments of American society. My purpose here is to examine the influence of America's escalating role in Vietnam on support for the Great Society, taking into account other factors, either generated primarily by the war or the reform program or largely extraneous to both. To assess the influence of the war, I will focus on congressional support for the Great Society in the crucial years 1966 and 1967. The Model Cities program, the last major Great Society initiative of the Johnson administration, will serve as a case study of congressional opinion during the period of American military escalation in Southeast Asia.

One of the pioneers of historical research on the subject of reform, Arthur M. Schlesinger, Sr., once stated that war cripples support for reform. In a widely reprinted lecture entitled "The Historical Climate of

Reform," Schlesinger noted that both the Civil War and World War I had set back various reform movements in their respective eras. His son would later make a similar observation on war and reform in the 1960s.[1] The Schlesingers were by no means alone in posting this link, and considerable evidence in subsequent periods points to the continuing existence of an adversary relationship. Early in World War II, President Franklin D. Roosevelt admitted that he had discarded "Dr. New Deal" in favor of "Dr. Win the War." Congressional conservatives were pleased by the change and during the war tried with mixed success to dismantle the reforms of the 1930s.[2] In his analysis of the influence of the Korean conflict on the Fair Deal, the historian Alonzo Hamby contended that the war, along with the rise of McCarthyism, subverted President Harry S. Truman's reform program. Hamby discerned, however, that other factors, such as weak support for many of Truman's key proposals and flawed legislative strategy by the administration, had hobbled the Fair Deal.[3] So the view that war is detrimental to reform efforts has a long and distinguished historical lineage.

President Johnson ascribed central importance to the Vietnam War as a factor undermining support for domestic reform. He told Congress in his 1967 State of the Union address that funding for the Great Society could not be expanded as fast as he would like owing to the costs of Vietnam. The imposed restraint, said Johnson, caused him special regret.[4] In an especially memorable passage from Doris Kearns's psychohistorical study of LBJ, Johnson himself underscored the shift from reform to war and emphasized his bitter feelings about it:

I knew from the start that I was bound to be crucified either way I moved. If I left the woman I really loved—the Great Society—in order to get involved with that bitch of a war on the other side of the world, then I would lose everything at home. All my programs. All my hopes to feed the hungry and shelter the homeless. All my dreams to provide education and medical care to the browns and the blacks and the lame and the poor. But if I left that war and let the Communists take over South Vietnam, then I would be seen as a coward and my nation would be seen as an appeaser and we both would find it impossible to accomplish anything for anybody anywhere on the entire globe.[5]

According to Johnson's memoirs, he believed all along that the opportunity to enact reform would prove fleeting. He concluded from historical experience that only for brief periods were Congress and the nation receptive to innovative legislation. Roosevelt's rebuff over court reorganization, in the aftermath of his 1936 landslide reelection, haunted LBJ. From the first, Johnson later wrote, he feared that his own massive win in 1964 "might be more of a loophole than a mandate."[6] Though never the type to propound formal theories, Johnson's long legislative experience led him to conclude that Congress quickly balked at being dominated by the White House. Signs of congressional displeasure over his own performance appeared early in 1965, when an administration bill to grant home rule to the District of Columbia was rejected. By winter, leaders of both parties were speaking openly of the need to pause and consolidate the Great Society. Events were soon to show that Johnson was determined to press further, but he was apprehensive about the possible impact of Vietnam on his domestic program. "The danger that we might have to slow that building [i.e., the Great Society] in order to take care of our obligations abroad, brought added anguish," he later wrote.[7] One must use caution in accepting Johnson's assessment. He was writing from hindsight. LBJ also viewed the Great Society as his public legacy. The claim that his beloved program fell victim to a foreign war was to a degree self-serving. It deflected attention from the shortcomings of the program itself and, hence, the man who brought it about. Johnson's explanation for America's involvement in Southeast Asia similarly excused him from blame. LBJ always insisted that he had merely fulfilled commitments made by his presidential predecessors whose policies had failed to achieve essential American aims in Vietnam. At bottom, Johnson's version made himself and his program tragic victims.

Many contemporaries shared the president's view that the Great Society would have to compete with the war in Vietnam. As early as February 1966, at an American Bankers' Association Convention, John R. Bunting, Jr., of the First Pennsylvania Bank and Trust Company, urged curtailment of the Great Society program in order to concentrate the talents, energies, and fiscal resources of the government on Vietnam.[8] In December, Tom Wicker of the *New York Times* suggested that the administration's recent request for an additional $10 billion for Vietnam would threaten future funding for the Great Society. Enemies of the program, said Wicker, would insist on compensating cuts in domestic spending as their price for approval of added monies for the war.[9] Shortly thereafter Martin Luther King, Jr., denounced the war for robbing the Great Society of vital funding.[10] So within a year and a half after the major American buildup began in Vietnam, observers of varying backgrounds and interests had come to agree that the war and the reform program were locked in a contest for the federal dollar.

Timing was one important aspect of this matter. Here, too, strong evidence exists to bolster the contention that Vietnam sapped support from domestic programs. The last major initiatives of the Great Society, including Model Cities, came in 1966, the second year of the massive U.S. buildup in South Vietnam. Thereafter, the Johnson administration focused on amending and consolidating existing programs and proposed nothing new of similar importance.[11] Thus the peak years of American expenditure in Southeast Asia began almost at the time when the Great Society lost impetus.

In fact, however, the Great Society did not collapse. Certain aspects, especially the Community Action programs (CAPs), were gutted, but aggregate spending on health, education, manpower training, community development, and housing rose 103 percent in fiscal year (FY) 1965, 60.8 percent in FY 1966, and 34.9 percent in FY 1967 and declined 2.2 percent in FY 1968. Thus the rate of increase fell steadily, but actual outlays increased dramatically. The figure for FY 1968, $20.1 billion, was 470 percent greater than the total for FY 1964, the last Kennedy budget. Most of the increase came in health programs and aid to education, which had middle-class constituencies. Programs targeted at the poor suffered more, especially the Community Action programs. In most cases, the Great Society suffered a loss of growth, rather than outright contraction, in the later Johnson years.[12] Taken together, the opinion of the president himself and the opinions of outside observers with diverse perspectives, combined with the trends in expenditures, constitute a formidable case that Vietnam supplanted the Great Society as the focus of national efforts and resources.

That it surely did, but to take center stage is not the same as to destroy or even to cripple the previous occupant of the spotlight. Moreover, to confirm a shift in the relative priority attached to events is not necessarily to establish causation between them. That is, the fact that the resources going to Vietnam were increasing while support for new domestic initiatives was waning does not establish that the fall in the latter was due to the rise in the former. Insofar as Congress was concerned, the Great Society fell victim to problems of its own making and to the changing political balance of power within the House of Representatives no less than to the rising costs of Vietnam.

In modern America the initiative for major legislative programs has tended to come from the White House, a fact that was never more true than during the Johnson period. Therefore, the place to begin analyzing the erosion of congressional support for the Great Society is at the lower end of Pennsylvania Avenue. Vietnam, according to Stanley Karnow's best-selling account of the war, had become Johnson's obsession by the beginning of 1966. If that is true, and if Congress relied on the White House to originate major proposals and to generate the support required to get them enacted, then Johnson's absorption with the war would itself be almost sufficient to halt further progress on the Great Society.[13]

However great Johnson's preoccupation with the war had become by the winter of 1965–66, it was not so severe as to preclude further efforts on behalf of reform. Although the bulk of the Great Society program was enacted in 1964 and 1965, the administration was still expanding both the program's scope and its funding through 1966. Johnson announced such major new proposals as Demonstration Cities and Fair Housing legislation in his 1966 State of the Union address, and he called for increased funding for the Teacher Corps and Rent Supplements. The president admitted that the twin demands of guns and butter were placing a squeeze on funds, but he insisted that an expanding economy would provide enough support for both. Furthermore, Johnson warned the legislators that the remedy for a deficit was a revenue increase rather than a cut in social programs. The tone of his address was confident. His was a call to continued action at home and abroad. "There are poor to be lifted up, and there are cities to be built, and there is a world to be helped," Johnson concluded.[14] America could accommodate both guns and butter.

The administration's handling of the Demonstration Cities bill, as Model Cities was first called, furnishes clear evidence that Johnson meant what he said in his State of the Union speech about selectively expanding the Great Society. The leader of the United Auto Workers (UAW), Walter Reuther, first raised the idea for a new urban program during a meeting at the White House in the summer of 1965. He called for something akin to an urban version of the Tennessee Valley Authority, which would establish models of neighborhood development in large cities. Although the details of Reuther's proposal were vague, he seems to have envisioned the creation of a few prototypical neighborhoods with refurbished dwellings, expanded social services, and enhanced cultural opportunities for the disadvantaged.[15] These prototypes would demonstrate the possibilities for improving life in the inner city and would serve as examples for similar local and state efforts around the country. The president was sufficiently impressed to order the formation of a special task force, headed by Professors Robert Wood of the Massachusetts Institute of Technology and Charles F. Haar of the University of Pennsylvania. Its purpose was in part to transform Reuther's ideas into more concrete form, as well as to reshape other aspects of the administration's urban policy.[16] The Wood-Haar group met secretly throughout the autumn of 1965 and sent its report to the Texas White House just before Christmas.[17]

98

A major conceptual ambiguity became apparent in both the report and the subsequent legislative embodiment of the Demonstration Cities proposal. Was the program intended to showcase the latest techniques developed by urban experts (presumably of proven value and effectiveness)? Or was it primarily to provide, in effect, neighborhood laboratories where innovations could be tested and good programs identified and publicized?[18] Academics on the task force leaned toward the second conception, while others, including a majority within the administration, favored the former approach. This fundamental lack of clarity in the original design of the program was by no means unique within the Great Society; indeed, it exemplified one type of shortcoming which bedeviled so much of Johnson's overall domestic program. Urban experts on the task force had the greatest doubts concerning the methods of attaining improvements in urban neighborhoods. Businessmen, labor leaders, and civil rights leaders on the task force, together with government officials who shaped the legislation, were impatient with such doubts and put the emphasis on action. Therefore, as Demonstration Cities proceeded toward enactment, it was increasingly defended as an answer to the nation's urban problems rather than as a means to experiment with potential answers.[19] By promising definitive results Johnson naturally attracted public and congressional support for the measure. The administration, however, had to promise more from the bill than the urban experts who helped to design it thought possible to deliver. In effect, the administration jeopardized the program's long-term future by burdening it with unrealistic expectations.

The most drastic change made in Reuther's original proposal concerned the number of projects included. The Wood-Haar Task Force had kept the UAW chief's initial figure of perhaps a half-dozen projects in as many cities. The administration raised the total to seventy. With so many more congressmen now able to anticipate money for their districts, the administration believed the prospects for passage would be greatly enhanced. The proposed funding level, however, was not raised commensurately, so the result was to dilute probable appropriations by spreading them across many additional projects. Thus the bill that Congress got differed from Reuther's original design in two fundamental aspects: the ostensible purpose of its projects and the amount of funding each would receive.

Of course any conceptual shortcomings in the program would be inconsequential if the Demonstration Cities bill failed to pass Congress, and by the middle of 1966 it appeared that the measure would die in committee. Introduced in February as part of the Omnibus City Demonstration, Metropolitan, and Urban Development Act, the bill languished in the House Subcommittee on Housing for three months. No one on the subcommittee, including its new chairman, William Barrett (D-Pa.), felt much enthusiasm for the bill. It attracted little active support outside of Congress as well.[20] Barrett and William Widnall (R-N.J.), the ranking minority member, accepted a substitute to the administration's version which would have effectively killed the measure. The substitute funded only planning and appropriated nothing for actual implementation of the program. Efforts by the newly formed Department of Housing and Urban Development (HUD) to salvage the original proposals achieved nothing. The representatives, used to Johnson's extensive activity in support of his recommendations, interpreted the lack of White House involvement as a sign that it was not seriously interested in the success of Demonstration Cities.[21]

Soon the members found differently. Despite the nation's steadily deepening involvement in Vietnam, the lack of rapid progress toward victory, and the growing controversy attending the escalation, the White House was able to intervene decisively in the latter half of 1966 to rescue Demonstration Cities. The precise nature and extent of Johnson's personal activities in this regard are unclear, although White House files suggest that he talked with many key congressmen and senators at critical junctures and that he set overall strategy to rescue the imperiled bill. Still, Johnson's enormous energies and his celebrated skills at lobbying have tended to obscure the fact that he assembled a domestic affairs staff of formidable talent. Those men—Joseph Califano, Henry H. Wilson, Jr., James Gaither, Harry McPherson, Harold "Barefoot" Sanders in the White House, and Lawrence O'Brien, the postmaster general—were shrewd and vigorous political operatives, whose time was not absorbed by Vietnam. Their success in resurrecting Demonstration Cities testifies that through the 1966 legislative session the White House was willing and able to do battle for its domestic program—and to win.

The administration set to work both on Capitol Hill and elsewhere to rescue its endangered proposal. The White House and HUD encouraged various parties which stood to benefit from Demonstration Cities—mayors, civil rights groups, the building trades, and others—to lobby Congress on behalf of the measure.[22] Within Congress, the White House spread the word that it had every intention of seeing the original bill enacted intact, and set about gathering votes and securing committed legislative sponsorship.[23] Of particular importance was the need to obtain a dedicated sponsor for the bill in the Senate. The administration wanted Edmund Muskie of Maine to assume this task. Muskie represented a mostly rural state and saw little benefit in becoming the champion of an urban bill, but the White House admired his legislative skills and took pains to enlist them for Demonstration Cities.

As the bill came to a vote in the fall, the White House continued to scrutinize its prospects. The AFL-CIO also worked in tandem with the administration to keep count of the bill's chances and to cultivate support. Together they compiled lists of undecided congressmen, which included comments not only on the likelihood of securing the doubtful vote but also on the possible means it would take to obtain an individual congressman's support. Of course there are no records of outright political horsetrading, but in such cases as that of an Illinois congressman, who needed campaign funds and who moved from indecision on the bill to strong support for it, the implication is clear. The memoranda of White House aides contain several references to "very good arrangements" with particular congressmen or to impending visits with others during which the aide intended to remind the representative of the recent "approval of a project in his district."[24] These efforts were successful. The bill which the *New York Times* had declared "dead" in May passed Congress the following October and was signed by the president on November 3. The original proposal had emerged substantially intact, owing to the impetus supplied by the White House.

But what obstacles had impeded its progress earlier in the session? Was Vietnam responsible in any significant way for the near defeat of Demonstration Cities? Had congressmen perceived the conflict between the war and reform which others at the time had begun to stress? Did such a perception make Congress reluctant to approve a program which would cost additional billions of dollars?

The best and most recent survey of the Johnson years, Allen J. Matusow's *The Unraveling of America,* notes that Wilbur Mills, the powerful chairman of the House Ways and Means Committee, pressed Johnson in 1967 to reduce domestic spending as the price for Mills's support of a tax surcharge. By that time inflationary pressures, to which the war contributed significantly, had become a serious concern. Johnson accepted the need to raise additional revenue with great reluctance precisely because he feared a quid pro quo such as Mills proposed. The Arkansas Democrat wanted the administration to announce publicly that it was choosing guns over butter. Interestingly, Mills had been the only congressman in 1966 to cite the cost of Vietnam as a reason for opposing Demonstration Cities.[25] Although Mills's chairmanship makes his views important, it is striking that no one else then in Congress cited Vietnam as the deciding factor in budgetary decisions. In the extensive and detailed records kept by the administration on individual congressmen's attitudes toward Demonstration Cities, the costs of Vietnam are almost wholly absent as a factor. So it was not until 1967 that the need to concentrate fiscal resources on the war emerged as an important factor in congressional decisions on appropriations.

Several factors explain the relatively small direct effect of Vietnam on domestic allocations in 1966. In contrast to previous wars, the United States entered Vietnam already possessing a large and modern army. Therefore a crash program to build up the military at the outset was unnecessary. The official estimate of the war's costs in May 1966, when Demonstration Cities seemed dead, was approximately $6 billion, less than 1 percent of the gross national product. The buildup had produced no credit crunch at that point and there were shortages of only a few raw materials. Indeed, the economic situation in 1966 seemed sufficiently healthy for certain economists to argue in favor of a new tax cut. Despite uncertainties over the course of the war—and it is well to remember that confidence died hard in American military strength and prowess, and hence in prospects for a quick victory—many experts did not regard Vietnam as an economic threat. Some critics did link the war to inflationary pressure and called for compensating cutbacks in domestic spending, but they tended to be conservative opponents of the Great Society, whose motives were suspect.[26]

If the war did not loom as especially ominous in 1966, Americans were growing worried about inflation. Concern surfaced in 1965 as the consumer price index began to rise at the fastest rate since the second Eisenhower term, and by early the following year business and financial circles, as well as the President's Council of Economic Advisers and the Bureau of the Budget, had come to see inflation as a serious threat to the nation's economic health.[27] The federal deficit had ballooned to $7 billion in fiscal year 1965 and the official forecast of a $1.8 billion shortfall for FY 1966 met wide skepticism on Wall Street, which predicted a figure closer to $9 billion. Yet the overall economic mood early in 1966 was very upbeat, according to various observers. "The prospects are *too* good," Malcolm Forbes told his readers.[28] The economy was in the fifth year of its longest peacetime expansion in history, and most experts expected the upward trend to continue. The outlook soured, however, as the year unfolded. By autumn the Business Council, composed of one hundred leading businessmen and economists, anticipated a sharp slowdown in activity over the coming year.[29] In December the gloom had deepened. Dun and Bradstreet found business leaders more pessimistic than at any time since 1963. Rising costs, slowing sales, shrinking profits, and the morass in Vietnam combined to dampen expectations of those surveyed.[30] The administration's announcement shortly thereafter that it would seek an additional $10 billion for the war must have added to Wall Street's gloom. Beyond actual costs, American escalation entailed continuing uncertainty over the course of the war, and Johnson's future plans for fighting and funding it troubled businessmen. They found it difficult to plan ahead.

Still, neither a pessimistic economic forecast nor Vietnam's role in producing it should be overemphasized for 1966. The Business Council's report in late October predicted at worst a slowdown, not a recession.[31] For much of the year, financial leaders were more concerned about the record deficit in the balance of payments. *Fortune*, which had chartered the fluctuating concern over inflation during 1966, was upbeat by year's end. So, cautiously, was *Forbes*.[32] Furthermore, not all inflationary worries were linked to Vietnam. The tremendous scale of the economic boom of the 1960s was itself sufficient to create fears among many businessmen that the economy was overheating.[33] Although Vietnam spending exacerbated this problem, the war did not create it. Moreover, the remedy, a tax increase, was obvious and not especially odious. No one knew then that the president would balk for so long at raising taxes.

Congress shared the growing fear of inflation, and this concern figured importantly in the attitudes of many members toward Johnson's Demonstration Cities bill. The president himself shared this view to a degree, and one of the things that had recommended the Reuther proposal to him was that its principal costs would be deferred for a full year after enactment.[34] By then, LBJ must have hoped, the war would be under control, he would be in a strong position for reelection, and the Great Society could regain full momentum. Members of the House faced the voters sooner, however, and to them, inflation and government spending were pressing concerns. Administration lobbyists repeatedly encountered congressmen who were reluctant to vote for new spending in the weeks immediately prior to the election.[35] To secure passage of Demonstration Cities, the administration had to accept reduced funding for the program, and it had to allow conservatives to demonstrate their fiscal responsibility to the electorate by initiating the cuts on the House floor.[36]

That the public's major concern was inflation, relative to other issues in the autumn of 1966, is doubtful. The Gallup Organization periodically asked Americans to name the most important problems facing the country. During 1965, Vietnam supplanted civil rights as the most pressing issue in the minds of most Americans. The war was, by a wide margin, the most cited problem in 1966, and by mid-year the cost of living had moved ahead of civil rights for the second position. When the Gallup Organization asked the same question in September, however, a summer of urban riots and the growth of the Black Power phenomenon had occurred, once again focusing concern on racial matters. Fifty-six percent of the respondents cited the Vietnam War as the nation's most important problem; 24 percent judged it to be racial concerns; 16 percent listed inflation.[37] Even before these results were published, political commentators had reached similar conclusions. Tom Wicker of the *New York Times* saw Vietnam as the salient issue in the 1966 campaign. He contended that controversy over the war had almost shattered the consensus Johnson had built in support of the Great Society, which in turn shifted attention from domestic achievements, weakened his influence in Congress, and rekindled liberal hostility toward the president.[38] Wicker probably overstated the war's influence in Congress—Johnson, after all, always got the majorities he needed in 1966—but the columnist was surely correct regarding Vietnam's importance as an issue.

The shattering blow to the fortunes of the Great Society in Congress came with the congressional elections of 1966. Republicans gained forty-seven seats and altered the ideological balance of power. Over half of the freshman Democratic class of 1964 failed to win reelection, and this group had lent Johnson staunch support on domestic matters.[39] Observers immediately noted that the election gave conservatives strength sufficient to block further reform.[40]

What influence Vietnam exercised in the Republican resurgence is impossible to gauge with precision. The party in the White House normally loses seats in off-year elections, but the total in 1966 was well above the average of thirty-two seats for the period since the 1930s. Still, the Johnson landslide of 1964 had produced the most lopsided Democratic majorities since the New Deal, so unusually large off-year losses were perhaps to be expected. Twenty-one of the new GOP members came from the party's traditional stronghold in the Midwest, which would seem to argue in favor of the theory that the 1966 results represented a normal correction.[41] The Democrats lost six seats in the Deep South, however, and that suggests other factors were at work. Nevertheless, given the degree of public concern over the war and the low opinions many people held of how Johnson was conducting it, Vietnam certainly was a factor in the vote, albeit of indeterminable importance.[42] Sensitive to the political winds, the president had announced two weeks prior to the election that he anticipated no major new programs for the Great Society. Instead, he intended to "fine tune" those already in existence by enhancing their efficiency and effectiveness.[43]

The more truculent attitude of the new Ninetieth Congress became apparent in the opening hours of its first session. The House declined to seat

Adam Clayton Powell, the controversial Harlem Democrat, pending resolution of a contempt citation against him for failing to pay a court-or-
dered settlement in a libel suit.[44] More ominous from Johnson's perspective, the House voted to reverse an earlier decision involving the Rules
Committee. No longer would the committee be given a maximum of three
weeks to pass along bills reported favorably out of committee. The vote
represented a major victory for conservatives, who dominated the Rules
Committee and were now in a position to control the tempo of the legislative process. Weaknesses within administration leadership in the House
compounded matters. Speaker John McCormick was aging and Majority
Leader Carl Albert had yet to recover from a long illness.[45] Electoral
defeats in 1966 led quickly to congressional defeat and disarray.

Johnson approached the new session warily. The White House maintained an uncharacteristic silence about its plans for the 1967 State of the
Union address. Throughout the previous year Republican forces in the
House had made plain their opposition to most of Johnson's domestic
reforms. Echoing conservative business circles, the GOP contended that
retrenchment was necessary to prevent inflation. Now their ranks were
swollen. The president's address reflected the changed political circumstances, but it also revealed his continuing commitment to reform. His
major theme was that America was undergoing a "time of testing." He
spoke now of limited resources and inflationary pressures exacerbated by
the war. The president also acknowledged flaws in some Great Society
programs. Yet he was by no means ready to abandon reform. Johnson
called for a 6 percent tax surcharge to reduce inflationary pressure. In a
subsequent news conference he would announce spending cutbacks in
such areas as road construction and public works. The Great Society was
not a target for cutbacks and the State of the Union address contained
new calls for action: government reorganization, aid to native Americans
and migrant workers, an antipollution program, campaign finance and
consumer protection legislation, a proposed educational television network, and a call to fund Demonstration Cities, now known as Model
Cities. Said Johnson, "At home the question is whether we will continue
working for better opportunities for all Americans." His answer was
plain.[46]

Yet the story of the appropriations battles of 1967 is not one of a
beleaguered administration trying to salvage what it could from a series
of hopeless situations. The cabinet departments, the White House staff,
and Johnson himself fought with skill and had surprising, if strictly limited, success in sustaining the Great Society. Still game to wage political
battles, the administration now faced congressional enemies more power-

ful than at any time since Kennedy's death. In such unpromising circumstances, the White House scotched virtually all requests from the cabinet for new programs, but the administration did not accede to the efforts of congressional enemies to dismantle existing operations.[47] Again, Model Cities illustrates the overall pattern.

The first year of the program's life was devoted to processing applications for grants to plan local programs and to the assembly of the necessary supervisory apparatus. Funding for this phase was a modest $11 million, $1 million less than Johnson had requested. To begin actual operations the White House asked for $412 million in FY 1968, supplemented by $250 million in urban renewal funds designated for use in Model Cities neighborhoods. Even HUD, a department with a record of excessive optimism, despaired of winning House passage of the full amounts. HUD's preliminary vote count is revealing. Of 163 congressmen considered favorable to Model Cities, only 5 were Republicans; 150 of the 190 anticipated votes against the bill came from the GOP. The 80 undecideds broke more evenly into 48 Democrats and 32 Republicans.[48] Anticipating criticism that it was foolish to inaugurate a major new program at a time of severe budgetary constraints, the administration chose to emphasize the original purpose of the Model Cities proposal with a new twist. It defended Model Cities as a program "to test out techniques and approaches to the problems of the cities so that when budgetary pressures do ease and more money is available to cities, that money can be efficiently and effectively utilized."[49]

The administration chose to push for passage first in the Senate, where its forces were stronger. Despite severe urban rioting that summer, which was rapidly eroding sympathy for ghetto dwellers, the bill made its way smoothly through the upper chamber. Warren Magnusun (D-Wash.) sponsored it, largely as a means of winning White House support for his own pet project, subsidizing development of a supersonic transport aircraft.[50] By August the Senate approved funding of $537 million for Model Cities, almost the full amount of Johnson's deliberately inflated formal request and more than he had expected to get.[51] This success was due in no small part to the strength of GOP moderates, centered in the Northeast, ten of whom voted in favor of Model Cities.[52]

The White House tried to employ the same ally when dealing with the much thornier situation in the House. Rejecting his aides' advice to take whatever the representatives would give him, Johnson refused to settle for "a dime less than the Senate" had approved.[53] At the president's prompting, Governor Nelson Rockefeller of New York quietly lobbied Minority Leader Gerald Ford and the influential New York Republican Charles

Goodell, urging them to fund the entire $537 million. Ford demurred and insisted that he would fight to cut every possible nickel.[54] The Michigan Republican made good his threat, and the House appropriated only $237 million for FY 1968.[55] The Joint Conference Committee resolved the funding discrepancy largely in favor of the House, agreeing to $212 million for Model Cities and an added $100 million for urban renewal. So confident was Ford of his strength that even the scope of this victory disappointed him, and he privately berated the ranking House Republican on the Conference Committee for undue generosity.[56] To Johnson the result was a bitter setback. Model Cities got only half of the $400 million he had hoped for, and the attendant urban renewal appropriation was a mere 40 percent of his expectation.[57]

The president could take greater satisfaction over other programs. Indeed, part of the reason Johnson did so poorly on Model Cities was that he had husbanded his remaining political capital for use on behalf of more established programs.

Surprisingly, the administration's biggest victory involved perhaps the most controversial element of the Great Society, the Office of Economic Opportunity (OEO). Almost from its beginning, OEO, and in particular its Community Action programs, had been the special target of conservatives and established local authority in most major cities.[58] Despite widespread hostility toward OEO, the Senate, led by Democrats Robert F. Kennedy and Joseph Clark and Republican Jacob Javits, approved $4.65 billion over two years for the poverty program. This amount actually exceeded administration requests by $200 million.[59] Again, the real battle was in the House, where Republicans and southern Democrats hoped to dismantle OEO. Instead, intense White House lobbying secured House agreement on a bill authorizing $100 million above the White House proposal. OEO paid a stiff price, in the form of an amendment which in effect ended the independence of the CAPs by giving control of them to city mayors. Even so it was a remarkable victory when one considers the intense hostility in the House to OEO as a whole.[60]

By 1968, President Johnson was a lame duck, no longer a decisive force in national political affairs. The impression made by the Tet offensive in Vietnam and the unexpected political showing of Senator Eugene McCarthy in the New Hampshire presidential primary combined to shatter Johnson's remaining stature. Insofar as the Great Society was concerned, the watershed had come one year earlier, in the winter of 1966–67. Until then, the Johnson administration had continued to expand its program of domestic reform. By 1966, concern about inflation had become a factor in congressional attitudes to new proposals, but Johnson could and did command the votes to obtain substantially what he wanted. By the end of 1966, he could no longer do so. Rising concern among congressmen and voters over the administration's handling of Vietnam and growing unease over the lack of progress there were important factors in producing the change, but other elements were involved as well. An overheating economy, rising inflation, ghetto unrest, and, most important, a predictable resurgence of a Republican opposition—bitterly hostile for the most part to the Great Society—contributed to the new political environment. In retrospect, Vietnam emerges as only one factor among many which caused the decline in congressional support for reform. To maintain that the war killed the Great Society is as misleading as to deny that Vietnam had any influence in the erosion of support for Johnson's reform program.

PART 3

Central America

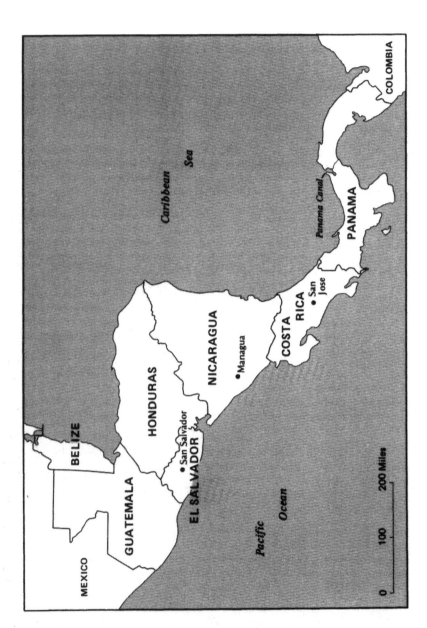

Central America

8

Revolt against the West:
The Nicaraguan Revolution
and Related Movements

RALPH LEE WOODWARD, JR.

IF THE American Revolution was a "revolt against empire," a revolution against colonialism, a war for national liberation; and if the French Revolution was a "revolt against privilege," a revolution against social injustice, a struggle of the capitalist bourgeoisie against a feudal aristocracy; then the Nicaraguan Revolution is part of a Latin American "revolt against the West," a revolution against both the feudal and capitalist traditions of North Atlantic civilization, and a movement to establish socialism as the dominant socioeconomic system. Such an understanding is necessary to the formulation of an American policy toward Nicaragua that will take into account the history of that country as well as its role in Cold War diplomacy.

The Sandinista revolution in Nicaragua is unique in some respects, yet it also is representative of the revolutions of the Third World that have occurred in Latin America and elsewhere throughout this century, beginning essentially with the Mexican Revolution of 1910. These revolutions are challenging the institutions and practices based on classical liberalism of the eighteenth century as institutionalized through the American and French Revolutions. Today, we have the ironic circumstance that the Nicaraguan Revolution is forced to defend itself against the United States, while receiving substantial aid and comfort from the government of France.

Prince Louis Napoleon Bonaparte observed in 1846, with an interoceanic canal through Nicaragua on his mind, that "there are certain countries, which, from their geographical situation, are destined to a

111

highly prosperous future: wealth, power, every national advantage flows into them, provided that where nature has done her utmost, man does not neglect to avail himself of her beneficent assistance."[1] The canal was never finished, and Nicaragua has yet to fulfill Napoleon III's expectations. Many others, foreigners and Nicaraguans, have repeated such glowing expectations for this city-state of about the size of Iowa and only slightly smaller in population. Now the Sandinista revolution has promised to create a new Nicaragua from the ashes of the Somoza dynasty. The Sandinistas have, during their first five years in power, launched the most sweeping changes ever in Nicaraguan society, although it remains to be seen if they can convert this land so often troubled by civil war, dictatorship, and social disruption, into a socialist showcase.

In many ways Central America is a microcosm of Latin America in general. There is a general pattern of modern Central American history that I shall only briefly summarize here.[2] Except for a few enclaves of capitalist agro-export development, the region, unified as the Spanish Kingdom of Guatemala for nearly three hundred years, followed neofeudal, subsistence-oriented patterns well into the eighteenth century. Spain's rivals, in the meantime, probed the isthmus with trade, stimulated by the industrial revolution. Spain's response—the Bourbon Reforms— promoted greater capitalist development and expanded export production.

Independence eliminated the Spanish bureaucracy and left creole landholding elites to dominate the five states, but they divided along lines already drawn in the late colonial period. Liberals advocated the policies of the Bourbon Reformers and the ideals of the American and French Revolutions, while Conservatives sought to retain the security and stability of traditional Hispanic practices and institutions. The political parties—Conservative and Liberal—reflected fundamentally different perceptions of how best to develop their country.

Conservatives, on the one hand, looked toward the maintenance of the two-class society that had long characterized both Spain and Spanish America. They defended the prerogatives of the landholding elite in their traditionally dominant roles, but also, in noblesse oblige fashion, assured the peasants of a degree of protection, especially against exploitation by the Liberal modernizers. They emphasized Hispanic values and institutions, especially the Roman Catholic church, and they rewarded loyal Indian and mestizo peasants with paternalism and respect for communal lands. Their demands on the peasants were real, but limited, and subsistence agriculture was at the heart of their economic philosophy. The Conservatives relied on the church, local chieftains, and landlords—in feudal style—for social control and to guarantee peace and security. Thus they defended states' rights against national unity and were xenophobic toward foreigners who threatened traditional society with Protestantism, democracy, and modernization. While they welcomed modest expansion of agricultural and mineral exports, which allowed them a few luxury imports, they were sensitive to the dangers of upsetting native labor and land-tenure patterns. They were essentially opposed to granting the nation's land and resources to foreign capitalists who did not share their religion, language, or social and cultural values, or who might threaten the preeminent place that they held in the social structure of the provinces.[3]

Liberals, on the other hand, represented that segment of the elite and an incipient bourgeoisie that wished to modernize Central America through emulation of the economic and political success of Western Europe and the United States. These "modernizers" rejected Hispanic values and institutions, especially the church, and espoused classical economic liberalism, opposing monopolies while encouraging private foreign trade, immigration, and investment. They emphasized the need for exports and treated the rural masses and their lands as the principal resources to be exploited in this effort. Although republican and democratic in political theory, they became much influenced by positivist materialism later in the century, and were contemptuous, even embarrassed, by the Indian heritage of their countries. Once in power they resorted to dictatorship to accomplish their economic goals and to defend their gains. Thus the professionalization of the military, which became their power base, was an important trend in the late nineteenth and early twentieth centuries. The absence of stronger middle sectors in the traditional two-class Central American societies and the persistence of elitist attitudes toward the masses meant that in practice the liberal element developed very differently from that in industrialized nations. What emerged were elite oligarchies of planters and capitalists who cynically, and without the noblesse oblige of their Conservative predecessors, continued to live off the labor of an oppressed rural population which shared little if any of the benefits of the expanded export production. On the contrary, the peasants found their subsistence threatened by encroachment on their lands for the production of export commodities.[4]

The Liberals triumphed in every Central American state late in the nineteenth century. Under Liberal guidance there was a boom in coffee exports, with urbanization, railway construction, and significant economic growth. The "coffee prosperity" assured not only Liberal political ascendancy (enforced by a strong military establishment), but the emergence of a new "coffee elite" and an allied urban national bourgeoisie in these "liberal states."[5]

A salient feature of the rise of these oligarchies was their ever-closer relationship with North American capital and the U.S. government. The charge of "dollar diplomacy" finds easy documentation in Central America from the 1860s forward, as U.S. economic interests grew and U.S. hegemony over the Caribbean Basin became a reality. A friendly relationship between the Liberal parties and the United States evolved from the time of independence, whereas Britain courted the Conservatives. By 1914 the Anglo-American rivalry on the isthmus had been decided clearly in U.S. favor. The United States became the principal market for Central American exports, especially bananas, which developed with U.S. capital, shipping, and technology. Industrial and agricultural exports from the United States flooded the Central American markets, and North American manufacturing and construction companies supplied the material and technology for modernization of Central America's city-state capitals. The International Railway of Central America and Tropical Radio and Telegraph, both subsidiaries of the giant United Fruit Company, monopolized transportation and communications throughout the isthmus and overcame (greatly aided by World War I) British and German competition.

The elites began to send their children to school in the United States, rather than to Europe as formerly. The offspring often returned with spouses who brought North American values directly into the social structure of the isthmus, blending more modern attitudes with traditional Hispanic values. The elites were part of the international capitalist upper class and had increasingly less in common with the working masses of their countries. The Liberals imitated U.S. political forms, if not realities, and the terminology of North American democracy filled the Liberal rhetoric. They rewrote the Central American constitutions to conform more closely to the U.S. Constitution of 1789, although in practice Central American chief executives retained more authority than their U.S. counterparts. Early in the twentieth century, U.S. politicians, businessmen, and academics pointed with pride to the enthusiasm with which Central American leaders were adapting to the U.S. model. Without actually hoisting the stars and stripes, Central America became a U.S. colonial dominion. United States embassies became inordinately large for such tiny countries, and basic economic and political decisions for these states were often made within the embassy walls. Military missions provided significant assistance toward the maintenance of the Liberal dictatorships through the training of national police forces to maintain internal security.

The Liberal pattern brought significant economic growth. Middle classes began to appear in the principal cities, but the emphasis on export agriculture deprived the rural peasants of land upon which to grow food, and their lot grew steadily worse, fueling migration into the cities where there were insufficient jobs to employ these mostly illiterate and unskilled displaced persons.

Serious challenges to these regimes began to appear in the 1920s as more modern political parties began to emerge, supported especially by the university communities and urban labor. These parties eventually ranged from Christian Democratic to Marxist-Leninist, but the Liberal dictatorships branded all opposition as "Communist." Only Costa Rica successfully made the transition from elite rule to social democracy. The old Liberal parties gradually succumbed to these more modern pressures in Guatemala, El Salvador, and Honduras, but the military and elite establishments jealously retained power, increasingly by force against the popular will. A Marxist-inspired peasant uprising in El Salvador was ruthlessly suppressed in 1932, with an estimated massacre of 30,000 peasants. The Guatemalan Revolution of 1944 began to establish progressive institutions and popular rule, but alignment with the Soviet Union and threats to expropriate United Fruit holdings saw it cut short by a U.S.-sponsored invasion from Honduras in 1954. Subsequently, and to the present day, counterinsurgency forces backed by the United States and Israel have checked recurrent leftist guerrilla forces in Guatemala. Military aid from the United States to other Central American countries has also been important in suppressing the challenge to liberalism, although in El Salvador the grass-roots development of the Christian Democratic party gained much support and apparently won the presidential election of 1972. The military regime brutally denied victory to the Christian Democrats, however, a move tacitly supported by the Nixon administration in Washington. Less dramatic manifestations of the growing challenge to the Liberal oligarchies occurred in the other states, as student and labor organizations formed the vanguard of efforts to replace the oligarchies with governments representing middle- and working-class interests. In Nicaragua, however, the Somoza dynasty continued Liberal party domination until 1979.

Nicaragua followed the general pattern of Central American development I have described at a somewhat slower pace than the other states and departed from it altogether in several important particulars. Bloody quarrels among Spanish conquistadores in Nicaragua set a tone of violence unmatched in the rest of Central America and initiated a continuing rivalry among the elite families of the two principal cities, León and Granada. The power of these families was based on landed estates, more feudal than capitalist, although a trickle of agricultural and mineral produce flowed from the colony. From the beginning, calculated terror was an accepted means of controlling the peasant population. With their superior weapons the conquerors quickly established a two-class society. The near-total destruction of the native population, however, created a labor shortage that nurtured a more paternalistic, noblesse oblige attitude toward the peasants, also encouraged by the clergy. As the industrial revolution brought increased trade (both legal and contraband) even to remote Nicaragua, however, and the eighteenth-century Bourbon Reforms began to place greater emphasis on exports, a new trend began toward exploitation of the peasant population by the elite. Yet visitors often described colonial Nicaragua as having a degree of prosperity and affluence not found in much of Spanish America. The population decline meant that land was abundant, allowing for both large cattle ranches and subsistence farming. There was plenty of land for all who wanted it. Near the end of the colonial period there was notable increase in exports of foodstuffs to the indigo-producing regions of El Salvador and Guatemala.[6]

Independence from Spain, however, ushered in a long period of civil war and revolution between the two factions of the elite. A Nicaraguan Constitution in 1826 laid the basis for government of the state along republican lines, but the real effect of independence was to remove the Spanish bureaucracy and place power entirely in the hands of the creole elite. The bitter struggles between León Liberals and Granada Conservatives decimated their ranks, but immigrants from Guatemala, such as Fruto Chamorro, provided new blood.[7]

The Liberal-Conservative struggle was burning hotly when Nicaragua became the focus of rivalry between the United States and Great Britain for control of an interoceanic route. Aggressive diplomats pursued each nation's interests, but eventually a railroad across Panama made the Nicaraguan route less attractive. The climax of this struggle, however, came when William Walker led a band of California filibusters to Nicaragua in support of the Liberals. Initially successful, Walker made himself president of the state in 1856, but a Conservative army led by Rafael Mora of Costa Rica and strongly supported by Rafael Carrera of Guatemala, with troops from all five states and with British assistance, routed Walker in April 1857. The Conservative alliance might have led to Central American reunion, but both Mora and Carrera were strong states' rightists.[8]

Mora's ouster two years later and Carrera's death in 1865 signaled Liberal resurgence everywhere in Central America with the notable exception of Nicaragua, where the Walker episode had thoroughly discredited the Liberals. Conservatives ruled more than thirty years longer in Nicaragua.[9]

Nineteenth-century accounts of Nicaragua document the slower pace of capitalist transformation of Nicaragua's economy. As late as 1898, a German observer, while noting the increased investment in agriculture and mining, commented on Nicaragua's relatively low level of development and the relative freedom of Nicaraguan agricultural labor. Compared with other Central American states, however, the transformation to modern society had only just begun.[10]

The Liberal reform finally came to Nicaragua with José Santos Zelaya beginning in 1893. Like other Liberal dictators, Zelaya encouraged accelerated foreign investments, and North Americans responded. The Conservative strength, however, and its alliance with some British and American economic interests, especially on the Caribbean coast, contributed to the overthrow of Zelaya in 1909.[11] In the turmoil that followed, U.S. economic interests were important in persuading the Taft administration to establish a customs receivership in 1911. Continued civil war led him to send the marines in 1912. They restored order and maintained the Conservative government backed by General Emiliano Chamorro.[12]

A marine guard remained to guarantee peace and deter revolution. Dana Munro, a doctoral candidate from the University of Pennsylvania who traveled through Nicaragua doing research for his dissertation, remarked that a hundred marines were "kept in one of the forts at Managua and a warship is stationed at Corinto as reminders that the United States will not permit another uprising against the constituted authorities. One hundred well-trained and well-equipped soldiers are in themselves no inconsiderable force in a country like Nicaragua."[13] Munro's first impressions of Central America, in 1914, confirm the suggestion that Nicaragua was modernizing more slowly than Costa Rica, Guatemala, or El Salvador, but he commented that even though the annual per capita income of Nicaragua probably did not exceed forty dollars, he had the feeling that the people were not "particularly unhappy about their poverty. They had food and shelter and such clothes as they needed without working very hard to obtain them." Yet he acknowledged that the economic situation was growing worse and that the currency reform established upon the advice of the American bankers "had increased the cost of living for the poor." Moreover, around Matagalpa and Metapa, where English and American coffee plantations had recently established themselves, he noted shortages of food and expanding misery among the peasants.[14]

Support of the Conservative party by the United States was relatively unique, for in most of Central America it was the Liberal party which had traditionally identified with this country. Eventually that would be the case in Nicaragua, too, but the Walker episode and the peculiar circumstances surrounding the overthrow of Zelaya contributed to a delay in that pattern in Nicaragua and, consequently, to the survival of the Conservative party. In 1925, with a compromise government in place made up of anti-Chamorro Conservatives and Liberals, the marines departed. Violence flared immediately between Conservatives and Liberals, with the result that the marines returned the following year. In 1927 Henry L. Stimson and General José Moncada, a Liberal, reached an agreement at Tipitapa to restore peace and to hold elections under U.S. supervision.[15]

In the ensuing election of 1928, the Liberals won control of the government, but one Liberal, Augusto César Sandino, refused to lay down his arms, launching a guerrilla struggle against the continued U.S. military presence that gained admiration throughout the hemisphere. This bloody chapter in relations between the United States and Nicaragua consumed an increasingly large number of marines and became unpopular in the United States, a forewarning of the Vietnam debacle a half-century later. The United States withdrew its forces in 1933, but in the meantime it trained a tough internal security force, the Guardia Nacional.[16]

Although Sandino had won his objective of removing U.S. forces, the victory was hollow, for soon after reaching agreements with the Nicaraguan government to lay down his arms, he was treacherously assassinated by members of the National Guard. The head of the guard, Anastasio Somoza García, was master of the country by 1935 and became president two years later. He and his sons would rule Nicaragua until July 19, 1979. The Somozas intensified a close relationship with the United States, similar to that which had been developing with Liberal dictatorships elsewhere on the isthmus. The Conservative party survived as the only important legal opposition party, but it divided over the question of collaboration with the Somozas. Eventually, many Liberals broke with the Somozas, as the regime became simply a family dynasty of economic and political power in the country. Nevertheless, the old Conservative and Liberal families continued to represent a privileged elite in a country which now proceeded on a path of modernization along nineteenth-century Liberal lines. This meant great expansion of export agriculture, some industrialization, a growth of financial institutions, and emergence of a middle class in Managua. The Somozas promoted development of that city to the detriment of the traditional elite centers of Granada and León. Having been destroyed in 1931 by earthquake and fire, Managua was an almost entirely new city, and its growth provided employment and opportunity for at least some of those who migrated from rural areas to escape exploitation. After a second destruction of the city by the earthquake of 1972, however, mismanagement of reconstruction funds by Tachito Somoza contributed to widespread disenchantment with the regime even among its former supporters.[17]

The Somoza dynasty was not the most brutal or repressive of Latin American dictatorships. Indeed, there were notable periods of free press, and the university campuses remained hotbeds of opposition, including openly Marxist faculties and students. The particular specialty of the Somozas was their skill in stealing from everyone in the country—so much so that the term "cleptocracy" has often been used to describe the regime.[18]

The Somoza government was not entirely unmindful of the needs of the people, and like other Central American Liberal dictatorships, it succeeded in bringing about a degree of modernization and some improvements in education, medical care, and social services. Nicaragua continued to produce a larger share of its food consumption than any other Central American country, but the trend toward exports was making it more dependent on foreign food imports, just as had happened in the other states. More and more land was devoted to coffee, cattle, cotton, and sugar instead of subsistence crops. Nicaragua's per capita annual income of about $900 placed it behind Panama, Costa Rica, and Guatemala on the isthmus, and poverty was growing rather than declining as real wages lagged behind inflation. Indeed, one of the most discouraging realities for the Liberal modernization model of the last hundred years in Central America is the apparent decline in standard of living for most Central Americans. By the 1970s, poverty was widespread in Nicaragua, and many of the undesirable effects of the Liberal-capitalist development had begun to fasten themselves on both rural and urban Nicaragua.

It was in this environment that the Frente Sandinista de Liberación Nacional (FSLN) developed after 1960, gaining strength especially at the National University in León. Led by Carlos Fonseca Amador and Tomás Borge, it was always dedicated to a socialist-oriented revolution. Of the original leaders of the movement, only Borge survived to taste victory. It gained few adherents until the late seventies, when opposition grew against Tachito Somoza's efforts to frustrate all legal political expressions. The assassination of Pedro Joaquín Chamorro, popular editor of the country's leading daily (the Conservative *La Prensa*), brought a dramatic upsurge in support for the Sandinistas. All segments of the country rallied to support the war against the dictatorship, resulting in its downfall in July 1979.

During the 1960s and early 1970s the Sandinistas developed close ties with Havana and Moscow, where they received advice, training, and moral and material support. Even though all were dedicated to the establishment of a Marxist state in Nicaragua, as the struggle wore on for nearly two decades, important divisions developed among the commanders regarding strategy and tactics as well as how to proceed once they had control of the government. The early Sandinistas favored direct transition to socialism with alignment to the Soviet bloc. The older commandants, notably Tomás Borge, but also including Henry Ruiz and Bayardo Arce, held to the Cuban revolutionary model glorified by Che Guevara's guerrilla tactics—the *foco* concept of rural guerrilla warfare, a strategy they called the Prolonged People's War. In the 1970s younger Sandinista revisionists, led by Jaime Wheelock, Carlos Núñez, and Luis Carrión, began to favor what was called the Proletarian Tendency, based more on the Chilean experience and emphasizing urban struggle and radicalization of the working class. Although they differed with the first group, they were just as dogmatic and also insisted on close alliance with the Soviet bloc. A third group, however, known appropriately as the Terceristas and led by Daniel and Humberto Ortega, argued for a more gradual transition to socialism and had a much broader concept of class alliances. Under their leadership, the FSLN formed alliances with Edén Pastora's Southern Front and with prominent Nicaraguan anti-Somocistas of the upper and middle class both within and outside of Nicaragua, including many members of the clergy. This pragmatic alliance with other interests and Cuban support became the dominant force and achieved victory in July 1979.

These moderates looked toward the establishment of a "Third Option," between East and West, something between social democratic Costa Rica and Communist Cuba, with an emphasis on nonalignment. This implied a more gradual transition to socialism, with maintenance of a strong private sector within the development of a welfare state. Such a policy, the moderates argued, would include continued support of leftists in neighboring states (El Salvador and Guatemala) while maintaining good relations with moderate allies—Panama, Costa Rica, Venezuela, and Mexico. The establishment of a government within a pluralist democratic framework would avoid isolation from the West and recognize the geopolitical reality of U.S. hegemony in the Caribbean Basin. For the moderates, Sandinismo would be simply a part of a social democratic synthesis between Marxism and capitalism, and it would count on the cooperation of the United States.

After the overthrow of Somoza there was some indication that these moderates were having an influence, and the early actions of the Carter administration reflected a tentative willingness to cooperate in the establishment of social democracy in Nicaragua. It soon became evident, however, that the moderate advisers had not prevailed, and that although the Sandinistas were willing to go slowly in actually transforming Nicaragua into a Marxist-Leninist state, they insisted from the beginning on a pro-Soviet foreign policy and alignment with the Soviets.

The intellectual framework of the FSLN commandants is crucial to this position. Nearly all were educated at the National University of Nicaragua in a strongly Marxist social science framework. This education was supplemented by frequent trips to Cuba, the Soviet Union, and the German Democratic Republic and by grants to study in those countries. They developed a worldview within a strongly Marxist mind-set that included deeply entrenched mistrust of the United States and the West. Imbued with "dependency theory," they insisted on a complete break with the capitalist world system. With the experience of Guatemala, Cuba, Chile, and other Third World countries that had attempted Marxist solutions to their problems, they were convinced that alliance with the East was the only way their revolution could survive. They were firmly committed to social justice and democracy, but they distrusted Western-style social democracy. Rather, their narrow ideological worldview called for democracy as that term is understood in the East rather than the West. Just as the Nicaraguan bourgeoisie vulgarly imitated the North Americans, the Sandinistas indiscriminately mimicked the rhetoric and tactics of the Cuban Revolution. Cuba offered an attractive alternative to the arrogant U.S. hegemony in Nicaragua.[19]

The moderate allies were initially included in the government, and a few still remain, such as Foreign Minister Father Miquel d'Escoto, but others defected or were pushed out. A major loss was the defection of Commandant Zero (Edén Pastora), who launched a major counterrevolutionary front, ARDE (Alianza Revolucionaria Democrática, or Democratic Revolutionary Alliance), from Costa Rica. Pastora's intense distrust of the United States precluded him from getting the kind of aid that the CIA gave to the Honduran-based FDN (Frente Democrático Nicaragüense, or Nicaraguan Democratic Front), which included about 7,000 members of Somoza's old National Guard. From an anti-Sandinista point of view this was unfortunate, for Pastora enjoyed far more prestige and popularity within Nicaragua than did the Somocista-linked FDN.

Once in power, the Sandinistas tried to put aside their old divisions, to some degree irrelevant now that the old regime had fallen. Fidel Castro played an important role in bringing about conciliation among the three Sandinista groups, encouraging them to concentrate on their common goal of establishing a socialist nation. The commandants reaffirmed their notion that the world was bipolar, and their distrust of the Western "liberals" became increasingly manifest. They decided that they had to convince the Soviets of their goodwill—that Nicaragua was, contrary to public statements, *not* nonaligned. The Soviets showed some reluctance to believe this; they were unwilling to provide massive economic aid as in the case of Cuba, nor did they wish to provoke confrontation with the United States in a region where the U.S. had an enormous geopolitical advantage. The Cubans also tried to prevent too strong a move toward the Left, fearing U.S. intervention.

The Sandinistas were and are convinced that military defense is essential to their survival, and they conceived this belief within a framework of alliance with the Eastern bloc. The question of whether the United States would allow a defenseless Nicaragua to carry out a socialist revolution remains unanswered, but the experience of Guatemala, Chile, and Grenada certainly helps to explain the apprehensiveness of the Sandinistas.

Within Nicaragua, the Sandinista revolution has brought sweeping changes and has moved toward the creation of a Marxist-Leninist state. The literacy campaign greatly raised the cultural level of most Nicaraguans while it also administered a strong dose of Marxist doctrine. Its economic program has brought a small increase in the production of foodstuffs but has met major obstacles in expanding agro exports, initially hurt by the war itself and later by the intransigence of the bourgeoisie. More than 60 percent of the economy remains in private hands in Nicaragua, but this segment of the economy is not healthy, and it remains to be seen whether Nicaragua can continue as a mixed economy. A major schism in the Catholic church has also occurred, with advocates of Liberation Theology and its "People's Church" now being opposed by the ecclesiastical hierarchy, which had opposed the Somozas but now opposes the Sandinistas and provides leadership for a growing opposition to Sandinismo within Nicaragua.[20]

The collapse of the Somoza dynasty represented the demise of nineteenth-century liberalism in Nicaragua and the beginning of a bold new experiment in which the interests of the masses would take precedence over those of the traditional elites. As in Cuba two decades earlier, this conflict would be complicated by East-West confrontation. That Nicaragua would move sharply toward socialism ahead of the rest of Central America, after lagging behind it for so many years, is historically a result of the Somozas' Liberal party failing to allow more moderate but progressive forces to develop and share in the political process during the last half century. As elsewhere on the isthmus, the elite repressed middle- and working-class interests, leaving violence and revolution as the only avenue for bringing change. That a tiny minority—the Sandinistas—was able to seize power and capture the imagination of the majority of the population is not unique in the history of revolution. The Sandinistas see themselves as a vanguard in the struggle to provide a better life for their compatriots.

Many of them are convinced that this means inevitable struggle against the United States and the West, the champion of nineteenth-century liberalism and defender of the old order. How their authoritarian means, the intervention of Soviet and U.S. interests into the struggle, and the development of legitimate opposition to the radical Sandinista approach will affect the course of the revolution and Nicaraguan history remains to be seen.

9

The United States, Costa Rica, and Nicaragua, 1980–1984

THOMAS M. LEONARD

COSTA RICANS enjoy being described as an industrious people who are not cursed by latifundia or racial strife. Considered a middle-class people, their peaceful political development stands in sharp contrast to that of their neighbors. Events since Costa Rica's civil war in 1948 did much to reinforce the popular image. The most important political party, the National Liberation party (PLN), has captured all but three presidential elections since 1948. Major opposition came from the Unity party (UP), which wrested the presidency from the PLN in 1958, 1966, and 1978, but once in power did not alter the economic and social programs set in motion by the PLN. A leftist coalition, the United People's party (PUP), included the Marxist-leaning Popular Vanguard party and the Socialist and People's Revolutionary parties. The first two groups competed for support from the majority of Costa Ricans, whereas the latter claimed support from the coastal banana workers, urban poor, intellectuals, and students. PUP, however, never gained more than 4 percent of the popular vote in elections since 1948. The army was outlawed after 1948, and a major portion of the national budget was spent on education and health care. Historically, Costa Rica remained aloof from the region's political conflicts. Given these factors, it enjoyed the label "Switzerland of the Americas."[1]

United States officials shared the view that Costa Rica was a tranquil haven surrounded by a sea of turmoil. In 1949 the State Department viewed San José as a place reserved for foreign service officers who had completed assignments in hardship posts elsewhere. In 1978 Senator George McGovern (D-S.D.) returned from Costa Rica greatly impressed by its "effective political system, its sensitive and profound social system."

A year later Assistant Secretary of State Viron Vaky remarked that Costa Rica was an exception to the region's authoritarian governments and was not plagued by wealth maldistribution.[2]

Two events in 1979, however, altered the perception of Costa Rican life and dragged it into the region's political and military conflict. First, increased petroleum costs, coupled with the loss of income from exports, created economic hardships within Costa Rica. Second, the overthrow of Anastasio Somoza in Nicaragua by the Sandinista revolutionaries severely strained Costa Rica's traditional neutrality from regional conflicts. After 1979, United States policy toward Costa Rica also changed, from one of indifference to one of coercing Costa Rica to join the battle against a Communist threat to the region.

Costa Rica: Caught in the Web of Events

From 1970 to 1979, Costa Rica enjoyed a high living standard, during which it consumed more than it produced. Importation of foreign goods was commonplace. Exports, primarily coffee, failed to keep pace with the cost of imports, and borrowing abroad became the means to make up the difference in the unfavorable trade balance. Among the imports was oil, on which Costa Rica was totally dependent in satisfying local needs. When the Organization of Petroleum Exporting Countries (OPEC) quadrupled the price of petroleum in 1979, Costa Rica's already unfavorable trade balance was adversely affected. The "oil shock" triggered a wave of international inflation and high interest rates. At the same time, world coffee prices plummeted and the demand by the Central American Common Market countries for Costa Rican manufactured goods slackened. Costa Rica's trade balance worsened. Vice President José Miguel Alfaro clearly illustrated the problem when he remarked that "in 1970 one bag of coffee bought 100 barrels of oil. Today one bag of coffee buys just three barrels of oil."[3]

These factors produced a drastic decline in Costa Rica's real economic growth (GDP, or gross domestic product) and doubled the official unemployment rate to almost 9 percent. The vast network of government agencies—including those dealing with land and colonization; municipal development; electric, water, and sewer; social security; and petroleum refinery—were hard pressed for income to carry on their services. The situation was so bad that one Costa Rican economist observed that the "fiesta is over. We've reached the bottom of the barrel." Television commentator Guido Fernandez charged that the politicians "haven't thought enough about how to pay for all this." Pessimists warned that unless the country quickly solved its economic problems, it would become vulnerable to the troubles of other Central American nations, or its people might even welcome a *caudillo* (strongman).[4]

President Rodrigo Carazo failed to face the crisis. Confronted with defections in his legislative coalition, he permitted the colon to float in December 1981. (See table 9.1.) It soon dropped from eight to forty for each U.S. dollar. Furthermore, by the end of 1981 Costa Rica was unable to pay interest on its $2.6 billion foreign debt. International banks rejected Carazo's proposals for rescheduling both short- and long-term debts unless the government accepted austerity measures imposed by the International Monetary Fund (IMF). Carazo refused, because such measures included an end to government subsidies for gasoline and public utilities and a cut in the size of the government bureaucracy. In response, the IMF canceled a current $300 million credit. Carazo's inaction was caused by fear of a popular backlash. Settlement of the financial crisis had to await the inauguration of a new president, scheduled for May 1982.[5]

As expected, the PLN candidate, Luis Alberto Monge, won the presidential election of February 4, 1982, capturing 57 percent of the popular vote. By the time of his inauguration in May, Monge inherited a bankrupt country. Neither interest nor principal had been paid to foreign creditors for nearly a year, although some multinational agencies, such as the World Bank, received token interest payments. Without reserves to support the colon, however, the exchange rate dropped to sixty-two for each U.S. dollar, and the GDP was estimated to shrink another 6 percent in 1982.

Most Costa Ricans anticipated Monge's austerity measures. He moved quickly after taking office. Government-owned agencies increased rates for electricity (56 percent), water (108 percent), and gasoline (70 percent).

Table 9.1. Costa Rican Economic Indicators

	1979	1980	1981
GDP increase (rate of growth, %)	4.9	0.6	−3.6
Consumer price increase (%)	9.2	18.1	37.0
Trade balance (in millions of dollars)	−315	−357	−62
External debt (in billions of dollars)	1.9	2.4	2.6

Source: Inter-American Development Bank, *Economic and Social Progress in Latin America, Report, 1982* (Washington: U.S. Government Printing Office, 1982), 227.

Government subsidies for basic foodstuffs disappeared, and there was a sharp cutback in public projects. For example, San José's new freeway system was halted in midstream. Taxes were increased on exports, and an export ministry was created to promote the sale of Costa Rican products.

Monge also sought to impress the international financial community. Officials from IMF, the World Bank, and the Inter-American Development Bank were invited to his inauguration. Realizing the economic and social consequences of IMF austerity demands, Monge put forth his own proposals. Together, the self-imposed austerity measures and the aggressive attitude toward the IMF had some positive results. A tentative agreement was reached on restructuring the government's debts with foreign creditors. In December 1982 the IMF approved a $100 million loan for economic stabilization programs for 1983. The IMF also advanced another $19.5 million in September 1983.

The austerity measures, credit restructuring, and advanced credits combined to bring down inflation to a 15 percent annual rate by December 1983 and permitted the government to make token interest payments on its foreign debt. The austerity program was expected to bring further improvements in 1986.[6]

Continued progress was minimal, however. Inflation did not abate, and unemployment was unofficially estimated at 20 percent. The international debt reached $4.1 billion, giving Costa Rica the highest per capita debt in the world. Domestic discontent increased, workers struck for increased wages, and coffee prices continued to fall. Demonstrations against increased costs for basic necessities prevented Monge from making further cuts in government programs, particularly education and health care, which received 28 percent of the annual budget. Economic assistance from the United States for 1984 totaled $110 million, which on a per capita basis was the eleventh highest in the world, but this was not enough to correct Costa Rica's economic chaos.[7]

While President Monge and others worried about the threat economic hardship posed to Costa Rica's social and political fabric, the country also began to experience terrorist activity. Historically a haven for political exiles, Costa Rica became a safety valve for many wanting to escape the violence of northern neighbors. Costa Rica granted asylum to refugees entering the country without arms and required only that they not engage in combat training or military activities while in the country. By January 1984 the government listed 2,901 official refugees in the country but claimed thousands more along its frontier with Nicaragua.

The exiles' activities resulted in violence and drew Costa Rica closer to the Central American conflict. In March 1981 a group called the Carlos

Agüerro Echeverria Command, which was named after a Costa Rican who died fighting with the Sandinistas in Nicaragua, claimed responsibility for wounding three U.S. marines and damaging the Honduran embassy in separate bomb attacks. The bombings were in protest of the support given by those countries to the Salvadoran government. In response, the Costa Rican government expelled thirty-six foreign exiles, mainly Nicaraguans and Salvadorans but also some Argentines and Hondurans. By year's end there was increased local pressure to reorient Costa Rica's security forces toward combating terrorist subversion. Some local civil guards were reportedly carrying automatic weapons.[8]

Throughout 1982 terrorist violence increased. In January, three terrorists, two of them Salvadoran, were killed in an unsuccessful attempt to kidnap a Salvadoran industrialist. Later in the year additional attempts were made to kidnap Salvadoran and Japanese businessmen, and an attempt to kidnap a U.S. diplomat was reported. The San José office of Tan-Sasha, the Honduran national airline, was bombed on July 3, and a similar explosion later rocked the apartment of the Nicaraguan political exile Fernando Chamorro. In San José, police discovered a "people's jail," which was a safe house stocked with arms, food, and medical supplies, thirty terrorist cells, and documents calling for efforts to undermine the Costa Rican government. Although the violence subsided in 1983 and 1984, threats continued against businessmen from the United States and elsewhere and against political exiles from Nicaragua and El Salvador. Residents near the Nicaraguan border were under constant threat of violence. The most notable example was in December 1983, when six people were killed amid heavy property damage caused by the fire bombing of Upala, two hundred miles north of San José.

The Costa Rican government responded to the violence by increasing border surveillance, tightening immigration laws, and expelling suspicious foreigners, mostly Nicaraguans. The terrorist activities also caused a heated national debate about rearming the civil and rural guards.[9]

Much of the violence was attributed to events in Nicaragua. Costa Ricans disliked the Somoza regime, sympathizing with those who wanted to oust him. President Carazo permitted the Sandinistas to base their operations in Costa Rica. Once in power, the Sandinista government moved leftward in philosophy and failed to implement a promised democracy, causing a dampening of Costa Rican sympathy for the revolution. A public opinion poll in 1984 showed that 84 percent of the Costa Rican people had turned sour on their neighbor's revolution.[10] As a result, by 1984 the government in San José sought to distance itself from its counterpart in Managua and to disassociate itself from the Salvadoran revolutionaries.

Although Costa Rica continued to send armaments to Salvadoran guerrillas, the activities of Edén Pastora drew it closer to the troubles in Central America. Pastora, an original Sandinista and popular military hero in the war against Somoza, deserted the Sandinista government in 1981. Charging that the Sandinistas strayed from the true revolutionary cause to Marxism-Leninism, Pastora set up camp in Costa Rica to conduct a not-so-secret war against them, an activity in violation of Costa Rican law. At the same time, the Honduran-based and CIA-financed National Democratic Front (FDN) openly recruited from ground-floor offices in San José.

Pastora received financial assistance from the CIA in establishing training camps and staging areas in northern Costa Rica. Despite promises to the contrary, President Monge lacked the military means to halt Pastora's activities. Although he assigned an additional seven hundred civil guardsmen to the northern sector, their service was limited to the discovery of vacated guerrilla camps. Suspicions mounted that landowners and local officials were bribed by Pastora, with CIA funds, to give warning of the advancing guardsmen. Pastora was left free to launch land and air attacks into Nicaragua, and to return to his confines inside Costa Rica. Following an unsuccessful assassination attempt against Pastora in May 1984, the Costa Rican government could not prevent his return in July after his recuperation in Venezuela. Unable to control its border, Costa Rica appealed to the Contadora group (Colombia, Mexico, Panama, and Venezuela), the Organization of American States (OAS), and directly to Nicaragua for a peacekeeping force on its northern border.[11]

From 1980 to 1984, Costa Rica was increasingly influenced by the events plaguing Central America. Its economy collapsed, creating domestic pressures for government action to alleviate hardship. To some, these internal pressures threatened Costa Rica's political stability. As violence and repression increased in El Salvador and Nicaragua, political refugees flooded into Costa Rica. Some became active terrorists and threatened Costa Rica's tranquility. Finally, the insurgency led by Pastora threatened to engulf Costa Rica in war. Financially strapped, under political pressure, and menaced by war, the Costa Rican government faced events beyond its control.

United States Policy:
Utilizing Another's Weakness

Historically, the United States found Costa Rica to be a staunch ally. A country where the president set the foreign policy direction, Costa Rica supported the U.S. effort in World War II and the battle against communism in the ensuing Cold War. More recently it supported President Jimmy Carter's human rights policies, opposed the Soviet invasion of Afghanistan, and shared the U.S. frustrations with the actions of OPEC and Iran. Costa Rica's relations with Nicaragua's Somoza regime were often strained. In 1948 and 1955 the two countries were at war. Both times the United States sided with Costa Rica. The Costa Ricans' sympathy for the Sandinistas was easy to understand.[12]

Problems mounted during the 1970s. Despite $5 million in assistance from the Carter administration for patrol boats to interrupt arms traffic to El Salvador, Costa Rica continued to be a base for the shipment of military supplies to the Salvadoran guerrillas.[13]

From 1979, following the overthrow of Somoza, until 1982, the United States gave minimal attention to Costa Rica. Policy was directed toward the Sandinistas in Nicaragua and the guerrillas in El Salvador. The San José government shunned the few overtures made by the Reagan administration.

On the eve of President Ronald Reagan's inauguration in January 1981, President Carazo expressed agreement with the mix of U.S. military and economic assistance to El Salvador and was confident that if it continued, a democratic government would emerge. He cautioned against a more rigid stance against the Sandinistas, whose rhetoric, Carazo believed, was extreme but whose policies at home were more moderate. Carazo also believed that the U.S. failure to provide economic assistance to the Nicaraguan government provided the Cubans and Soviets more leverage in the country and that further aggressive actions by the United States would drive the Sandinistas into the Communist camp.

Carazo's advice was ignored by the incoming Reagan administration, which placed the Central American conflict within the context of the East-West struggle. The White House emphasized a military solution in El Salvador and used all means short of direct confrontation to topple the Sandinista regime. From 1981 to 1984, President Reagan warned that communism threatened the entire Central American region. Costa Rica was under pressure to join the crusade against its spread.[14]

In August 1981, while in San José, the ambassador to the UN, Jeane Kirkpatrick, repeated Reagan's theme. She charged that Costa Rica's economic disruptions were directly linked to the Soviet Union, that Soviet diplomats were responsible for fomenting labor unrest, and that leftist guerrillas were encamped throughout the country. Kirkpatrick offered U.S. assistance with military training. Two months later, also in San José, Assistant Secretary of State for Latin American Affairs Thomas O. Enders pressed President Carazo to support U.S. policy in Central America more openly. Carazo resisted, however, protesting that both emissaries exaggerated the Communist threat, and he emphasized that economic and not military aid was needed. The former vice president José Miguel Alfaro later recalled that Kirkpatrick's offer of economic assistance was contingent upon acceptance of military aid.

Apparently the Reagan administration had no plans to assist Costa Rica with its economic problems. In December 1981, responding to Representative Gerry E. Studds's (D-Mass.) question, "What are we going to do—wait until there is open insurgency there and then pour in aid?" an administrator in the Agency for International Development (AID), M. Peter McPherson, remarked, "we are trying to do a lot to try to figure out the Costa Rica situation." The administration initially sought only $2.9 million in economic assistance for Costa Rica in 1982. Some Costa Ricans interpreted this to be punishment for Carazo's recalcitrant position.[15]

The presidential election of Luis Alberto Monge signaled a closer relationship between San José and Washington. Although the PLN historically supported the U.S. position in world affairs, Monge recognized Washington's need to maintain Costa Rican democracy in troubled Central America, and thus could afford to resist becoming a totally committed ally. For the next two years, conflicting signals came out of San José in response to the Reagan administration's pressure for support of U.S. policy in Central America.

Reagan welcomed Monge's election in 1982 by dispatching Agricultural Secretary John Block and Assistant Secretary Enders to head the U.S. delegation attending Monge's May inauguration. They promised economic assistance if Costa Rica accepted IMF austerity measures. Monge also was invited to Washington. After meeting with Reagan in June, the two presidents expressed fuller appreciation of the other's problems, particularly with regards to Central America. Reagan returned the visit in December 1982, a gesture to reaffirm the U.S. commitment to Costa Rica.[16]

President Monge's austerity efforts at home won the approval of both the IMF and the United States. While the IMF made $119.5 million available, the United States advanced $266 million through 1983 and another $110 million was scheduled for 1984. Costa Rica also became one of the first eleven nations designated to receive assistance under the Caribbean Basin Initiative when it was passed by Congress in 1983. The largest segment of the economic assistance program was to help businessmen purchase raw materials abroad. Critics charged that the United States was failing to address local food production and other self-sufficiency measures which would defuse social and political tension.[17]

While the merits and demerits of economic assistance were debated, the primary U.S. objective was to keep Nicaragua isolated. Officials continually blamed the Sandinistas for terrorist activities and border incidents in Costa Rica, which had no army and only 7,000 civil and rural guards, who performed police functions. According to U.S. law no aid could be given to foreign police organizations, which the Kissinger Commission found to be a "particularly absurd situation" with regards to Costa Rica.[18] Rather than change the law, the administration sought to circumvent it.

In June 1982 President Monge decided to increase border security by professionalizing a 500-man unit of the civil guard. To assist with the project, the United States forwarded $2 million in nonlethal military gear—uniforms, boots, radios, and field equipment. (See table 9.2.) Ammunition for the guard's M-14 rifles came from Venezuela. The United States also agreed to train Costa Rican officers at its Southern Command Headquarters in Panama. A total of seventy guards soon enrolled at the School of the Americas for basic infantry training and a course specifically designed for patrolling border areas in mountainous jungle regions. The Costa Rican government also increased its naval patrol of Salinas Bay between itself and Nicaragua. A voluntary organization, OPEN, was formed to deal with potential national disasters and emergencies. Critics quickly charged that Monge caved in to U.S. demands out of economic necessity. Frank McNeill, U.S. ambassador to Costa Rica, countered that Monge was acting only in response to Sandinista threats.

Border incidents increased, largely owing to the activities of ARDE, which were Pastora's guerrilla forces operating from northern Costa Rica.

Table 9.2. United States Assistance to Costa Rica (in millions of dollars)

	1962–1979	1980	1981	1982	1983
Economic aid	199.0	16.0	15.2	51.7	214.3
Military aid	6.9	0.5	0.2	2.1	4.6

Sources: Agency for International Development, *U.S. Oversees Loans and Grants, July 1, 1945–September 30, 1981*, 43; House Committee on Foreign Affairs and Senate Committee on Foreign Relations, "Country Reports for Human Rights Practices for 1983," 98th Cong. 2d sess., 523.

To help secure the area, the chief of the U.S. Command in Panama, General Paul Gorman, suggested to Monge and his cabinet in September 1983 that about a thousand U.S. National Guardsmen be brought to Costa Rica for constructing roads similar to those built by U.S. servicemen in Honduras. Secretary of State George P. Shultz attempted to disguise the proposal as one of economic development to help accelerate AID agricultural programs. The Costa Ricans backed off.

Border clashes continued, and so did U.S. threats and pressure, despite denials in both Washington and San José. In 1984 the new ambassador, Curtin Winsor, charged that "something more had to be done" to preserve democracy in the region. Under Secretary for Defense Fred C. Ikle called for increased military assistance to combat the leftist threat to Costa Rica.[19]

In the late spring of 1984, at the same time reports surfaced that U.S. military advisers from Panama were secretly teaching Costa Ricans how to train their own people, Foreign Minister Carlos Gutierrez approached the U.S. embassy in San José with a request for $7.5 million in military assistance. The shopping list included 4,000 M-16 rifles, 24 mortars, and 120 M-60 machine guns to be used for improving border surveillance. Public Security Minister Angel Edmundo Solano denied that the aid would further antagonize relations with Nicaragua. In Washington the State Department recommended quick approval, believing that such assistance would force Costa Rica from its "neutralist tightrope act and push it more explicably and probably into the anti-Sandinista camp." Although no clear connection was established, the Costa Rican request came at about the same time AID suspended a $58 million loan in an effort to have the Costa Rican legislature approve a change in banking laws that would avoid the National Bank by permitting foreign loans to go directly to private business. Such actions caused Senators Jim Sasser (D-Tenn.) and Jeff Bingaman (D-N.M.) to charge the Pentagon in Washington and the embassy in San José with coercing Costa Rica into following U.S. policy.[20]

From 1982 until late 1984, Monge attempted to maintain a sense of independence from the United States. The invitation of IMF, World Bank, and Inter-American Development Bank officials was deliberate; the United States did not have pervasive influence over those agencies. To spur regional peace negotiations, Monge used the U.S.-sponsored American Democratic Community (Costa Rica, El Salvador, and Honduras), which had been formed in February 1982 to give credibility to the Salvadoran presidential elections of March 1982. Monge complained about Ambassador Winsor's continual comments urging Costa Rica to take a stronger stand against Nicaragua. At the United Nations, Costa Rica joined the vast majority in censuring the 1983 U.S. invasion of Grenada. At the same time, Monge refused to send one thousand men to the U.S.-built Regional Military Training Center in Honduras. Unable to secure his Nicaraguan border with an international peacekeeping force, Monge declared his country's neutrality in international affairs in December 1983.[21]

Before the national legislature acted on Monge's neutrality proclamation, however, it made the $7.5 million military aid request to the United States. This action provoked anti–United States demonstrations in San José and sent Monge on an eleven-nation European tour to reaffirm Costa Rican neutrality.[22]

Just as the pressure increased on Costa Rica in 1982 to join the U.S. crusade against Nicaragua, that pressure quickly dissipated in late 1984. U.S. congressional opposition choked off, at least for the moment, President Reagan's military solution to the Central American crisis and, with it, efforts to force a change in Costa Rica's neutral stance.

Conclusion

From 1980 to 1984, U.S. and Costa Rican policies toward Central America were at odds. The United States sought to force Costa Rica into following its anti-Sandinista policy. At the same time, Costa Rica wished to maintain its traditional neutral stance from regional conflicts. Circumstances largely beyond Costa Rica's control forced it to succumb to U.S. pressure.

Costa Rica confronted economic adversity—inflation and staggering international debt—set off by the 1979 "oil shock," loss of export income from depressed coffee markets, and demand at home for manufactured goods. Furthermore, events in Nicaragua and El Salvador brought increased violence to Costa Rica. Most important, however, Pastora's military activities against the Sandinista regime in Nicaragua hurt the Costa Rican economy. Lacking a military of its own, Costa Rica was unable to control Pastora's activities or secure its own borders.

The United States meanwhile increased efforts to eliminate the Sandinistas from Nicaragua and utilized Costa Rica's economic adversity to force compliance with this objective. Despite efforts to exhibit a neutral stance, Costa Rica was slowly drawn into the American camp.

PART 4

Nuclear War and Deterrence

10

Prospects for Ballistic Missile Defense toward the Year 2000

DONALD M. SNOW

AFTER ROUGHLY a decade of near seclusion from widespread public attention, active defense against ballistic missiles has reemerged as a major part of the strategic debate. Advances in ballistic missile defense (BMD) technologies have played an important role in this revival of interest. Prospects for antiballistic missiles (ABMs) have brightened considerably since opponents declared missile defense dead in the early 1970s, and so-called exotic technologies involving such things as directed energy transfer (DET) in the form of space-based lasers (SBL) and charged-particle beams (CPB) offer the possibility of dramatic breakthroughs in the ability to defend against a nuclear attack.

While considerable scientific and engineering progress (allowed under the ABM Treaty of 1972) took place during the middle to late 1970s, President Ronald Reagan's forceful adoption of ballistic missile defenses put the area into the forefront of a national debate over strategic nuclear policy. That debate had lain fallow during most of the decade, but it began to revive in the furor surrounding President Jimmy Carter's adoption of a counterforce targeting strategy through Presidential Directive (PD) 59 in August 1980 and was given further fuel by President Reagan's aggressive advocacy of offensive force modernization in his major speech on the subject in October 1981. The president's speech on March 23, 1983, which included reference to the exotic systems and was instantly dubbed the "star wars" speech, brought BMD into the debate.[1]

In some important ways, BMD is at the center of the ongoing national disagreement over appropriate nuclear deterrence strategies for the future. At least within the public realm, advocacy has centered on the opposing poles of continued adherence to assured destruction on the one

137

hand, and, on the other, strategies emphasizing limited nuclear options and giving some attention to possible nuclear war fighting. To proponents of assured destruction, BMD always has been and always will be anathema. From their position the central reality of the nuclear balance is that a nuclear war would be an unmitigated, probably civilization-ending catastrophe, and it is the knowledge of that outcome that enlivens deterrence. Any suggestion that the disaster might be mitigated, as in the case of successful BMD, simply removes useful inhibitions and deserves only opposition, particularly because the protection might prove illusory.

The assured-destruction view largely held sway during the 1970s but has met increasing intellectual opposition, a part of which entails advocacy of BMD. In this revised view the kind of nuclear war that is least improbable would not be the horrible assured-destruction scenario but some more limited form. Recognizing both that deterrence is the crucial purpose of nuclear strategy and that deterrence could fail through accident or inadvertence, these analysts argue for strategies of limited nuclear war. From this position a major thrust of strategy is nuclear war termination at the lowest possible levels of destruction, such that society would survive and recover. Thus the attempt to defend against a nuclear attack, as part of the effort to limit a nuclear war's effects, is not only natural but the only prudent and responsible course to follow.

The lines are thus clear, with BMD as a possible lightning rod for the future debate. To understand how that debate will come out and thus what the likely role of BMD will be toward the turn of the century, we must, first, learn more about the process leading to the current state of BMD in official policy (the Strategic Defense Initiative, or SDI, of the Reagan administration); second, we must examine some of the principal arguments underpinning current advocacies of BMD and some of those in opposition. I will then suggest some conclusions.

From the ABM Treaty to the Strategic Defense Initiative

The idea of active defenses against nuclear-tipped ballistic missiles is as old as the missile age, and, in fact, scientists solved the theoretical problems associated with BMD before they first successfully tested the ballistic missile. The problems in defending against a rocket attack have been practical, largely involving engineering difficulties arising from the theoretical base. The issue of BMD in the form of antiballistic missiles flared up during the 1960s, when opponents were in the majority. The result was the ABM Treaty of 1972 as the centerpiece of the Strategic Arms Limitation Talks (SALT) I, which precluded the deployment of effective defenses by the Soviet Union and the United States against attacks by one another.[2] To many adherents of assured destruction, the question of BMD was effectively foreclosed at that time, and, as one contemporary commentator observed, "The ABM Treaty probably averted a costly competition in defensive systems."[3]

Those opponents of BMD who thought they had averted active defenses for all times were premature in their judgment. The ABM Treaty prohibited deployment of all but minor ABM systems, but it did not (and because of verification problems, could not) ban research and development efforts short of actual systems testing, and such efforts continued apace outside the spotlight of public scrutiny. Research, largely justified by counterpart programs in the Soviet Union, focused on two levels that Secretary of Defense Harold Brown identified in his final annual report to Congress: "We continue treaty-permitted R&D on Ballistic Missile Defense (BMD) as a hedge against Soviet breakthroughs or breakouts that could threaten our retaliatory capability, and as a possible point defense option to enhance the survivability of our ICBM force."[4]

Brown's statement encompassed both areas where progress had occurred. His reference to point defenses was an allusion to ABM programs, such as the Low Altitude Defense System (LoADS), that would incorporate nonnuclear tipped interceptor rockets to attack incoming Soviet reentry vehicles aimed at American retaliatory forces. Research on point defenders received additional impetus because difficulties in finding a suitable basing mode for the MX missile system suggested that a point ABM defense would be the most plausible means to ensure the rocket's invulnerability. The other focus, suggested by the reference to a possible Soviet breakthrough, was in so-called exotic defenses based in the physical properties associated with high-energy laser beams and charged-particle beams. The Carter administration created an office within the Department of Defense specifically for the various services to oversee research into these technologies, generically known as directed-energy transfer. Research on the program-weaponizing laser beams, the most publicly visible of these efforts, has focused on the basing of BMD systems incorporating lasers in space to intercept and destroy rising Soviet missiles.[5] This latter possibility led President Reagan to issue his now-famous entreaty on the subject: "I call upon the scientific community in our country, those who gave us nuclear weapons, to turn their great talents now to the cause of mankind and world peace: to give us the means of rendering these nuclear weapons impotent and obsolete."[6]

The Reagan Pentagon, at least as reflected in the statements of Secretary of Defense Caspar W. Weinberger in his reports to Congress, did not instantly adopt an aggressive pro-BMD stance. Weinberger's first annual report contained a note of caution and even a tone of skepticism: "For the future, we are not yet sure how well ballistic missile defenses will work; what they will cost; whether they would require changes in the ABM Treaty; and how additional Soviet ballistic missile defenses—which would almost certainly be deployed in response to any U.S. BMD system—would affect U.S. and allied offensive capabilities."[7] In his second report the message was cryptic but somewhat more optimistic, although it contained no reference to exotic systems. His entire discussion of BMD in a 350-page document was: "Our extensive work with Ballistic Missile Defense (BMD) components has demonstrated that an active defense could protect some high-value strategic assets from ballistic missile attack. The program is structured, therefore, to sustain our understanding of this technology so that we could field an advanced and highly effective BMD system quickly should the need arise."[8]

Sometime between the release of that report on February 1, 1983, and the president's speech on March 23, 1983, the administration embraced directed-energy-transfer BMD. Certainly government leaders did not discover the technology; references and advocacies began to appear in the public literature in such quasi-official sources as *Aviation Week and Space Technology* during the middle 1970s,[9] and, as mentioned earlier, the Carter administration had announced a formal program in the area. If dramatic breakthroughs in terms of technical feasibility had occurred in the interim, they were not apparent in the public record.

Regardless of the conversion process, the president embraced the concept of BMD, including exotic defenses, in his March speech, declaring, "Current technology has attained a level of sophistication where it is reasonable for us to begin this effort. It will take years, probably decades, of effort on many fronts."[10] His announcement had been presaged by the commissioning of two studies on the subject in June 1983, which were completed in October.[11] These studies, when integrated, recommended the expenditure of $18 billion to $27 billion between fiscal years 1985 and 1989 for research and development and for a total deployment by the year 2000 of a system with a total cost estimated in the range of $95 billion.[12]

President Reagan formally accepted these recommendations on January 6, 1984, in the form of National Security Decision Directive 119. The Strategic Defense Initiative was thus born, later reflected in the now-enthusiastic advocacy of the program by Weinberger in his report for fiscal year 1985 and beyond. He wrote: "The study concluded that advanced defense technologies could offer the potential to enhance deterrence and to help prevent nuclear war by reducing significantly the utility of Soviet preemptive attacks and by undermining an aggressor's confidence in the probability of a successful attack against the United States *and* its allies" (emphasis in original).[13] To this end, the secretary recommended $1.74 billion in research and development funding for fiscal year 1985.[14]

This evolution clearly suggests that advocates of BMD have the upper hand in the Reagan administration. Whether even the spirited leadership of the administration can prompt a movement toward active defense is not so clear, however, nor is the wisdom of doing so entirely obvious. SDI defenses do not, after all, exist, and the technologies may never mature. To reach some judgment on those technologies and the desirability of moving toward defenses, we will find it helpful to examine the arguments on either side of the issue.

The Desirability of Active Defenses

Contemporary proponents of ballistic missile defense make a number of arguments in support of their advocacy. Although different adherents cite or emphasize different reasons, the arguments can be grouped around five related points, ranging from the feasibility of constructing effective defenses to the mandate for self-protection resulting from the emergence of knowledge about the so-called "nuclear winter" phenomenon.

The first argument, in direct contradiction to the most telling negative argument in the old ABM debate, is that active defenses are now technically feasible because of technological advances since the 1960s. In that earlier time, opinion centered on President John F. Kennedy's misleading analogy that the problem of missile defense was akin to "hitting a bullet with another bullet." Rather, a leading proponent argues, the task is conceptually much simpler than that: "A missile launched at the U.S. travels so fast that if you tossed an ice cube at it and hit it, you would divert it sufficiently to render it impotent. . . . [A] missile's high speed makes it vulnerable."[15]

This conceptual simplicity has, of course, been dogged by practical problems (e.g., how do you find the missile to throw the ice cube at it?). In essence, the problem is one of target acquisition and tracking (a radar problem), trajectory determination (a computing problem), and interception (a weapons problem). Proponents argue that advances in radar (especially space-based radar), in computing capabilities (notably speed in processing), and in interceptor sophistication have, or soon will, overcome all of these difficulties. The recent test of a successful ABM is cited as evidence of this, as is progress in systems such as LoADS and, in the longer run, the prospects of DET BMD devices that could produce a so-called layered system that could be essentially impenetrable.[16]

The second and third arguments fly in the face of "conventional wisdom" as it emerged from the ABM debate. The second argument is that missile defenses reinforce, rather than detract, from deterrence, especially if substantial offensive arms reductions accompany deployment of those defenses. If the first premise of both American and Soviet foreign policies is the avoidance of nuclear war because of mutually recognized certain catastrophe, then the problem of deterrence is to avoid changes in the perceptions producing inhibitions. As Herman Kahn put it, "One significant indication of the effectiveness of deterrence is that the Soviet Union and the United States share the belief that a nuclear war would only begin out of desperation or inadvertence."[17] Put another way, a major goal of deterrence is to ensure that neither side determines that it could profit by using nuclear weapons. An important element in thwarting such calculations is in raising uncertainties about the potential profitability of attacks that would cross the nuclear threshold. As Keith Payne and Colin S. Gray noted, "Even . . . limited conventional defensive coverage for U.S. retaliatory forces would create enormous uncertainties for Soviet planners considering the effectiveness of a strategic first strike."[18] Daniel O. Graham and Gregory A. Fossedal presented the same argument in the form of a rhetorical question: "Would a defense be adequate if it provided no rock-bottom guarantees at all—but did throw so much uncertainty into the calculations of someone contemplating an attack on the U.S. that they would decide not to?"[19]

Those who argue that even a residually effective defense is better than none have always faced the criticism that arsenal sizes are so great that a partial dilution of effect would make no difference and that offensive weapons could easily overwhelm any defense. This criticism is recognized at official levels and has led Weinberger to conclude that a movement toward defense would be most beneficial if accompanied by reductions in offensive forces. "For the longer term, offensive force reductions and defensive technologies can be mutually reinforcing. Effective defenses that reduce the utility of ballistic missiles and other offensive forces have the potential for increasing the likelihood of negotiated reductions of those offensive forces."[20] Offensive arms reductions, quite obviously, reduce the quantitative (and possibly the qualitative) problems faced by defenses. If deployed and orchestrated properly, the result could be a movement toward a strategy of "assured survival," under which "we can reasonably project that strategic defense would be more likely to prevent all-out war—with the added, crucial advantage that if it does not, we are not totally without defense."[21]

The third and related argument, once again in direct contradiction to assured-destruction thought, is that defensive systems stabilize rather than destabilize the deterrence system and nuclear balance. The reason for this assertion is that BMD is nonprovocative in the sense that a weapon deployed in an unambiguously defensive manner does not put any offensive system at risk (it cannot be used to attack and destroy an offensive weapon before the offensive system is used). Thus, a defensive system has two salutary effects in terms of avoiding a first strike, which is the primary reason for American-based deterrence. First, because the system cannot be used preemptively, it avoids putting the adversary in a perceived "use them or lose them" situation during a crisis that might provide the incentive to launch first. Second, to the degree that such systems protect retaliatory forces, they reinforce the feasibility of second striking, or retaliatory, strategies and stress disincentives to attack first.

The fourth argument is that it is irresponsible, and even morally reprehensible, not to make some effort to defend against potential nuclear attack, a point made repeatedly by Reagan and Weinberger in defending SDI. This position arises from the realization that while deterrence is the major concern, it can fail. "The central problem of nuclear deterrence is that no offensive deterrent, no matter how fearsome, is likely to work forever, and the consequence of its failure would be intolerable for civilization."[22] Ballistic missile defense thus emerges as a prudent hedge against that failure that could mitigate the disaster should it occur. As Barry J. Smernoff put it in regard to laser-based defenses, "the emergence of SBL technology creates a new alternative for coping with the seemingly inscrutable problems and ethical dilemmas of nuclear war and nuclear weapons and the open-ended nature of the strategic arms competition."[23] This argument has particular appeal in the professional military community, because defenses aimed at protecting society from the ravages of war, which this argument supports, represent a traditional military value absent from most thinking about nuclear weapons.

The fifth argument is of recent vintage and relates to the evidence that a nuclear war could trigger a phenomenon known as "nuclear winter."[24] Briefly, the idea of nuclear winter is that at some level of exchange (as yet unspecified but being studied in a number of independent investigations), the result would be massive firestorms that would inject large amounts of microscopic soot into the stratosphere. This soot would in turn create a dense cloud that would encircle the globe and block out the sun's rays. The effect would be to lower the average temperature of the earth by up to twenty degrees Fahrenheit, thereby destroying crops, freezing large portions of the globe's surface water, and making the earth essentially uninhabitable for up to a year. The result would be ecocide on a global scale and the possible extinction of life as we know it.

Although the scientific community is coming to accept the fact of nuclear winter, the point at which it is triggered remains elusive and, in any precise way, probably will continue to do so (the only reliable way to locate the nuclear winter threshold is to exceed it, which would be calamitous). In a general climate of uncertainty about the winter threshold, anything that could mitigate the extent of a thermonuclear exchange by reducing the number of detonations has some appeal. Ballistic missile defenses thus have the potential to keep any exchange at a level below the threshold by disabling a percentage of incoming forces. This effect would be especially enhanced if combined with a reduction in offensive arms, as Payne and Gray point out in their rebuttal to Carl Sagan's assertion that knowledge of the winter has mandated extremely deep cuts in offensive arsenals: "Advocates of a radical scale of nuclear disarmament need to appreciate that truly deep reductions in offensive nuclear arsenals would be feasible only in the event of a heavy deployment of strategic defensive systems."[25] The force of this argument depends to some extent on what level of exchange would induce the winter; the lower the level, the greater the need to take all measures to ensure that the threshold is not exceeded. The relative recency of investigation of the winter, however, ensures that this fifth argument will be the source of considerable future debate and disagreement.

The Undesirability of Active Defenses

Anyone who surveys the sweep of the missile age finds that opponents of strategic active defenses have dominated American discussions. This domination was most evident in the period surrounding SALT I and the adoption of the defense-crippling ABM Treaty as its centerpiece. In that debate, the basic arguments against active defenses were articulated, and they are being reiterated, if in slightly different form, in contemporary discussions. In essence, these arguments break into three positions.

The first negative argument is associated with adherents of assured destruction, who characterize BMD as a destabilizing chimera. It is destabilizing because, to the extent people believe that active defenses will improve the chance of surviving nuclear war, such systems loosen useful inhibitions to begin nuclear war. Moreover, most of these critics are deeply suspicious that such systems would not work well enough to make a substantial difference in the event of all-out nuclear war (which is the form they believe such a war would take). This limitation is particularly true regarding the protection of populations, since even a minor "leakage" in urban-protecting systems would result in large-scale devastation. Thus BMD in principle is to be opposed because it weakens the "hostage effect" central to assured destruction (an inhibition to start nuclear war because it would be suicidal—an execution of the hostages).[26] Also, the protection apparently provided by such systems would possibly prove illusory in the real event anyway, which would be the cruelest irony of all.

The second negative argument, which also speaks to the question of stabilization versus destabilization, is the problem of the transition from a defenseless world to one in which active defenses play at least some part. This dilemma is also known as the "how do we get from here to there" problem,[27] and it refers to the difficulties and sources of instability that might accompany the addition of active defenses by one or both sides to nuclear arms competition.

There are, of course, two basic possibilities in this regard. The least troublesome is the situation where both sides more or less simultaneously develop and decide to deploy systems of roughly similar capabilities (at whatever level of effectiveness). In that circumstance, it is possible that arms control processes could effect an orderly mutual deployment of such systems, so that the changeover would be symmetrical and would maintain similar force structures throughout for both sides. Whether the result at the end of this process (some offensive-defensive mix) would be stable or unstable is, of course, a matter of more or less theological beliefs about whether BMD is stabilizing.

The more troublesome potential situation is where one side or the other makes a substantial breakthrough that would allow it to field a system for which the adversary had either no counterpart or one that was markedly inferior. A dramatic advance in some form of DET-based weaponry would seem to offer the best likelihood of such a situation, and if exploited, could provide significant advantage for the possessor. This prospect is apparently particularly troubling to the Soviets and may well explain their violent opposition to SDI.

The potential source of instability arises from the realization by the disadvantaged state that its situation will be substantially weakened once deployment has been completed by the other. Especially if the defenses are formidable, the nonpossessor may be left with a largely useless offensive force which would be picked off and destroyed before reaching its target should that force be launched, transforming the "use them or lose them" problem to a potential "use them or *leave them useless*" dilemma that is equally intractable.

This latter potential difficulty may prompt the nonpossessor to decide that his only recourse is to fire his missiles before the other side's defenses are operational. In other words, the weaker state may decide it is expedient and rational to "fire when you can" rather than accept an inferior position wherein the opponent can threaten attack without having to fear the consequences of retaliation.

Not all observers, one should add, believe the problem to be severe. Graham and Fossedal, in particular, dismiss it: "Would the Soviets attack as we complete our ground-based defense? Of course not; no fundamental change in the balance of power is threatened. . . . The stronger the U.S. defenses become, the less sense a Soviet strike makes—but the process is marginal, not an all-for-one shot."[28]

The final argument against active defenses is their cost. When the original ABM system was proposed in the late 1960s, its price tag was what now seems to be a modest $5 billion or so; depending on the source one consults and the kind of system one envisages, the costs for the kinds of defenses that could be deployed now are far higher.

There is substantial disagreement on this issue. The most enthusiastic proponents of BMD argue that effective defenses based on existing technologies could be fielded at comparatively modest cost. In their advocacy, Graham and Fossedal make such assertions. At one point they argue, "At a cost of $2 billion . . . the U.S. could protect the MX missile in existing silos in North Dakota."[29] At another point they allege, "Within five years, at a cost of $12 billion, the United States could deploy a two-layered fleet of satellites that would filter out 98 percent of a Soviet missile launch."[30] Most experts, including the Weinberger Pentagon, reject these estimates as far too low.

Other observers, and especially those looking at systems that incorporate laser and particle-beam components, are less sanguine at the modesty of cost that the defense entails. Hard information about cost estimates is not available in the public domain, but guesses abound. As one observer catalogs, "Estimates of the amount needed to make the new system both operational and effective range from $10 billion to $500 billion."[31] That represents a substantial spread; another observer provides a range for the installation of a layered system incorporating lasers and particle beams as well as ABMs: "The goal . . . is to have a multilayered ballistic missile defense in place within 20 years at a cost estimated at between $250–500 billion."[32]

Such guesses are, of course, no more than that and could be affected by factors such as technological complications and inflation. The higher end of the cost spectrum is probably the more realistic, or at least that is the impression that officials give off the record. The question is whether the American public would support such expenditures (particularly in an era of large budget deficits and legislative mandates to reduce or eliminate those deficits), and certainly there will be opposition on these grounds alone. Two associated difficulties, in turn, will buttress that opposition.

The first problem is that supporters of deployment will not, with any precision, be in a position to demonstrate the effectiveness of the systems they are proposing in advance of decisions to deploy them. Testing of these systems will always be modest, and whether such results can confidently be extrapolated to all-out exchange scenarios will always be hotly contested. Opponents will be able to claim the possibility that the American people are being asked to spend a half trillion dollars or more for a program not susceptible to testing.

The second bedeviling factor is the possibility that the expense will be open-ended, because the defense will simply open a new arena for arms race competition. This prospect is most often associated with a race in space, where BMD satellites invite counterdeployment of antisatellite (ASAT) weaponry and redundancy of systems. Beyond weaponizing the last medium, this whole area of competition could be extremely expensive and long term, meaning that even high initial cost estimates could represent no more than the tip of the investment iceberg.

Conclusions

The discussion to this point has focused on the reasons to develop and the reasons not to develop ballistic missile defenses. As one might expect from a debate that spans most of the nuclear missile age, the arguments on both sides are extensive and impressive. Still, which set of arguments carries the ultimately greater weight? and how will those arguments affect eventual decisions about whether to deploy missile defenses?

Those decisions will not be made exclusively on the basis of weighing one set of arguments against another and deciding on the objective balance between them. If the debate about ABM nearly two decades ago is any guide (which it undoubtedly is), the decisions will also have a large political content that goes beyond the technical merit of argumentation.

There are similarities in the two settings. In the late 1960s, ABM was defeated largely on two grounds: it was expensive, and there was substantial expert community disagreement over whether it would work. The question of expense was made more difficult because the proposals for ABM came on the heels of an extensive offensive nuclear force modernization program (e.g., Minuteman III, Polaris/Poseidon) and because the Vietnam War was placing a considerable drain on defense resources.

Clearly, there are parallels today. If ultimate decisions had to be made now, substantial disagreement would exist about the feasibility of BMD, especially of exotic DET-based defenses, which currently do not exist. Proposals for BMD come on the heels of President Reagan's aggressive offensive force modernization program announced in 1981, and the systems proposed will apparently be highly expensive. One can even argue that there is a parallel between the Vietnam War and the present huge federal deficits, since each represents a politically and economically debilitating drain on resources.

Prospects for President Reagan's Strategic Defense Initiative and for BMD generally would thus seem to rely on the extent to which his administration can overcome economic and technical objections. If it can surmount those objections, BMD can become politically feasible. If it cannot overcome or at least moderate them, the current advocacies of BMD will likely go the way of ABM in the 1960s. Overcoming these problems is neither easy nor impossible, and there is at least one approach currently entering discussions that may have some appeal at least on the American side of the debate. That is the idea of a "defense-protected build-down" (DPB) of offensive forces.[33]

The basic notion behind this proposal is to combine advocacies for a reduction in offensive armaments with a phased introduction of strategic defenses. Using arms control negotiations (such as those currently under way at Geneva) to provide schedules and timetables, we could gradually draw down the number of offensive missiles and replace them with BMD components to protect against the remaining offensive weapons. Defenses would allow protection and security for remaining retaliatory systems and would thus reinforce deterrence; they would also make the consequences of the failure of deterrence less disastrous (including, perchance, keeping detonation levels below the threshold for the nuclear winter). This basic scenario closely matches Reagan's image of a defense-dominant world in which nuclear weapons are rendered impotent and obsolete.

There is no unanimity within the expert community about the synergism between the offense and defense in this scheme nor in the details of the process. Alton Frye, for instance, is ambivalent about the basic relationship, stating that "the sharp reduction in offensive warheads . . . might tend to reduce the incentive to seek some new 'impregnable' defense—or conversely it might tend to make such a defense seem more attainable."[34] At the same time, a certain level of additional uncertainty enters into strategy because of the proposal. According to Alvin W. Weinberg and Jack N. Barkenbus, "the difficulty in estimating the effectiveness of a defensive system is a serious shortcoming of a DPB strategy."[35] Furthermore, the administration's own criterion for fielding defenses is that they be "cost effective," by which it means that additional increments of defense must be cheaper to deploy than offensive countermeasures. Some form of DPB offers potential for addressing these economic and technical difficulties that form the political objection to BMD.

The major element in the technical objection to BMD is the difficulty of handling anything as massive as an all-out Soviet launch at the United States combined with the prospect of overwhelming any system by offensive warhead proliferation. That objection is at least moderated by a build-down of offensive weapons that would both reduce the defensive problem quantitatively and place restrictions on proliferation that could overwhelm the system. The problem for the defense becomes simpler when combined with an offensive build-down, although one must admit that the exact performance capability improvement could never be precisely known in advance. Economically, a build-down would create some marginal reductions in expenditures on offensive systems that could be devoted to the defenses. Given the enormous costs of proposed defenses and the relative modesty of expenditure on offensive forces, reductions in offense would not cancel out increased spending on defense, but the symbolism of the effort could make the process politically attractive.

This combination has been widely accepted as desirable and possibly as a sine qua non for making defenses attractive. A movement toward defense would energize the support of the pro-BMD community, and arms reduction supporters would find it difficult to oppose the scheme. To the extent that the proposal revitalizes a currently moribund arms control community, there is further basis for support.

Any change in the shape of the nuclear balance must, of course, be a two-actor drama that includes the Soviet Union, and there is reason for at least short-term caution about how the Soviets would greet a movement toward defense. First, the Soviets have sharply rebuked the SDI and have made the abandonment of the program (which they label as aimed at producing "space-strike weapons") a prerequisite for progress on offensive arms reductions.[36] These objections are not the same thing as a total rejection of missile defenses; the Soviets, after all, possess around Moscow the world's only operational BMD system, which they have recently upgraded. Their rejection of SDI space elements must be confronted and overcome, however. Second, the Soviet Union has made a serious commitment to offensive nuclear armaments which has produced for it superpower status that would be questionable otherwise. The role of strategic offensive arms as a backdrop for Soviet power is indeed important, even critical, and the Soviets are unlikely to negotiate away that source of their strength easily or casually. This factor raises some question about the sincerity of Mikhail Gorbachev's disarmament proposal of January 15, 1986. Third, a movement toward strategic defenses is most attractive if both sides can build roughly equivalent systems simultaneously. At this point it is not clear whether research and development efforts in both countries will produce such equivalent systems in a simultaneous manner, especially in the space-based systems the Soviets appear to fear and are attempting to ban.

The nuclear missile age ushered in the apparently total dominance of offensive strategic weaponry against which there were no defenses, and many arguments about those weapons implicitly maintained that that relationship was immutable. Such a view ignores the history of weaponry, which has been one of fluctuation between offensive and defensive superiority. History has suggested that for every ultimate offense, there emerges a defense, and vice-versa. As Payne and Gray put it, "For the strategic defense to achieve a very marked superiority over the offense over the next several decades would be an extraordinary trend in light of the last 30 years, but not of the last hundred or thousand years."[37] Strategic defense is an idea whose time may not have arrived but which may be on the way.

American Nuclear Weapons Programs and Strategies during the 1980s: Comparative United States and Soviet Perspectives

DANIEL S. PAPP

IN RECENT YEARS, academic experts and strategic analysts have devoted considerable attention to the roles of perceptions in international affairs.[1] Although the two groups have often used different methodologies and examined unrelated issue areas, many individuals have presented persuasive evidence that international actors frequently perceive the same event, action, trend, or policy differently. Perhaps more important, analysts also found that those actors then assume that the perceptions they adopt are accurate and base their actions and policies on them. The necessities of accuracy and understanding are especially important when the subjects are nuclear weapons programs and strategies. To err may be human, but in nuclear matters, to err may be the end of mankind.

Given this elementary fact, it is surprising that experts and analysts have devoted relatively little effort to comparing and contrasting the perceptions of nuclear matters held by the United States and the Soviet Union.[2] In this study I hope to facilitate an understanding of the differences between these perspectives and thus to help lessen the dangers of miscalculation flowing from misunderstanding and misperception.

Several caveats complicate an examination of the nuclear perspectives of the United States and the Soviet Union. First, given their different historical experiences, geopolitical realities, political-social philosophies, and ecotechnical capabilities, the two nations have different conceptions of how the international system works, why it works as it does, and what threats it poses to each country's security. These differences in worldview have been examined elsewhere and need not be repeated here.[3] For the present, suffice it to say that these differences contribute to differing perceptions of nuclear programs and strategies and undermine each side's ability to understand—and grant legitimacy to—the other's perspectives.

This difference in worldview causes a second major problem for those who seek to contrast and compare U.S. and Soviet outlooks on nuclear matters. Put simply, experts and analysts themselves can never be certain that their appraisals of the opposing positions on nuclear matters are being interpreted through accurate and appropriate perceptual filters. Try as they might, experts and analysts can never guarantee that their interpretations of U.S. or Soviet views are correct.

These problems are further compounded by the propensity of both nations to posture on nuclear issues. Statements on nuclear issues by the United States and the Soviet Union may or may not be accurate reflections of actual perceptions that exist in Washington or Moscow; policy statements may be declaratory or actual; and procurement and deployment patterns may be as much or more the products of past perceptions as current outlooks. Determining actual perceptions is difficult, even if the analyst succeeds in overcoming the complications caused by the author's ethnocentric and ideological outlooks, or if he or she discerns the differences in the historical, geopolitical, political-social, and ecotechnical points of departure that the United States and the Soviet Union themselves bring to the issue areas of nuclear affairs.

New U.S. Nuclear Delivery Systems: The Soviet Viewpoint

Even before the Reagan administration took office in January 1981, the United States had embarked on a number of nuclear modernizations and improvements that included development of a new intercontinental ballistic missile (ICBM, the MX), two new bombers (the B-1, production of which was canceled by President Jimmy Carter, and an advanced technology bomber incorporating "Stealth" technologies), and a new fleet ballistic submarine and missile (both called Trident). Additionally, the United States pursued development and in some cases deployment of new technologies that improved accuracy (the Mark 12A warhead), enhanced penetration capabilities (multiple independently targetable reentry vehicles [MIRVs], maneuverable reentry vehicles [MaRVs], and "Stealth" technologies) and bettered survivability (super-hardened ICBM silos, quieter fleet ballistic submarines [SSBNs], and longer-range submarine-launched ballistic missiles [SLBMs]). Work meanwhile continued on a nuclear delivery vehicle called the cruise missile, which could arguably be seen as introducing a "fourth leg" of the American nuclear triad.

Not surprisingly, official and unofficial Soviet spokesmen alike saw these initiatives as methods by which the United States sought to reobtain nuclear superiority.[4] Americans, again not surprisingly, rejected these Soviet charges and claimed that nuclear improvements were needed to offset qualitative and quantitative advances in Soviet offensive nuclear forces and passive and active strategic defenses.

Despite these disagreements before the 1980s, the tone and temper of argument over U.S. nuclear systems rapidly escalated after Reagan took office. In part, escalated disagreements were a function of his preelection and postelection anti-Soviet rhetoric, and in part, they were a function of increasing U.S.-Soviet tension caused by the U.S.S.R.'s invasion of Afghanistan and the Carter administration's responses to that invasion. The most critical factor contributing to heightened disagreement over U.S. nuclear systems, however, was Reagan's clear and immediate intent to accelerate the pace of development and deployment of those systems.

Soviet commentary centered on six programs: the MX, the revived B-1, Stealth technologies, cruise missiles, the Trident programs, and the nuclear forces of the North Atlantic Treaty Organization (NATO). Soviet authorities also paid particular attention to U.S. efforts to improve C^3I for nuclear forces, revitalize U.S. civil defense efforts, and, by 1983, develop defensive technologies for space-based and earth-based deployments.

THE MX

American policymakers used a variety of arguments to defend the need for the MX during its decade of development. The MX was and is defended as a replacement for obsolescent Minuteman IIs and IIIs that constitute the bulk of the nation's ICBM force; as a bargaining chip that will strengthen the position of the United States at Strategic Arms Limitation Talks (SALT); as a weapon that in any one of a number of alternate basing modes would overcome the problem of ICBM vulnerability brought about by improved accuracies of Soviet ICBMs; as a tool that would strengthen the deterrent capabilities of the United States because of its precise accuracy, which in turn would contribute to the MX's utility as a credible war-fighting instrument; and as a needed balance in both psychological and military terms to the 308 large SS-18 ICBMs that the U.S.S.R. has deployed.[5]

Soviet spokesmen have rejected all of these arguments, maintaining instead that the real drive for the MX comes from either the desire of the so-called military-industrial complex to acquire profit, or, more dangerously and insidiously from the Soviet perspective, from an attempt on the part of "unrealistic" segments in American political-military circles to reestablish nuclear superiority.[6]

The Soviets have several concerns about the MX. First, the MX's accuracy makes it a potential first-strike weapon.[7] While the Reagan administration undoubtedly pleased the Kremlin by deciding to seek only one hundred MXs instead of the two hundred that the Carter administration had sought, the fact remained that those one hundred MXs alone with their ten reentry vehicles apiece could give the United States a one-warhead-per-silo coverage of over 70 percent of the U.S.S.R.'s deployed ICBM forces.[8] Even though the Kremlin had already obtained greater coverage of U.S. ICBM forces on a two-warhead-per-silo basis with its SS-18s by the time Reagan took office,[9] the improved exchange ratio that the MX would give the United States was—and is—undoubtedly unsettling to the Kremlin.

Second, given the age of U.S. Minuteman II and Titan ICBMs, the Kremlin may view the MX as a meaningful response to block obsolescence. Although Soviet public commentaries have never discussed the Kremlin's view of the role of age and obsolescence in strategic missile forces, new Soviet ICBMs have appeared almost annually in one mode or another throughout the 1970s and 1980s; the most modern U.S. ICBM, the Minuteman III, was deployed first in 1970 and then updated with the addition of the Mark 12A warhead in the late 1970s. Although Soviet updating may be the product of modernizing inadequate earlier technology, it may also be the result of a Soviet belief that new is better. If so, then the U.S.S.R. may view the MX as a major threat to national security simply because of its "newness."

Finally, from the Soviet perspective, the MX may eliminate from the Kremlin's psychological arsenal whatever political and diplomatic utility it may derive from international awareness that Soviet ICBMs are bigger than American ICBMs. Although in military terms this may be a specious and fatuous awareness, in political and diplomatic terms, size may have a perceptual impact, even if that size is only an ICBM perceived on paper as opposed to a battleship or carrier cruising offshore.

One of the most telling arguments used by Western opponents of the MX—that it would be a high-value, high-threat target that would contribute to crisis instability—has apparently never been used by the U.S.S.R. in its perorations against the MX. The reason that the Soviets never make that argument is straightforward: they have pledged never to be the first to use nuclear weapons. Although declaratory policy is made to be broken, the Soviets could never make the high-value, high-threat argument, since whatever political utility a no-first-use statement may have as a declaratory policy would be eliminated if the Kremlin were to argue that the MX contributed to crisis instability. Such an argument would, of course, imply that in a crisis the U.S.S.R. intended to strike first.

The Kremlin, then, may actually see the MX as a legitimate military and political-diplomatic danger, even though in most respects it is little more than an American counterpart to the Soviet SS-18. The ethnocentric nature of this perceptual blind is equally apparent in Soviet assessments of America's other nuclear programs, even as it is apparent in America's own assessments of those programs.[10]

THE B-1

American perspectives on the need for the B-1, a new penetration strategic bomber, to replace B-52s have centered on three factors: the age of the B-52s, the capabilities of the B-1, and continuing requirements to deploy a credible, flexible arm of the strategic nuclear triad.[11] President Reagan most artfully posed the age question—even if his accuracy was debatable: B-52s, he said, are older than the men who flew them.[12] Regardless of the accuracy of his statement, the age of B-52s remains a potent political argument for the B-1.

Military arguments for the B-1 are more persuasive. The B-1 presents a smaller radar cross section than the B-52. Combining this with its advanced avionics and the Stealth technologies that have been incorporated into its airframe, the B-1 promises to be able to penetrate Soviet air defense through the rest of this century.[13] To the Reagan administration, the claimed penetration ability of the B-1 makes it an attractive weapon.

At the same time, the Reagan administration perceives penetration of Soviet airspace in the event of a conflict as important not only in delivering weapons but also in allowing armed reconnaissance and changing target sets. Standoff weapons delivered by B-52s would not afford this capability. Thus, unlike the Carter administration, Reagan sees a pressing requirement for the B-1.[14]

The Soviets, in contrast, see the B-1 as a profit center for the American military-industrial complex and as another ratchet upward in arms competition. Although Soviet sources continually ensure that their air defense forces are equal to the task of defending airspace, air defense personnel themselves must doubt their own capabilities, if only because of the time they took and the degree of difficulty they had both in 1978 and 1983 in intercepting unidentified Western aircraft that had penetrated Soviet airspace. If Soviet air defense forces found it difficult to intercept unarmed passenger aircraft without penetration devices, how many more problems would the Kremlin encounter in attempting to destroy a fleet of B-1s with advanced avionics aboard and rudimentary Stealth technologies incorporated into their design? For the Kremlin, the B-1 program presents a significant addition to the U.S. nuclear threat.[15]

"STEALTH" TECHNOLOGIES

American decisionmakers have continually emphasized that Stealth technologies incorporated into future manned bomber airframes will give the United States a new ability to retaliate against the U.S.S.R. in the event of a Soviet first strike. The Soviets, of course, view Stealth differently; from the time the Carter administration first revealed the development of new technologies to overcome radar identification, the Kremlin has expressed concern that those technologies would enable the United States to launch a secret and disarming first strike.[16]

From the American perspective, such an outlook is absurd, but from the Soviet side, it is less preposterous, especially when viewed in conjunction with other ongoing U.S. strategic nuclear programs. Indeed, all of the arguments that lend credibility to Soviet fears of American first use of the B-1 are multiplied in the Stealth program, even though the threat of such technologies on a post-B-1 airframe designed specifically to incorporate such technologies is more than a decade away. From the Soviet perspective, Stealth technologies do not present an immediate threat, but they do underline the dangers of U.S. nuclear policies.

STRATEGIC CRUISE MISSILES

America's development of strategic cruise missile technology was important for several reasons.[17] It extended the life of older bombers; increased the military usefulness of both old and new bombers; and heightened the likelihood that deterrence would not fail, at least according to the nation's policymakers.[18] While some Americans recognized that such missiles would seriously complicate arms control efforts, no meaningful opposition developed against them for this or other reasons.[19] Indeed, from the American perspective, many analysts maintained that the slow speed of first generation strategic cruise missiles made them ideal second-strike weapons and useless first-strike weapons.

Again not surprisingly, the Kremlin viewed these weapons differently. Even during the Carter administration, the Soviets decried ongoing cruise missile development as an American effort to open a "fourth channel" in the strategic nuclear arms race while simultaneously circumventing the SALT I agreement.[20] Later Soviet commentary on long-range cruise missiles indicated the specific areas of Kremlin concern, including the cruise missile's accuracy, its ability to penetrate Soviet defenses, and the secrecy of its approach.[21] Given the rudimentary quality of the U.S.S.R.'s look-down-shoot-down capability and the apparent difficulty that Soviet radars have in identifying low-flying targets, Soviet concern is understandable. To pessimistic Soviet defense authorities, U.S. cruise missile capabilities probably appeared to negate much of the Kremlin's expenditure on air defense. Thus it should come as no surprise that one of the primary Soviet objectives in post–SALT I nuclear negotiations was to limit U.S. deployment of strategic cruise missiles. To the Kremlin, first-generation strategic cruise missiles may not appear to be credible first-strike weapons, if only because of their slow speed, but they could serve as follow-up weapons to a first strike begun by other strategic systems. This, to the Kremlin, is a grim possibility.

THE TRIDENT PROGRAMS

To most Americans, SLBMs are the most secure and therefore most credible leg of the country's strategic nuclear deterrent. Probably because of this, the Trident SSBN and SLBM programs have generated little opposition in the United States, especially when compared with the MX and B-1. The Trident SSBN's greater quietness and the Trident SLBM's greater range contribute significantly to the survivability of the sea-launched leg of the American deterrent, and this ability strengthens deterrence, at least from most Americans' perspectives. Americans rarely noted that the improved accuracy of the Trident II (D-5) missile will also give it a potentially destabilizing hard-target kill capability.

In comparison, the Soviets include both the Trident I (C-4) missile and the D-5 missile as part of the American drive to reattain strategic nuclear superiority. They view the D-5 in particular as a dangerous weapon that will heighten the danger of nuclear war because of its range and accuracy.[22] The Kremlin is concerned about the greater range of both the C-4 and D-5 as compared with older U.S. SLBMs, because of the complications it raises for Soviet antisubmarine warfare capabilities. Soviet concern about the "nuclearization" of oceans not previously patrolled by U.S. or Soviet fleet ballistic submarines may be for military rather than political reasons. Even so, the political utility of the nuclearization issue should be immediately apparent, especially as it relates to bodies of water such as the Indian Ocean whose littoral states are almost without exception nonaligned.[23]

Accuracy, the Kremlin's second concern about the D-5, becomes especially disconcerting when the D-5 is considered in conjunction with the accuracy of MX ICBMs. The combined D-5/MX force, from the Soviet perspective, will give the United States 3,400 warheads on 340 launchers, each of which has prompt hard-target kill capabilities. From Moscow's view, this scene cannot be pleasing.

THE NUCLEAR FORCES OF THE NORTH ATLANTIC TREATY ORGANIZATION

From the American standpoint, NATO's nuclear modernization was a policy response specifically undertaken to offset an exponential improvement in Soviet intermediate nuclear forces dedicated to the European theater. As the U.S.S.R. replaced its old and inaccurate single-warhead SS-4s and SS-5s with new and accurate three-warheaded SS-20s during the late 1970s, first Western European and then American policymakers became increasingly concerned that SS-20s could lead to a decoupling of the U.S. strategic arsenal from European defense and to Soviet dominance on the so-called escalation ladder. To prevent these occurrences, in December 1979 NATO decided to deploy U.S. Pershing II missiles (P-IIs) and ground-launched cruise missiles (GLCMs) in Europe beginning in December 1983.

As far as NATO was concerned, these intermediate nuclear forces (INF) did nothing more than offset Soviet gains brought about by the SS-20 deployment. NATO INF deployment would ensure coupling, prevent Soviet escalation dominance, forestall the "Finlandization" of Europe, and, most important, enhance deterrence.[24] Although diverse forces in the West ardently opposed INF deployment, it began as scheduled.

Throughout the period preceding and following INF deployment, the Kremlin launched a stream of invectives against the P-IIs and GLCMs. Its accusations were many and diverse: the INFs were part of NATO's drive to attain military superiority in Europe; their mere presence lowered the nuclear threshold; they could serve as first-strike weapons because of proximity to the U.S.S.R.; they were part of a broader Western offensive against the U.S.S.R. Each Soviet rationale deserves commentary.

The Kremlin maintained that NATO's INFs could be seen only in conjunction with French and British nuclear modernization programs, as well as, of course, various other U.S. programs having some utility for European purposes. With France and Great Britain proceeding with their own nuclear modernization programs, and with some of the new C-4 SLBMs in the American arsenal possibly assigned to NATO use, Soviet military planners may have feared that whatever nuclear advantage they had derived from the SS-20 was being quickly eroded, eliminated, or reversed. Thus, Moscow may have seen NATO's INFs as more than an effort to offset SS-20s; from its perspective the INFs probably appeared as part of Western efforts to reacquire nuclear superiority.[25]

Additionally, given the increased quantity of nuclear launch vehicles deployed in Europe and the decreased time available for Kremlin authorities to make decisions in the event of a reported attack from Western Europe, the Soviets may have been legitimately concerned that they would have to make quicker nuclear-release decisions, thereby lowering the nuclear threshold. This concern, of course, emanates directly from the eight-to-ten-minute launch-to-impact time of NATO's P-IIs.[26] From the Soviet perspective, the P-II's primary purpose may have been to attack Soviet command, control, and communication facilities, thus necessitating a Soviet move, because of the P-II's shorter flight time, to a launch-on-warning or a launch-through-attack strategy. Indeed, again from the Soviet perspective, the fact that the West intends to deploy only 108 P-IIs may have contributed to a conclusion that it would use them against C^3 facilities. With only 108 missiles, and despite their great accuracy, they could scarcely be useful against Soviet ICBM sites, because of both the number and the location of those sites, most of which lie beyond the P-II's range.

The P-IIs may therefore imply to the Soviets a U.S-NATO intention to launch a decapitating first strike. Given U.S. refusal to make a no-first-use declaration, and given NATO's doctrine of flexible response, such a conclusion may seem warranted to the Soviets. Assurances from the United States that the P-II's range falls just short of that required to hit Moscow probably carry little weight in the Kremlin, which in turn makes the P-IIs seem even more threatening. With the Soviet Union's refusal to recognize its own role in bringing about NATO's INF modernization through its SS-20 program, the U.S.S.R. may believe its line that NATO's INF in general and P-IIs in particular are indicative of NATO first-strike intentions.[27]

Indeed, some Soviet sources even view INF as part of a broader Western military, ideological, economic, and diplomatic strategy to "decouple" Eastern Europe from the socialist world.[28] In this view some Kremlin authorities see Eastern European indebtedness, the rise of Solidarity in Poland, West German calls for rapprochement with East Germany, and other U.S. and Western European overtures to Eastern Europe as integrally linked to INF, with the overall Western strategy being to "Finlandize" Eastern Europe in reverse.

Related Issues: C³I, CD, SDI, and Strategy

COMMAND, CONTROL, COMMUNICATION, AND INFORMATION

During the 1970s, decisionmakers in Washington became increasingly concerned that their ability to communicate with America's nuclear forces would be impaired in a post-Soviet first-strike environment. This concern stemmed both from the growth of Soviet nuclear capabilities and from an increased awareness of the effect that electromagnetic pulses (EMP) could have on electronic circuitry. As concern grew, presidential administrations took steps to improve the survivability of command, control, communication, and information (C³I) capabilities in a post-nuclear environment. President Reagan further accelerated these efforts.

As far as the Reagan administration was concerned, improved and hardened C³I capabilities contributed to deterrence, and should deterrence fail, they enhanced the nation's ability to fight a controlled nuclear exchange. Convinced, as the president's advisers were, that the Soviet Union was prepared to "fight and win a nuclear war,"[29] they reasoned not illogically that if the Soviets believed that fighting and winning a nuclear war was possible, then deterrence would be degraded. To enhance deterrence, the United States required a countervailing ability to fight a nuclear war and prevent the Soviets from thinking they could win. America therefore needed secure and survivable C³I capabilities. Creating those capabilities became a leading priority of the Reagan administration.[30]

Again, Soviet authorities saw a different chain of logic. Stressing America's refusal to adopt a no-first-use statement and the Reagan administration's emphasis on controlled nuclear exchanges, the Soviets argued that improvements of C³I by the United States were clear indications that it intended to fight and win a nuclear war.[31] As in the case of NATO's intermediate nuclear forces and other U.S. weapons programs, Soviet written sources refused to acknowledge that an action-reaction phenomenon had led to C³I improvements. They viewed these changes as proof that the United States had adopted a war-winning strategy.

CIVIL DEFENSE

As postulated by Reagan security strategists, Soviet civil defense efforts had gained a psychological-political advantage that enabled the Kremlin to apply political and diplomatic pressure during crisis situations. The Reagan administration believed that the Soviet Union could begin to evacuate its cities during a crisis, thereby sending a signal that it was prepared to fight. The United States, with its urban population still in place, would have two choices: capitulate to the Soviet Union, or fight and suffer devastating human losses. If it chose the second option, the Soviet Union would sustain far fewer casualties than the United States, the reasoning went, since the Soviets had already removed residents from their cities. Even if the Soviets never ordered urban dwellers to leave, the reasoning continued, they were in a superior position because they had a marginally viable civil defense program and the United States did not.[32]

To administration strategists, then, both for humane and national security considerations, the development of U.S. civil defense capabilities and a crisis relocation plan became important parts of national security policy. Although many Americans derided the plans as futile because of their views that no one could survive nuclear war, the administration considered the programs necessary to enhance deterrence. Moreover, should deterrence fail, they would lessen death and destruction.

The Soviet response to U.S. civil defense programs was little different from its response to America's C[3]I improvements. Again, the Soviet Union accused the Americans of preparing to fight a nuclear war that they believed they could win.[33] This reaction, while expected, was particularly disingenuous given the Soviets' own extensive civil defense program, which predated the American effort of the 1980s. Indeed, the line of logic that the Soviets themselves used to condemn U.S. civil defense programs served to legitimize in part the arguments used by Reagan strategists to charge that Soviet civil defense programs indicated that its authorities believed nuclear war winnable.

To be sure, the Soviets probably were concerned that whatever advantage they may have acquired because of their civil defense program had been diminished because of America's civil defense efforts, and they may have been equally concerned that U.S. efforts could contribute to its war-fighting options. On the whole, however, it is probable that Soviet verbal responses to the U.S. civil defense program of the 1980s were less a product of honest concern than of efforts to fan antinuclear sentiment in Western Europe and the United States.

THE STRATEGIC DEFENSE INITIATIVE

Since President Reagan's March 1983 speech calling upon the scientific community to develop defenses that would render nuclear weapons "impotent and obsolete," the U.S. Strategic Defense Initiative (SDI) has been a subject of heated debate. Opponents view SDI as an expensive and ultimately futile waste of money that could be strategically destabilizing. Proponents admit that SDI will be expensive, but they maintain that technical breakthroughs could eventually produce a highly reliable low-leakage defense system that could allow the world to move beyond the present dangerous balance of nuclear terror.

Although the United States substantially reduced research and development of strategic defensive technologies following the 1972 ABM Treaty, the Reagan administration showed increased interest in such technologies almost as soon as it entered office. Expenditures on research and development of defensive technologies actually went up even before Reagan's "Star Wars" speech.[34] To the president, strategic defense provided a potentially viable alternative to the condition of ensured mutual destruction under which the world had lived for more than a decade.

Once again, however, the Soviets took a different view of SDI. Their commentary on all aspects of ballistic missile defense from ground based to space based was immediate and vitriolic. They have decried research and development efforts for ground-based systems as violations of the 1972 ABM Treaty, and as ways for the United States to achieve strategic superiority.[35] Soviet commentary on space-based missile defense has been even more extreme, calling the concept of ABMs in space an "inseparable element of a course aimed at achieving a first-strike potential, at achieving military superiority," and an effort to "upset the existing equilibrium of strategic forces."[36]

Soviet concern about the impact of ballistic missile defenses on the strategic balance may be legitimate; as Western opponents of BMD pointed out, BMD could have destabilizing consequences, especially if deployment were nonsymmetric. Nevertheless, even though Soviet expressions of concern about the militarization of space may be honest in some circles, the Kremlin's own military space programs suggest that these concerns are not universally shared.[37] Additionally, of course, the Soviet Union may be concerned about the possibility that the United States will acquire a notable lead in ground-based or space-based BMD. Although to the Soviets a "breakout" effect would probably be difficult to achieve with ABM deployment, it may not seem to be beyond the realm of American possibilities. Finally, and most frighteningly from the Soviet perspective, space-based BMD may be part of a more comprehensive American strategy of attaining strategic nuclear superiority, even as Reagan intimated during the 1980 presidential campaign.

Although Soviet perceptions of the bellicosity of U.S. nuclear strategies escalated after President Reagan took office, Soviet commentaries throughout the last half of the 1970s showed gradually increasing concern about the direction of U.S. nuclear strategy. These concerns continued to heighten as various officials of the new Reagan administration observed that nuclear superiority was desirable, that nuclear war could be limited, that nuclear conflicts could be survived, and that nuclear war could be fought and won.

Several observations by the new U.S. officials were taken out of context, and several were irresponsible or unwise. Nevertheless, despite these qualifying caveats, the Reagan administration brought to the White House an undeniably different perspective on nuclear weapons from that of previous administrations—including the post-PD 59 Carter months. The new administration was convinced that the Soviet Union believed that both limited and central nuclear wars could be fought and won, and it believed that the best way to dissuade the Soviets of that belief was to develop its own strategy to fight and prevail in a nuclear conflict. Highly accurate and capable new systems would be necessary in fighting such a conflict, and they would have to be under secure control and command. The new systems would soon become available—the MX, the B-1, the Trident systems, Stealth technologies, cruise missiles, and P-IIs—and technologists could develop C^3I capabilities to employ them flexibly. From the perspective of the Reagan administration, these steps would enhance the credibility of deterrence.

But when seen from the vantage point of the Reagan administration, the new systems provided more than enhanced deterrence. Should deterrence fail, the new strategic systems also provided the United States with credible opportunities to respond to a partial Soviet strike with a partial American strike, and selectively to target those strikes on Soviet counterforce capabilities. Thus to Reagan strategists, the systems furnished the chance to limit the scope of nuclear war should deterrence fail; at the same time the systems reduced the odds that deterrence would fail.

The Kremlin totally rejected this reasoning. Although Soviet sources as yet have not offered an integrated assessment of how the Kremlin sees the different components of U.S. nuclear systems fitting with each other, such an assessment is not difficult to construct.[38] First, given the combination of Reagan's anti-Sovietism, his willingness to pursue across-the-board nuclear modernization programs, and the movement of strategy from a primarily ensured-destruction outlook to a primarily war-fighting outlook, Soviet authorities may have concluded that Reagan, in the back of his mind, contemplated a first strike against the Soviet Union. His "bomb the Russians" gaffe in August 1984 only added to this Soviet perception.[39] Second, from a Soviet worst-case perspective, the new American systems presented an awesome first-strike potential.

How may the Soviets see such a strike developing? In many ways, their analysts may envision an American first strike as a mirror-image of the much-discussed "bolt-out-of-the-blue" scenario developed by worst-case American strategists during the late 1970s about the possibility of a Soviet surprise attack on the United States. In other ways, however, the Soviet outlook may be even more frightening than the American outlook. From the Soviet perspective, an American first strike may proceed as follows.

First, U.S. anti-satellite weapons would blind Soviet surveillance satellites. Then, U.S. P-IIs deployed in Europe would be launched shortly after the one hundred MX missiles and most of the D-5 SLBMs. The 108 P-IIs would be targeted on Soviet C³I sites, including those in and beyond Moscow. (Soviet military analysts probably reject U.S. claims that P-IIs have insufficient range to strike Moscow.) While the P-IIs prevented Soviet command center communication with missile command sites, the highly accurate MX and D-5 warheads would strike their targets only a few minutes later, with target coverage possibly as high as 2.5 warheads to one target.[40] B-1 and Stealth bombers would then conduct nuclear and conventional armed reconnaissance flights over the U.S.S.R., seeking surviving counterforce targets. Although these flights would arrive hours after the first salvo, they could conceivably find counterforce targets still on land, frozen there by the P-IIs' first strike against C³I sites. Those few ICBMs that survived the MX and D-5 assault and were launched would become relatively easy targets for even a moderate-leakage, space-based BMD, and America's casualties from those few warheads that struck its cities would be minimized because of civil defense programs. Soviet SSBMs on patrol would of course survive, but Soviet leaders would then face the same dilemma that the "bolt-out-of-the-blue" scenario earlier postulated for American presidents: would the Soviet national command authority, knowing that its economic and population base remained essentially intact, launch its relatively inaccurate surviving SLBMs? Would it do this, knowing that the enemy had withheld roughly 90 percent of its ICBM force and many of its SLBMs, using them to threaten a retaliatory third strike against Soviet cities in the event of a countervalue Soviet second strike from surviving SLBMs?

From an American perspective, such reasoning is ludicrous. Even under extreme provocation, no American president would launch a cold-blooded, calculating, dangerous, and highly uncertain attack. From the Soviet perspective, however, as preceding pages argue, realities are seen differently. Indeed, as the Soviets have known for the past few years at least, the United States during an earlier era had planned to turn the U.S.S.R. into a "smoking, radiating ruin at the end of two hours" in the event of war between the countries.[41]

These possible Soviet outlooks about U.S. nuclear strategies during the 1980s clearly come into conflict with the hopeful and even encouraging outlooks adopted by the Reagan administration. This is not to argue that either the United States or the Soviet Union is lying about its perception of American nuclear strategies. Rather, from the evidence presented here, both about U.S. and Soviet perceptions of American nuclear weapons and nuclear weapons–related programs, and about U.S. and Soviet perceptions of U.S. nuclear strategies, both sides may have reached their differing perceptions honestly and legitimately. That is the most frightening observation of all.

Although one may argue that differences in perception are either benign or present little threat to peace, the weight of historical evidence suggests otherwise. Hitler believed that Poland was unimportant to France and Great Britain, but France and Great Britain felt differently. North Korea believed that the United States had abandoned South Korea; it had not. Argentina convinced itself that the Falkland Islands meant little to Great Britain, but the British considered them critical for prestige. Even though one could cite many instances where differences in perception did not lead to war, different perceptions between nations of those issues that divide them almost certainly increase the possibility of war.

In relations between the United States and the Soviet Union, nuclear issues are central. The extreme differences in perspectives on American nuclear programs and strategies may prove unimportant in the broader scope of their relations, but given the greater likelihood of war when significant differences in perception exist, neither Americans nor Soviets can afford to be sanguine about the possibility of avoiding conflict, especially with the stakes so high. What, then, can be done to overcome or at least reduce these differences in perspective?

It may be true that nothing can be done. As argued at the beginning of this study, both the United States and the Soviet Union carry with them the baggage of different historical experience, geopolitical realities, political-social philosophies, and ecotechnical capabilities, and both view the world and global issues through lenses tinted by these factors. Perceptions will inevitably differ.

Still, need they be diametrically opposed? The answer is no. Improved efforts by leadership of both sides—and failing that, either side by itself—to educate itself about the other side's capabilities and perceptions would be a useful first step. It is ridiculous, for example, that Soviet leaders cannot understand the role that they themselves had in bringing cruise missiles and P-IIs to Western Europe; conversely, so too is it ridiculous that an American president could not realize until nearly three years into his term that the other side viewed his arms control proposals as slanted because he, the president, did not understand the structures of Soviet nuclear forces when he made the proposals. Both sides can and must do better; failing that, one side by itself could improve its efforts and thus add measurably to global security without jeopardizing its own security.

Functionally speaking, both sides could benefit from exchanges of viewpoints on nuclear issues that take place outside the glare of summit meetings or nuclear arms control negotiations. Such talks may yield nothing, and they may degenerate into forums for propaganda and recrimination. Nevertheless, the failures of such talks would cost little or nothing; the benefit derived from successful talks could be immense.

These are not utopian suggestions. They are low-cost, potentially high-yield concepts. The probability of significant changes resulting from them is low; the possibility of some changes resulting from them is high. Even if the probability of important change is low, however, any improvement in understanding between Washington and Moscow on nuclear issues may be the difference between global disaster and, if not peace, the absence of war.

Notes

CHAPTER 1: THE IMPORTANCE OF STUDYING MILITARY
HISTORY, BY ROBERT H. FERRELL

1. See the excellent study by Daniel F. Harrington, "American Policy in the Berlin Crisis of 1948–49" (Ph.D. diss., Indiana University, 1979); Harrington is now an air force historian.

2. See Robert H. Ferrell, ed., *The Eisenhower Diaries* (New York: Norton, 1981), and *The Diary of James C. Hagerty: Eisenhower in Mid-Course, 1954–1955* (Bloomington: Indiana University Press, 1983).

3. Ferrell, *Diary of James C. Hagerty*, 101–2.

4. Ferrell, *Eisenhower Diaries*, 311–12.

5. Matthew B. Ridgway, *Soldier: The Memoirs of Matthew B. Ridgway* (New York: Harper, 1956); Maxwell D. Taylor, *The Uncertain Trumpet* (New York: Harper, 1959).

6. Marquis W. Childs, *Eisenhower, Captive Hero: A Critical Study of the General and the President* (New York: Harcourt, Brace, 1958).

Part 1. The War in Vietnam

CHAPTER 2: PRELUDE TO VIETNAM: THE EROSION OF THE U.S.
ARMY'S RAISON D'ÊTRE, 1945–1962,
BY COLONEL HARRY G. SUMMERS, JR.

1. Even the navy recognized land power as decisive. As its then basic doctrinal manual put it, "The final outcome [of war] is dependent on ability to isolate, occupy or otherwise control the territory of the enemy, for land is the natural habitat of man" (*Sound Military Decisions* [Newport: U.S. Naval War College, 1942], 8).

2. Russell F. Weigley, *History of the United States Army* (New York: Macmillan, 1967), 486.

3. Ibid., 493–94.

4. See the discussion of Kennan's containment theory in Henry A. Kissinger, *White House Years* (Boston: Little, Brown, 1979), 61–63. For Kennan's "X" articles, see his "The Sources of Soviet Conduct," *Foreign Affairs* 25 (July, 1947):566–82.

5. Harry S. Truman, "Statement on the Korean War," 27 June, 1950,

quoted in Henry Steele Commager, comp., *Documents of American History* (New York: Appleton-Century-Crofts, 1963), 2:560–61.

6. T. R. Fehrenbach, *This Kind of War* (New York: Macmillan, 1963), 426–27.

7. Dean Acheson, quoted in U.S. Senate, *Military Situation in the Far East,* Hearings Before the Committee on Armed Services and the Committee on Foreign Relations, 82d Cong., 1st sess. (Washington: U.S. Government Printing Office, 1951), pt. 3, pp. 1734–35, 2257–58.

8. Russell F. Weigley, *The American Way of War: A History of United States Military Strategy and Policy* (New York: Macmillan, 1973), 390–91.

9. Douglas MacArthur, quoted in *Military Situation in the Far East,* pt. 1, pp. 39–40, 68.

10. The extent of demoralization was revealed by the army's rejection of the concept of victory in its post–Korean War rewrite of its basic doctrinal manual. See *Field Service Regulations: Operations,* Field Manual 100-5 (Washington: U.S. Government Printing Office, Sept. 25, 1954), 6.

11. Colmar, Baron von der Goltz, *The Conduct of War: A Brief Study of Its Most Important Principles and Forms,* trans. 1st Lt. Joseph T. Dickman (Kansas City: Franklin Hudson Publishing, 1896), 32.

12. Maxwell D. Taylor, *Swords and Plowshares* (New York: Norton, 1972), 135–36.

13. See John Foster Dulles, *Department of State Bulletin* 30 (12 Jan. 1954):107–10.

14. Maxwell D. Taylor, *The Uncertain Trumpet* (New York: Harper, 1959), 4, 17.

15. Weigley, *American Way of War,* 418.

16. Matthew B. Ridgway, *Soldier: The Memoirs of Matthew B. Ridgway* (New York: Harper, 1956), 271–77.

17. Stephen Peter Rosen, "Vietnam and the American Theory of Limited War," *International Security,* Fall 1982, p. 84.

18. The army's basic doctrinal manual had been rewritten in 1962 to reflect the new emphasis on counterinsurgency. See *Field Service Regulations: Operations,* Field Manual 100-5 (Washington: U.S. Government Printing Office, Feb. 19, 1962), 4–5.

19. Rosen, "Vietnam and the American Theory of Limited War," 85.

20. Secretary of State Dean Rusk, quoted in Michael Charlton and Anthony Moncrieff, *Many Reasons Why: The American Involvement in Vietnam* (New York: Hill & Wang, 1978), 115.

21. Rosen, "Vietnam and the American Theory of Limited War," 89.

22. Alain C. Enthoven and K. Wayne Smith, *How Much Is Enough?*

Shaping the Defense Program, 1961–1969 (New York: Harper & Row, 1971), 89, 92, 106.

23. Corelli Barnett, "Outsider's Influence on Defense Policy, Part 2," *RUSI (Royal United Service Institute Journal)*, June 1982, p. 7.

24. See Harry G. Summers, Jr., *On Strategy: A Critical Analysis of the Vietnam War* (Novato: Presidio Press, 1982), chap. 6, "Friction: The Dogma."

25. Douglas S. Blaufarb, *The Counterinsurgency Era: U.S. Doctrine and Performance, 1950 to the Present* (New York: Free Press, 1977), 52.

26. Lloyd Norman and John B. Spore, "Big Push in Guerrilla Warfare," *Army,* Mar. 1962, pp. 33–34.

27. Karl von Clausewitz, *On War,* trans. and ed. Michael Howard and Peter J. Paret (Princeton: Princeton University Press, 1976), 88–89.

CHAPTER 3: "IN THE LANDS OF THE BLIND": EISENHOWER'S
COMMITMENT TO SOUTH VIETNAM, 1954,
BY GEORGE C. HERRING

1. See, for example, Gary R. Hess, "Franklin D. Roosevelt and Indochina," *Journal of American History* 49 (Sept. 1972):353–68; George C. Herring and Richard H. Immerman, "Eisenhower, Dulles and Dienbienphu: 'The Day We Didn't Go to War' Revisited," *Journal of American History* 71 (Sept. 1984):343–63; and Larry Berman, *Planning a Tragedy: The Americanization of the War in Vietnam* (New York: Norton, 1982). The best overall discussion of Vietnam decisionmaking is Leslie Gelb with Richard Betts, *The Irony of Vietnam: The System Worked* (Washington: Brookings, 1978). For a good introduction to the debate, see Gelb and Betts, *Irony of Vietnam,* 14–24.

2. The best account of the decisions of 1949–50 is Robert M. Blum, *Drawing the Line: The Origins of the American Containment Policy in East Asia* (New York: Norton, 1982), esp. 198–213.

3. Herring and Immerman, "Eisenhower, Dulles and Dienbienphu," passim.

4. See, for example, record of National Security Council (NSC) meeting, July 15, 1954, *Foreign Relations of the United States, 1952–1954* (cited hereafter as FRUS), multi-vols. (Washington: U.S. Government Printing Office, 1979), 13:1840, and Walter Bedell Smith to State Department, July 18, 1954, *FRUS, 1952–1954,* 16:1427.

5. William J. Duiker, *The Communist Road to Power in Vietnam* (Boulder, Colo.: Westview, 1981), 172–73.

6. For vivid descriptions of post-Geneva South Vietnam, see memoran-

dum by acting special assistant for intelligence, Aug. 10, 1954, *FRUS, 1952–1954,* 13:1934–35, and National Intelligence Estimate, Aug. 3, 1954, ibid., 1905–14.

7. Navarre's comments are in Robert McClintock to State Department, May 8, 1954, ibid., 1519.

8. Cyrus L. Sulzberger, diary entry, May 9, 1950, in Sulzberger, *Seven Continents and Forty Years: A Concentration of Memoirs* (New York: Quadrangle, 1977), 102–3.

9. John Foster Dulles, Memorandum of conversation with Douglas MacArthur, May 11, 1954, *FRUS, 1952–1954,* 13:1528.

10. Memorandum of conversation of W. M. Gibson and Robert Hoey of State Department with Ngo Dinh Diem, Jan. 15, 1951, doc. no. 3051, William J. Donovan Papers, U.S. Army Military History Institute, Carlisle Barracks, Pa., box 8(a) (cited hereafter as Donovan Papers); Dean Acheson to Legation, Saigon, Jan. 16, 1951, *FRUS, 1951* (Washington: U.S. Government Printing Office, 1977), 6:348, and Edmund Gullion to secretary of state, Jan. 24, 1951, ibid., 359–60.

11. Richard Casey diary, June 17, 1954, in Thomas B. Millar, ed., *Australian Foreign Minister: The Diaries of R. G. Casey, 1951–1960* (London: Collins, 1972), 159.

12. Douglas Dillon to State Department, May 24, 1954, *FRUS, 1952–1954,* 13:1608–9.

13. Robert McClintock to State Department, July 4, 1954, ibid., 1783–84.

14. Leo Cherne to William J. Donovan, Sept. 23, 1954, doc. no. 4060, Donovan Papers.

15. James Lawton Collins, *Lightning Joe: An Autobiography* (Baton Rouge: Louisiana State University Press, 1983), 379.

16. Memorandum, acting secretary of state to president, Sept. 23, 1954, *FRUS, 1952–1954,* 13:2053–54.

17. Vice Adm. Arthur Davis to Dulles, Oct. 20, 1954, ibid., 2146.

18. Record of NSC meeting, Oct. 26, 1954, ibid., 2184–86.

19. John Foster Dulles, memorandum of conversation with Eisenhower, Aug. 17, 1954, ibid., 1953, and Dulles to Wilson, Aug. 18, 1954, ibid., 1954–56.

20. Record of NSC meeting, Oct. 22, 1954, ibid., 2154.

21. Douglas Dillon to State Department, Nov. 15, 1954, ibid., 2246–50.

22. Dulles, memorandum of conversation with Eisenhower, George Humphrey, Charles Wilson, and Harold Stassen, Mar. 24, 1953, ibid., 419–20.

23. John Foster Dulles, record of State Department–Joint Chiefs of Staff meeting, Jan. 28, 1953, ibid., 361–62.

24. J. Lawton Collins, in record of Joint Chiefs of Staff meeting, Apr. 24, 1953, ibid., 500.

25. Eisenhower to E. E. Hazlett, Apr. 27, 1954, Dwight D. Eisenhower Papers, diary series, box 4, Dwight D. Eisenhower Library, Abilene, Kans.

26. John W. Allison, memorandum of conversation with Arthur Radford, Feb. 4, 1953, *FRUS, 1952–1954,* 13:385.

27. Arthur Radford, record of State Department–Joint Chiefs of Staff meeting, Oct. 1, 1954, ibid., 2109.

28. Walter Bedell Smith, memorandum of conversation with Cambodian leaders, June 20, 1954, ibid., 16:1205, and with Prince Buu Loc, May 25, 1954, ibid., 915.

29. Record of NSC meeting, Feb. 4, 1954, ibid., 13:1014–15.

30. James Hagerty, diary, July 23, 1954, James Hagerty Papers, Dwight D. Eisenhower Library.

31. See Stephen E. Ambrose, *Ike's Spies: Eisenhower and the Espionage Establishment* (Garden City, N.Y.: Doubleday, 1981), 189–214, and Richard H. Immerman, *The CIA in Guatemala* (Austin: University of Texas Press, 1982).

32. Eisenhower to Diem, Oct. 22, 1954, in George M. Kahin and John W. Lewis, *The United States in Vietnam* (New York: Dial, 1969), 456–57.

33. Dulles, memorandum of conversation with Eisenhower, Aug. 17, 1954, *FRUS, 1952–1954,* 13:1953.

34. Donald Heath to State Department, Sept. 29, 1954, ibid., 2093.

35. Ronald H. Spector, *Advise and Support: The Early Years—The U.S. Army in Vietnam* (Washington: U.S. Government Printing Office, 1983), 228–30.

36. Gelb and Betts, *Irony of Vietnam.*

37. Gordon Wood, review of Barbara Tuchman, *The March of Folly,* in *New York Review of Books* 31 (Mar. 29, 1984):8.

CHAPTER 4:
APPLYING AIR POWER IN VIETNAM: THE 1972 LINEBACKER
BOMBING CAMPAIGNS, BY MARK CLODFELTER

Materials maintained at the Albert F. Simpson Historical Research Center (AFSHRC), Maxwell Air Force Base, Alabama, are referenced with their respective file numbers. Although many of the sources remain classified, the Air Force Office for Security Review has declassified the extracts I have used.

1. Karl von Clausewitz, *On War*, trans. and ed. Michael Howard and Peter J. Paret (Princeton: Princeton University Press, 1976), 87.

2. David Mac Isaac, ed., *The United States Strategic Bombing Survey*, 10 vols. (New York: Garland, 1976), vol. 1: *Overall Report (Europe)*, 38; vol. 7: *Summary Report (Pacific War)*, 26.

3. Ibid., vol. 4: *The Effects of Strategic Bombing on German Morale; vol 1: Overall Report (Europe)*, 108; vol. 7: *Summary Report (Pacific War)*, 21.

4. Ibid., vol. 7: *Summary Report (Pacific War)*, 28.

5. For a discussion of Nixon's desire for an honorable settlement and the outline of the Oct. 1971 proposal, see "A Plan for Peace in Vietnam: The President's Address to the Nation, Jan. 25, 1972," *Weekly Compilation of Presidential Documents* 8, no. 5 (Jan. 31, 1972):120–25.

6. Richard M. Nixon, "A Plan for Peace in Vietnam," 124. The United States had 139,000 troops in Vietnam at the time of the president's address. He scheduled the removal of an additional 70,000 by May 1.

7. Richard M. Nixon, *RN: The Memoirs of Richard Nixon*, 2 vols. (New York: Warner, 1978), 2:60–61.

8. Henry A. Kissinger, *White House Years* (Boston: Little, Brown, 1979), 1109.

9. Guenter Lewy, *America in Vietnam* (New York: Oxford University Press, 1978), 411.

10. Edgar Ulsamer, "Air Power Halts an Invasion," *Air Force*, Sept. 1972, p. 60.

11. Kissinger, *White House Years*, 1333. Le Duc Tho confirmed this assertion in talks with French Communists in May 1972. He stated: "One unknown for us at the time of the launching of the [Easter] offensive turned out to be a surprise: The position taken by Nixon. We had considered it, but had eliminated this eventuality as impossible during the year of the Peking and Moscow visits and during a presidential election year in the USA. This was a mistake, but not a catastrophic one. The only disadvantage is that military action will be slowed down and in order to win a political victory we will have to step up our diplomatic activities" (message, "Comments of Le Duc Tho," from Maj. Gen. Keegan, chief of air force intelligence, to Gens. Clay and Vogt, 242137Z, May 1972, in *PAVE AEGIS and Miscellaneous Messages, SEA, June 1971–June 1972*, AFSHRC file no. K717.03-219, vol. 5, Secret; this message is a transcript of a report sent by the U.S. delegation in Paris to the secretary of state).

12. On Aug. 9, 1972, Adm. John S. McCain, Jr., commander in chief, Pacific Command (CINCPAC), directed three carriers in the Gulf of Tonkin to devote all of their sorties to Operation Linebacker. He also ordered the air force to schedule a minimum of forty-eight strike sorties per day against its areas of responsibility in the North Vietnamese heartland. The bombing increase resulted from "growing concern here [Pacific Command Headquarters] and in Washington that insufficient effort is being applied against the North Vietnamese heartland." The bombing's purpose was "to signal Hanoi in the strongest way possible that our air presence over their country will not diminish" (message, CINCPAC to COMUSMACV, CINCPACAF, CINCPACFLT, CINCSAC, 090225Z, Aug. 1972, in *Message Traffic, May–December 1972,* AFSHRC file no. K168.06-229).

13. Robert Thompson, *Peace Is Not at Hand* (New York: McKay, 1974), 121.

14. Message, "Comments of Le Duc Tho," 242137Z, May 1972, in *PAVE AEGIS and Miscellaneous Messages, SEA, June 1971–June 1972,* Secret.

15. Thompson, *Peace Is Not at Hand,* 123; Joseph Alsop, "Hanoi's Strategy Changed," *Washington Post,* Jan. 24, 1973.

16. On Oct. 13, Nixon reduced the number of daily attack sorties to 200 and restricted the scope of B-52 operations. This reduction resulted in no decrease in air force sorties sent against the North Vietnamese heartland. Three days later, as Kissinger journeyed from Washington for a "final" session with Communist negotiators, Nixon cut the number of daily strikes to 150. This measure reduced by 10 the number of air force strike sorties against the heartland. See Headquarters 7th Air Force, *7 AF History of Linebacker Operations, 10 May 1972–23 October 1972,* n.d., AFSHRC file no. K740.04-24, 32.

17. Message, "Comments of Le Duc Tho," 242137Z, May 1972, Secret.

18. Kissinger, *White House Years,* 1365–66.

19. Nixon, *RN,* 2:195.

20. Thompson, *Peace Is Not at Hand,* 121.

21. Headquarters PACAF, *Corona Harvest: The USAF in Southeast Asia, 1970–1973: Lessons Learned and Recommendations: A Compendium* (June 16, 1975), AFSHRC file no. K717.0423-11, 65, Secret.

22. William C. Westmoreland, in W. Scott Thompson and Donaldson D. Frizzell, eds., *The Lessons of Vietnam* (New York: Crane, Russak, 1977), 61.

23. Gen. John W. Vogt, Jr., U.S. Air Force oral history interview by Lt. Col. Arthur W. McCants, Jr., and Dr. James C. Hasdorff, Aug. 8–9, 1978, AFSHRC file no. K239.0512-1083, 87, Secret.

24. Kissinger, *White House Years*, 1393.

25. Headquarters PACAF, *Linebacker II USAF Bombing Survey* (Apr. 1973), AFSHRC file no. K717.64-8, 1.

26. Brig. Gen. Harry Cordes to Brig. Gen. James R. McCarthy, n.d., AFSHRC file no. K416.04-13, vol. 12, p. 3. (Cordes was deputy chief of staff for Intelligence at SAC headquarters during Linebacker II.)

27. U.S. Congress, House Committee on Appropriations, Subcommittee on DOD, *DOD Appropriations: Bombings of North Vietnam*, hearings, 93d Cong., 1st sess., Jan. 9–18, 1973, p. 18.

28. Nixon, *RN*, 2:244.

29. Maj. George Thompson (Ret.), interview with author, Omaha, Neb., Oct. 27, 1982.

30. Vogt interview, Aug. 8–9, 1978, 90–91, Secret.

31. Admiral Moorer, interview by newsmen, Apr. 4, 1973; Maj. John R. Allen, interview with author, Osan AB, Korea, Sept. 22, 1981; audiotape from Major Allen to author, June 1982. In January 1973, Moorer made this same statement during the Senate hearings, following testimony before the House Appropriations Committee, Subcommittee on Defense. See *DOD Appropriations: Bombings of North Vietnam*, 51.

32. "Terror Bombing in the Name of Peace," *Washington Post*, Dec. 28, 1972.

33. Tom Wicker, "Shame on Earth," *New York Times*, Dec. 26, 1972.

34. "Outrage and Relief," *Time*, Jan. 8, 1973.

35. *DOD Appropriations: Bombings of North Vietnam*, 51.

36. Nixon, *RN*, 2:247.

37. Kissinger, *White House Years*, 1453.

38. Nixon, *RN*, 2:245–46.

39. Kissinger, *White House Years*, 1459–62.

40. Ibid., 1469.

41. Ibid., 1470.

42. Nixon, *RN*, 2:222–23; Kissinger, *White House Years*, 1467–70.

43. Allan Goodman, *The Lost Peace: America's Search for a Negotiated Settlement of the Vietnam War* (Stanford: Hoover Institution Press, 1978), 157.

44. Thompson, *Peace Is Not at Hand*, 138.

45. Nixon, *RN*, 2:257–58.

46. Murrey Marder, "North Vietnam: Taking Pride in Punishment," *Washington Post*, Feb. 4, 1973; Michael F. Herz, *The Prestige Press and*

the Christmas Bombing, 1972 (Washington: Ethics and Public Policy Center, 1980), 54. In contrast, 334 American B-29 bombers killed 83,793 persons in a *single* raid against Tokyo on Mar. 9, 1945. See Russell F. Weigley, *The American Way of War: A History of United States Military Strategy and Policy* (New York: Macmillan, 1973), 364.

47. Tammy Arbuckle, "Bombing Was Pinpointed," *Washington Star,* Apr. 1, 1973.

48. Michael Allen, "Sharing the Agony of Hanoi," *Christian Century,* Jan. 24, 1973, pp. 92–93; *Linebacker II USAF Bombing Survey,* 37.

49. Address by James B. Stockdale to the Armed Forces Staff College, Apr. 9, 1975, quoted in U.S. Grant Sharp, *Strategy for Defeat: Vietnam in Retrospect* (San Rafael: Presidio Press, 1978), 258.

50. "North Viet Bombing Held Critical," *Aviation Week and Space Technology,* Mar. 5, 1973, 13; *DOD Appropriations: Bombings of North Vietnam,* 4; Kissinger, *White House Years,* 1417, 1445–46; Nixon, *RN,* 2:231; H. E. Rutledge, "A POW View of Linebacker II," *Armed Forces Journal International* 115 (Sept. 1977):20; Herz, *The Prestige Press and the Christmas Bombing,* 19; Joseph Alsop, "Hanoi's Strategy Changed," *Washington Post,* Jan. 24, 1973.

51. "North Vietnam's Statements on the Paris Talks, December 17 and 21, 1972," in Herz, *The Prestige Press and the Christmas Bombing,* 84.

52. Kissinger, *White House Years,* 1457–59; Nixon, *RN,* 2:250.

53. Nixon wrote: "There was no doubt that the Communists had infiltrated the Saigon government" (*RN,* 2:240).

54. Lt. Gen. Gerald W. Johnson, U.S. Air Force oral history interview by Charles K. Hopkins, Apr. 3, 1973, Andersen Air Force Base, Guam, AFSHRC file no. K239.0512-831, 23. Johnson was commander of the Eighth Air Force and its vast B-52 fleet during Linebacker II.

55. Henry A. Kissinger, "Agreement on Ending the War and Restoring Peace in Vietnam: News Conference, January 24, 1973," 71. In *Weekly Compilation of Presidential Documents,* vol. 9, no. 4 (Jan. 29, 1973), p. 71.

56. Nixon, *RN,* 2:259.

57. Kissinger, *White House Years,* 1461.

58. "What Admiral Moorer Really Said about Airpower's Effectiveness in SEA," *Air Force,* Nov. 1973, p. 25.

59. Howard Silber, "SAC Chief: B-52s Devastated Viet Air Defenses," *Omaha World Herald,* Feb. 25, 1973; Vogt interview, Aug. 8–9, 1978, 69, Secret.

60. Col. Clyde E. Bodenheimer, interview with author, Maxwell Air Force Base, Ala., Jan. 7, 1983.

61. Col. Robert D. Clark, interview with author, Robins Air Force Base, Ga., Jan. 7, 1983.

62. Thompson, *Peace Is Not at Hand,* 105.

63. Kissinger, *White House Years,* 1470.

Part 2: The Home Front

CHAPTER 5:

COLD WAR, LIMITED WAR, AND LIMITED EQUALITY: BLACKS IN
THE U.S. ARMED FORCES, 1945–1970, BY ROBERT F. BURK

1. For overviews of racial policies in the twenty-five years after World War II, see Harvard Sitkoff, *The Struggle for Black Equality* (New York: Hill & Wang, 1981); William C. Berman, *The Politics of Civil Rights in the Truman Administration* (Columbus: Ohio State University Press, 1970); Donald R. McCoy and Richard Ruetten, *Quest and Response: Minority Rights and the Truman Administration* (Lawrence: University Press of Kansas, 1973); Peter J. Kellogg, "Civil Rights Consciousness in the 1940's," *Historian* 42 (1979):18–41; Robert F. Burk, *The Eisenhower Administration and Black Civil Rights* (Knoxville: University of Tennessee Press, 1984); and Carl M. Brauer, *John F. Kennedy and the Second Reconstruction* (New York: Columbia University Press, 1977). For overviews of the treatment of racial minorities in the armed forces, consult Richard M. Dalfiume, *Desegregation of the U.S. Armed Forces: Fighting on Two Fronts, 1939–1953* (Columbia: University of Missouri Press, 1969); Jack D. Foner, *Blacks in the Military in U.S. History* (New York: Praeger, 1974); and Richard J. Stillman II, *Integration of the Negro in the U.S. Armed Forces* (New York: Praeger, 1968).

2. See Alonzo L. Hamby, *Beyond the New Deal: Harry S. Truman and American Liberalism* (New York: Columbia University Press, 1973), chap. 10; Henry Lee Moon, *Balance of Power: The Negro Vote* (Garden City, N.Y.: Doubleday, 1948).

3. McCoy and Ruetten, *Quest and Response,* 6–12; John M. Blum, *V Was for Victory* (New York: Harcourt Brace Jovanovich, 1976), 219.

4. Kellogg, "Civil Rights Consciousness," 26–31.

5. Hamby, *Beyond the New Deal,* 344–46; George H. Gallup, ed., *The Gallup Poll: Public Opinion, 1935–1971* (New York: Random House, 1972). See polls of Aug. 25, 1943; July 25, 1948; Apr. 29, 1949; Jan. 8, 1950; and Aug. 16, 1952.

6. Jack Greenberg, *Race Relations and American Law* (New York: Columbia University Press, 1959), 356.

7. See *To Secure These Rights: The Report of the President's Committee on Civil Rights* (New York: Doubleday, 1947); Barton J. Bernstein, "America in War and Peace: The Test of Liberalism," in Barton J. Bernstein, *Towards a New Past: Dissenting Essays in American History* (New York: Vintage, 1967), 305.

8. Bernstein, "America in War and Peace," 305–6; McCoy and Ruetten, *Quest and Response,* 123–26.

9. Foner, *Blacks in the Military,* 193.

10. William Peters, *The Southern Temper* (New York: Doubleday, 1959), 129–30.

11. Lee Nichols, *Breakthrough on the Color Front* (New York: Random House, 1954), 212.

12. Herbert S. Parmet, *Eisenhower and the American Crusades* (New York: Macmillan, 1972), 438.

13. Ibid., 419; *New York Times,* Mar. 26, 1953; Robert J. Donovan, *Eisenhower: The Inside Story* (New York: Harper, 1956), 155–56.

14. Morris J. MacGregor and Bernard C. Nalty, eds., *Blacks in the Armed Forces: Basic Documents,* vol. 12: *Integration* (Wilmington, Del.: Scholarly Resources, 1977), 353–81; Greenberg, *Race Relations and American Law,* 367.

15. Donovan, *Eisenhower,* 159; Nichols, *Breakthrough on the Color Front,* 213; Dwight D. Eisenhower, *The White House Years: Mandate for Change* (Garden City, N.Y: Doubleday, 1963), 235; NAACP, *Annual Report* (1954), 42 (1957), 39.

16. Donovan, *Eisenhower,* 161; Greenberg, *Race Relations and American Law,* 363.

17. Rep. Charles C. Diggs, Jr., to Sec. of the Air Force Dudley C. Sharp, July 7, 1960, in MacGregor and Nalty, *Blacks in the Armed Forces,* 316–46.

18. Brauer, *John F. Kennedy,* 85–86.

19. Ibid., 86; Stillman, *Integration of the Negro,* 109–12; John P. Davis, ed., *The American Negro Reference Book* (Englewood Cliffs, N.J.: Prentice-Hall, 1966), 658.

20. Davis, *American Negro Reference Book,* 659–61; Stillman, *Integration of the Negro,* 111–22; Dalfiume, *Desegregation of the U.S. Armed Forces,* 222–23.

21. James C. Evans, quoted in Stillman, *Integration of the Negro,* 63.

22. Congressman Adam Clayton Powell, Jr., to Asst. Sec. of the Navy

for Air John Floberg, June 29, 1953; Floberg to Powell, July 17, 1953; Cdr. Durward Gilmore et al., to chief of Bureau of Naval Personnel, Vice Adm. J. L. Holloway, Aug. 31, 1953; "Memorandum, Chief of Naval Personnel for the Secretary of the Navy, Sept. 1, 1953"; "Statement of the ACLU Concerning Segregation and Discrimination in the U.S. Navy, June 1955"; American Civil Liberties Union Exec. Dir. Patrick M. Malin to Sec. of the Navy Thomas S. Gates, Jr., Nov. 26, 1957, all in MacGregor and Nalty, *Blacks in the Armed Forces,* 303–10.

23. Headquarters, U.S. Army, Europe, Historical Division, "Integration of Negro and White Troops in the U.S. Army, Europe, 1952–1954," in MacGregor and Nalty, *Blacks in the Armed Forces,* 270.

24. NAACP, *Crisis* 62 (1955), 517; Greenberg, *Race Relations and American Law,* 361–66.

25. Bureau of Naval Personnel, "Memorandum on Discrimination of the Negro, 24 Jan., 1959," in MacGregor and Nalty, *Blacks in the Armed Forces,* 132–40.

26. Charles C. Moskos, Jr., "Racial Integration in the Armed Forces," in Norval Glenn and Charles M. Bonjean, eds., *Blacks in the United States* (San Francisco, Calif.: Chandler, 1969), 562–63.

27. John Hope Franklin, *From Slavery to Freedom: A History of Negro Americans* (New York: Vintage, 1967), 651; Harry F. Rosenthal, "Viet Vets Still Pay Price," *Zanesville* (Ohio) *Times Recorder,* July 24, 1985.

28. Excerpts from Wallace Terry, "Black Power in Vietnam," *Time,* Sept. 19, 1969, in Leslie Fishel, Jr., and Benjamin Quarles, eds., *The Black American* (New York: Scott, Foresman, 1970), 583–86.

29. Terry, "Black Power in Vietnam," 586–87; Benjamin Quarles, *The Negro in the Making of America* (London: Collier, 1969), 287.

CHAPTER 6:
THE ANTIWAR MOVEMENT IN AMERICA, 1955–1965,
BY CHARLES DEBENEDETTI

1. Charles Chatfield, *For Peace and Justice: Pacifism in America, 1914–1941* (Knoxville: University of Tennessee Press, 1971), pt. 1; Charles DeBenedetti, *Origins of the Modern American Peace Movement, 1915–1929* (Millwood, N.Y.: KTO Press, 1978), pt. 1; C. Roland Marchand, *The American Peace Movement and Social Reform, 1898–1918* (Princeton: Princeton University Press, 1972), chaps. 5–10. Using the insights of the historical sociologist Charles Tilly, the present chapter understands the word "movement" to signify "a political product" engaged in "sustained *interaction* in which mobilized people, acting in the

name of a defined interest, make repeated demands on powerful others via means which go beyond the current prescriptions of the authorities" (Charles Tilly, "Social Movements and National Politics," in Charles Bright and Susan Harding, eds., *Statemaking and Social Movements: Essays in History and Theory* [Ann Arbor: University of Michigan Press, 1984], 313, emphasis in the original).

2. Lawrence S. Wittner, *Rebels against War: The American Peace Movement, 1933–1983* (Philadelphia: Temple University Press, 1984), 235–41; Charles DeBenedetti, *The Peace Reform in American History* (Bloomington: Indiana University Press, 1980), 157–64.

3. Sanford Gottlieb, quoted in Godfrey Hodgson, *America in Our Time* (New York: Random House, 1978), 276. Estimates of the size of the movement are drawn from Charles Bolton, "A Program for the Future," *Nation* 197 (Nov. 2, 1963):279; and "Turn Toward Peace: The First Sixteen Months, A Report from the Staff," p. 1, issued by Turn Toward Peace, May 1963, folder 1, box 8, Student Peace Union Records, Archives Division, State Historical Society of Wisconsin, Madison (cited hereafter as SHSW).

4. George F. Kennan, "Overdue Changes in Our Foreign Policy," *Harper's Magazine* 213 (Aug. 1956):27; Jerome D. Frank and Earl H. Nash, "The Making of a Peace Activist," *War/Peace Report* 5, no. 4 (Apr. 1965):9.

5. C. Wright Mills, *The Causes of World War III* (New York: Simon & Schuster, 1958), 2.

6. Reprinted in Seymour Melman, ed., *Disarmament: Its Politics and Economics* (Boston: American Academy of Arts and Sciences, 1962), 18–19.

7. Erich Fromm, *The Sane Society* (New York: Holt, Rinehart & Winston, 1955), 357.

8. Stephen Cary and Robert Pickus, "Reply to the Critics," *Progressive* 19 (Oct. 1955), 24. For the full Quaker position, see American Friends Service Committee, *Speak Truth to Power: A Quaker Search for an Alternative to Violence* (Philadelphia: American Friends Service Committee, 1955).

9. Mills, *Causes of World War III*, 47, 81; C. Wright Mills, "Program for Peace," *Nation* 185 (Dec. 7, 1957):420, 424.

10. Editorial, *Journal of Conflict Resolution* 1 (Mar. 1957):2.

11. Bradford Lyttle, *You Come with Naked Hands: The Story of the San Francisco to Moscow March for Peace* (Raymond, N.H.: Greenleaf, 1966), 1. For the CNVA, see Neil H. Katz, "Radical Pacifism and the Contemporary American Peace Movement: The Committee for Non-

violent Action, 1957–1967" (Ph.D. diss., University of Maryland, 1974); Milton S. Katz and Neil H. Katz, "Pragmatists and Visionaries in the Post-World War II American Peace Movement: SANE and CNVA," in Solomon Wank, ed., *Doves and Diplomats: Foreign Offices and Peace Movements in Europe and America in the Twentieth Century* (Westport, Conn.: Greenwood, 1978), 275–79; Jo Ann Ooiman Robinson, *Abraham Went Out: A Biography of A. J. Muste* (Philadelphia: Temple University Press, 1982), 162–76.

12. James T. Shotwell, in minutes of meeting of Dec. 2, 1957, SANE logbook for 1957–59, SANE National Offices, Washington, D.C. For the full story of the test-ban struggle, see Robert A. Divine, *Blowing on the Wind: The Nuclear Test-Ban Debate, 1954–1960* (New York: Oxford University Press, 1978).

13. Mills, *Causes of World War III*, 6.

14. Charles E. Osgood, "The Case for Graduated Unilateral Disengagement," *Bulletin of the Atomic Scientists* 16 (Apr. 1960):128.

15. Lewis Mumford, "Moral Emergency," *Fellowship* 24 (Jan. 1, 1958):22; Kenneth E. Boulding, *Conflict and Defense: A General Theory* (New York: Harper, 1963), 332.

16. "The Committee of Correspondence: A Statement," pamphlet dated Mar. 1960, in Committee of Correspondence folder, Social Protest Project, Bancroft Library, University of California, Berkeley.

17. Erich Fromm, *May Man Prevail?: An Inquiry into the Facts and Fictions of Foreign Policy* (Garden City, N.Y.: Doubleday, 1964), 248.

18. Henry A. Kissinger, *The Necessity for Choice: Prospects of American Foreign Policy* (New York: Harper, 1960), 213; Thomas C. Schelling and Morton H. Halperin, *Strategy and Arms Control* (New York: Twentieth Century Fund, 1961), 141–42. For the origins of deterrence strategizing and arms control, see Lawrence Freedman, *The Evolution of Nuclear Strategy* (New York: St. Martin's, 1981); and Robin Ranger, *Arms and Politics, 1958–1978: Arms Control in a Changing Political Context* (Toronto: Macmillan, 1979), 3–49.

19. Fromm, *May Man Prevail?* 203; Seymour Melman, *The Peace Race* (New York: Ballantine, 1961), 24; Amitai Etzioni, *The Hard Way to Peace: A New Strategy* (New York: Collier, 1962), 127.

20. Fromm, *May Man Prevail?* 203.

21. Seymour Melman, "The 'Arms Control' Doctrine," *Nation* 192 (Feb. 11, 1961):114; Post War World Council, *Newsletter*, Mar. 1961.

22. Michael Maccoby, "Social Psychology of Deterrence," *Bulletin of the Atomic Scientists* 17 (Sept. 1961):278, 281.

23. Charles E. Osgood, "Reversing the Arms Race," *Progressive* 26

(May 1962):30; Erich Fromm, "The Case for Unilateral Disarmament," in Donald G. Brennan, ed., *Arms Control, Disarmament and National Security* (New York: Braziller, 1961), 188.

24. Fromm, "Case for Unilateral Disarmament," 188.

25. A. J. Muste, "Politics on the Other Side of Despair," *Liberation* 7 (Apr. 1962):8.

26. Paul Goodman, "Declaring Peace against the Governments," *Liberation* 7 (Mar. 1962):7.

27. Melman, *Peace Race*. Also, see George McGovern, "Planning for Peace," *Progressive* 27 (Dec. 1963):23–26; Emile Benoit and Kenneth E. Boulding, *Disarmament and the Economy* (New York: Harper, 1963); and Kirkpatrick Sale, *SDS* (New York: Random House, 1974), 152–53.

28. "The Committee of Correspondence: A Statement." Also see Sidney Lens, *Unrepentant Radical: An American Activist's Account of Five Turbulent Decades* (Boston: Beacon, 1980), 254–55; and, for the Student Peace Union, George R. Vickers, *The Formation of the New Left: The Early Years* (Lexington, Mass.: Heath, 1975), chap. 3.

29. Norman Thomas form letter, Sept. 11, 1961, and attached "Memorandum Outlining a Major National Campaign to Build Support for Alternatives to the Threat of War as the Central Thrust of American Foreign Policy," folder 5, box 8, Student Peace Union Records, SHSW.

30. Leo Szilard, "A Way to Get Off the Road to War," *War/Peace Report* 2 (Mar. 1962):8.

31. "Women Strike for Peace," *New University Thought* 2 (Spring 1962):147.

32. George H. Gallup, *The Gallup Poll: Public Opinion, 1935–1971*, 3 vols. (New York: Scholarly Resources, 1972), 3:1826.

33. "The 1962 Political Peace Race," *War/Peace Report* 2 (Sept. 1962):9–10.

34. "Why and How Did Peace Break Out?" *I. F. Stone's Bi-Weekly* 11 (Sept. 2, 1963):1.

35. Students for a Democratic Society, "America and the New Era," June 1963, p. 14, Social Protest Project, Bancroft Library.

36. Ibid.

37. Richard Flacks, "Some Thoughts on the Current Scene," *Prep Newsletter*, no. 1 (May 1963):10.

38. A. J. Muste, "The Peace Movement 1963," *Our Generation against Nuclear War* 2 (ca. Summer 1963):5.

39. Bolton, "Program for the Future," 280.

40. "Vietnam: Documentation of Disaster," Oct. 1963, box 25a, Social Protest Project. Also see Nancy Zaroulis and Gerald Sullivan, *Who*

Spoke Up?: American Protest against the War in Vietnam, 1963–1975 (Garden City, N.Y.: Doubleday, 1984).

41. "Algeria, Vietnam and Punta Del Este," *Monthly Review* 13 (Mar. 1962):500; Annalee Stewart, "Undeclared War in Vietnam," *Four Lights* 22 (June 1962):3; "Vietnam Again," *New Republic* 147 (Dec. 15, 1962):5.

42. "Barbed Wire and Bamboo," *New University Thought* 2 (Autumn 1962):13.

43. Youth against War and Fascism flyer, "Stop the Slaughter in Vietnam!" Apr. 1, 1963, carton 20, World without War Council Records, Bancroft Library.

44. Women Strike for Peace, *National Information Memo* 2 (June 28, 1963):4.

45. *New York Times,* July 14, 1963, sec. 6, p. 2.

46. *Congressional Record,* 88th Cong., 1st sess., Sept. 10, 1963, p. 16599.

47. "Will New Chances for Peace Be Another Lost Opportunity?" *I.F. Stone's Bi-Weekly* 11 (Oct. 28, 1963):7.

48. A. J. Muste and David McReynolds, "Memo on Vietnam: A Statement Prepared for the War Resisters League," attached to Charles Bloomstein form letter, Aug. 7, 1964, carton 15, World without War Council Records, Bancroft Library. Also see Ronald Steel, *Walter Lippmann and the American Century* (New York: Random House, 1980), 541–56, passim.

49. *Congressional Record,* 88th Cong., 2d sess., June 3, 1964, p. 12609.

50. "U.S. Press and Vietnam," *National Guardian,* Oct. 17, 1964, p. 2.

51. Alfred Hasler to Mildred and Ivan Potts, Aug. 25, 1964, transfile 4, Fellowship of Reconciliation Records, Peace Collection, Swarthmore College, Swarthmore, Pa.

52. Rev. Daniel Berrigan, "In Peaceable Conflict," *Catholic Worker* 31 (Mar. 1965):1.

53. "Declaration of Conscience," *Catholic Worker* 31 (Feb. 1965):2.

54. Benjamin Spock to Hubert H. Humphrey, Feb. 15, 1965, box 8, Benjamin Spock Papers, Manuscripts Division, George Arents Memorial Library, Syracuse University.

55. Paul Boyer, "From Activism to Apathy: The American People and Nuclear Weapons, 1963–1980," *Journal of American History* 70 (Mar. 1984):821–44.

56. Roger Hagan, "Peace at the Polls," *Nation* 196 (Feb. 2, 1963):84.

57. Robert Paul Wolff, "A Challenge to the Peace Movement," 5, attached to Marc Raskin to Arthur Waskow, Mar. 7, 1962, box 8, Arthur I. Waskow Papers, Archives Division, SHSW.

CHAPTER 7:
GUNS VERSUS BUTTER: VIETNAM'S EFFECT ON CONGRESSIONAL
SUPPORT FOR THE GREAT SOCIETY, BY JAMES C. SCHNEIDER

1. Arthur M. Schlesinger, Sr., *The American as Reformer* (Cambridge, Mass: Harvard University Press, 1951), 18; Arthur M. Schlesinger, Jr., *Robert F. Kennedy and His Times* (Boston: Houghton Mifflin, 1978), 842–43.

2. John Morton Blum, *V Was for Victory: Politics and American Culture during World War II* (New York: Harcourt Brace Jovanovich, 1976), 234–45; Richard Polenberg, *War and Society: The United States, 1941–1945* (Philadelphia: Lippincott, 1972), 73–99.

3. Alonzo L. Hamby, *Beyond the New Deal: Harry S. Truman and American Liberalism* (New York: Columbia University Press, 1973), 307, 309, 418–22.

4. *New York Times*, Jan. 11, 1967, pp. 1, 17.

5. Doris Kearns, *Lyndon Johnson and the American Dream* (New York: New American Library, 1976), 263.

6. Lyndon B. Johnson, *The Vantage Point: Perspectives on the Presidency, 1963–1969* (New York: Holt, Rinehart & Winston, 1971), 322–23.

7. Ibid., 324.

8. *New York Times*, Feb. 8, 1966, p. 50.

9. Ibid., Dec. 8, 1966, p. 46.

10. Ibid., May 12, 1966, p. 39; Dec. 16, 1966, p. 33.

11. The most comprehensive and recent history of the period is Allen J. Matusow, *The Unraveling of America: A History of Liberalism in the 1960s* (New York: Harper & Row, 1984). Also essential are Eric F. Goldman, *The Tragedy of Lyndon Johnson* (New York: Dell, 1968); Jim F. Heath, *Decade of Disillusionment* (Bloomington: Indiana University Press, 1976); and Schlesinger, *Robert F. Kennedy*. The literature on the Great Society has proliferated even faster than the programs themselves. Among the best works are Robert D. Plotnick and Felicity Skidmore, *Progress against Poverty: A Review of the 1964–1974 Decade* (New York: Academic Press, 1975); Robert A. Levine, *The Poor Ye Need Not Have with You: Lessons from the War on Poverty* (Cambridge, Mass.: Harvard

University Press, 1970); Henry Aaron, *Politics and the Professors: The Great Society in Perspective* (Washington: Brookings, 1978); and Sar A. Levitan and Robert Taggert, *The Promise of Greatness: The Social Programs of the Last Decade and Their Major Achievements* (Cambridge, Mass.: Harvard University Press, 1976). See also the appropriate section of James T. Patterson, *America's Struggle against Poverty: 1900–1980* (Cambridge, Mass.: Harvard University Press, 1981).

12. Bureau of the Census, *Historical Statistics of the United States: Colonial Times to 1970,* pt. 2 (Washington: U.S. Government Printing Office, 1975), 1116.

13. Stanley Karnow, *Vietnam: A History* (New York: Viking, 1983), 479.

14. *Public Papers of the Presidents of the United States: Lyndon B. Johnson, 1966* (Washington: U.S. Government Printing Office, 1967), 1:3–12.

15. Memorandum, Walter P. Reuther to Lyndon B. Johnson, May 13, 1965, Presidential File, Legislative Background—Model Cities, box 1, "Early Origins," Lyndon B. Johnson Presidential Library, Austin, Tex. (Hereafter Presidential File will be referred to as PF; the Lyndon B. Johnson Presidential Library as LBJPL.)

16. Transcript of an interview with Robert C. Wood, Oct. 19, 1968, PF, Oral History Collection—"Wood," LBJPL (cited hereafter as Wood interview).

17. Memorandum, Harry M. McPherson, Jr., to Joseph Califano, Dec. 13, 1965, PF, Legislative Background—Model Cities, box 1, "Origins and Deliberations of Wood-Haar II," LBJPL; the report is attached to this memorandum.

18. Ibid.

19. See, for example, the Department of Housing and Urban Development Section-by-Section Summary of the Demonstration Cities Act of 1966, PF, Aides—Wilson, box 13, "Demonstration Cities," LBJPL.

20. Wood interview; Robert Weaver to the president, May 22, 1966, PF, Legislative Background—Model Cities, box 2, "The Legislative Struggle," both in LBJPL.

21. Robert Weaver to the president, May 22, 1966, PF, Legislative Background—Model Cities, box 2, "The Legislative Struggle"; memorandum, Sidney Spector to Robert Weaver, May 24, 1966, PF, Legislative Background—Model Cities, box 2, "The Legislative Struggle," LBJPL.

22. Memorandum, Henry H. Wilson, Jr., to the president, May 30, 1966, PF, Legislative Background—Local Government, box 139,

"LE/LG 4/28/66–7/31/66"; memorandum, Charles Schultz to Joseph Califano, June 6, 1966, PF, Legislative Background—Model Cities, box 2, "The Legislative Struggle," LBJPL.

23. Joseph Califano to the president, June 6, 1966, PF, Legislation—Local Government, box 139, "LE/LG 4/28/66–7/31/66," LBJPL.

24. Robert C. Wood to Joseph Califano, Oct. 5, 1966; memorandum, Sidney Spector to Henry Wilson, Sept. 10, 1966, both in PF, Legislative Background—Model Cities, box 2, "Legislative Struggle II," LBJPL.

25. Matusow, *Unraveling of America*, 170–72.

26. *Baron's* 46, no. 1 (Jan. 3, 1966):4; *New York Times*, May 26, 1966, pp. 1, 67, and Aug. 8, 1966, p. 1.

27. *Baron's* 46, no. 1 (Jan. 3, 1966):4; *New York Times*, Jan. 17, 1966, pp. 1, 15, and May 21, 1966, p. 49.

28. *Forbes* 97, no. 1 (Jan. 1, 1966):13; *New York Times*, Jan. 17, 1966, pp. 1, 15.

29. *New York Times*, Oct. 22, 1966, p. 35.

30. Ibid., Dec. 8, 1966, p. 74.

31. Ibid.

32. *Fortune* 73, no. 2 (Feb. 1966):37–44, no. 5 (May 1966):31–38, and 74, no. 6 (Dec. 1966):39–46; *Forbes* 99, no. 1 (Jan. 1, 1967):23.

33. *New York Times*, June 26, 1966, sec. 3, p. 1.

34. Wood interview, LBJPL.

35. *New York Times*, Oct. 16, 1966, sec. 4, p. 2; memorandum, Sidney Spector to Henry Wilson, Sept. 10, 1966; Robert C. Wood to Joseph Califano, Oct. 5, 1966, both in PF, Legislative Background—Model Cities, box 2, "Legislative Struggle II," LBJPL.

36. *New York Times*, Nov. 4, 1966, p. 44.

37. See vol. 3 of the collected surveys: George H. Gallup, *The Gallup Poll: Public Opinion, 1935–1971* (New York: Random House, 1972).

38. *New York Times*, Aug. 9, 1966, pp. 1, 4.

39. Ibid., Nov. 10, 1966, pp. 1, 28.

40. Ibid., Nov. 11, 1966, pp. 1, 25.

41. Ibid., Nov. 10, 1966, pp. 1, 28.

42. Gallup, *Public Opinion*, vol. 3.

43. *New York Times*, Oct. 23, 1966, p. 84.

44. Ibid., Jan. 15, 1967, sec. 4, p. 1.

45. Ibid.

46. *Public Papers of the Presidents, 1967*, 1:2–7; *New York Times*, Jan. 8, 1967, sec. 4, p. 1.

47. There are many examples of the Republicans' opposition to the

Great Society. See *New York Times,* Jan. 18, 1966, pp. 1, 8; Feb. 6, 1966, sec. 4, p. 5; Feb. 21, 1966, pp. 1, 32; Mar. 3, 1966, p. 17; Oct. 1, 1967, sec. 4, p. 2.

48. Memorandum, Henry Wilson to the postmaster general, May 1, 1967, PF, Aides—Wilson, box 14, "Memos to the PMG," LBJPL.

49. Memorandum, Robert Weaver to Lawrence O'Brien, Apr. 21, 1967, ibid.

50. "Model Cities Fact Sheet," unidentified, n.d., PF, Aides—Gaither, box 265, "Model Cities," LBJPL.

51. Memorandum, Mike Manatos to the president, Aug. 21, 1967, PF, General Federal Aide 3, box 16, "FA 4, 8/20/67–5/8/68," LBJPL.

52. Attachment to speech by Senator Mike Mansfield, "Our Promise to Urban America," author unidentified, n.d. [Aug. 1967], PF, Aides—Califano, box 47, "Model Cities," LBJPL.

53. Memorandum, Mike Manatos to the president, Sept. 19, 1967, PF, General Federal Aide 3, box 16, "FA 4, 8/20/67–5/8/68," LBJPL.

54. Memorandum, Harold Sanders to the president, Oct. 23, 1967, ibid.

55. Memorandum, Joseph Califano to the president, Oct. 24, 1967, ibid.

56. Ibid.

57. Memorandum, Harold Sanders to the president, Oct. 24, 1967, ibid.

58. Matusow, *Unraveling of America,* 243–75.

59. *New York Times,* Oct. 6, 1967, p. 1.

60. Ibid., Nov. 14, 1967, p. 1; Dec. 25, 1967, pp. 1, 26.

Part 3: Central America

CHAPTER 8: REVOLT AGAINST THE WEST: THE NICARAGUAN
REVOLUTION AND RELATED MOVEMENTS,
BY RALPH LEE WOODWARD, JR.

1. N. L. B. (pseudonym for Louis Napoleon Bonaparte), *Canal of Nicaragua: or, a Project to Connect the Atlantic and Pacific Oceans by means of a Canal* (London: Mills, 1846), 4.

2. For a fuller summary of Central American history, see Ralph Lee Woodward, Jr., *Central America, a Nation Divided,* 2d ed. (New York: Oxford University Press, 1985). Portions of this summary were published

previously in "Roots of Revolution: Socioeconomic Perspectives on Nicaraguan History," *Athenaeum Society Review* 1, no. 1 (Fall 1984):7–20.

3. On the colonial background of political party development in Central America, see Miles Wortman, *Government and Society in Central America, 1680–1840* (New York: Columbia University Press, 1982); Mario Rodriguez, *The Cádiz Experiment in Central America, 1808–26* (Berkeley: University of California Press, 1978); and Ralph Lee Woodward, Jr., "The Social and Economic Origins of the Guatemalan Political Parties (1773–1823)," *Hispanic American Historical Review* 45 (1965):544–66. Revealing editorials reflecting Central American Conservative philosophy may be found in *El Tiempo* (Guatemala, 1839–41); *Gaceta Oficial* (Guatemala, 1841–46); *Gaceta de Guatemala* (Guatemala, 1847–71); and *La Gaceta, Diario Oficial* (Managua, 1860–90).

4. The Liberal approach to development is evident in Central American historical writing from 1870 through the mid-twentieth century. See Lorenzo Montúfar, *Reseña histórica de Centro América*, 7 vols. (Guatemala: El Progreso, 1878–87), upon which many other pro-Liberal accounts of the nineteenth century were based. This literature is discussed in William J. Griffith, "The Historiography of Central America since 1830," *Hispanic American Historical Review* 40 (1960):548–69. See also Robert Wauchope and Margaret Harrison, eds., *Applied Enlightenment: 19th Century Liberalism* (New Orleans: Middle American Research Institute, Publication no. 23, 1972).

5. See D. J. McCreery, *Development and the State in Reforma Guatemala* (Athens: Ohio University Press, 1983); David Browning, *El Salvador: Landscape and Society* (London: Oxford University Press, 1971); Carolyn Hall, *El Café y el desarrollo historico-geográfico de Costa Rica* (San José: Editorial Costa Rica, 1976); Alberto Lanuza, *Estructuras socioeconómicas, poder y estado en Nicaragua, de 1821 a 1875* (San José: Tesis de Grado, Universidad de Costa Rica, 1976); and C. F. S. Cardoso, "Historia económica del café en Centroamérica (siglo XIX)," *Estudios Sociales Centroamericanos* 4, no. 10 (1975):9–55.

6. Germán Romero-Vargas, *Les structures sociales du Nicaragua au XVIIIe siècle* (Doctorat d'état diss., Université de Paris, 1976; Lille: Atelier de Reproduction des Theses, 1977).

7. See Pedro Joaquín Chamorro, *Fruto Chamorro* (Managua: Unión, 1960); see also Joaquín Zavala Urtecho, "Huellas de una familia vasco-centroamericana en 5 siglos de historia," 2 vols., *Revista del Pensamiento Centroamericano* 23, nos. 111 and 112 (Dec. 1969 and Jan. 1970):1–316, for a detailed history of another important Nicaraguan Conservative family.

8. See Mario Rodríguez, *A Palmerstonian Diplomat in Central America: Frederick Chatfield, Esq.* (Tucson: University of Arizona Press, 1964); and C. L. Stansifer, "Ephraim George Squier, diversos aspectos de su carrera en Centroamérica," *Revista Conservadora del Pensamiento Centroamericano* 20, no. 98 (1968):1–64. There is a voluminous literature on the Walker episode, but among the best remains W. O. Scroggs, *Filibusters and Financiers* (New York: Macmillan, 1916). Among useful recent works are David Folkman, *The Nicaragua Route* (Salt Lake City: University of Utah Press, 1972); Frederick Rosengarten, *Freebooters Must Die!* (Wayne, Pa.: Haverford House, 1976); C. H. Brown, *Agents of Manifest Destiny, the Lives and Times of the Filibusters* (Chapel Hill: University of North Carolina Press, 1980); and James T. Wall, *Manifest Destiny Denied* (Washington: University Press of the Americas, 1982).

9. See Francisco Ortega Aranciba, *Cuarenta años (1838–1878) de la historia de Nicaragua* (Managua: Banco de América, 1974); and Lanuza, *Estructuras*.

10. Gustavo Neiderlein, *The State of Nicaragua of the Greater Republic of Central America* (Philadelphia: Philadelphia Commercial Museum, 1898), 85.

11. See C. L. Stansifer, "José Santos Zelaya: A New Look at Nicaragua's Liberal Dictator," *Revista Interamericana* 7 (Fall 1979):468–85; see also J. J. Morales, *De la historia de Nicaragua de 1889–1913: la dictadura del Presidente General José Santos Zelaya* (Granada: Editorial Magys, 1963) for a Conservative party viewpoint; and B. I. Teplitz, *The Political and Economic Foundations of Modernization in Nicaragua: The Administration of José Santos Zelaya* (Ph.D. diss., Howard University, Washington, 1973).

12. See Dana Munro, *The Five Republics of Central America* (New York: Oxford University Press, 1918), 227–64, and *Intervention and Dollar Diplomacy in the Caribbean, 1900–1921* (Princeton: Princeton University Press, 1964), 160–216.

13. Munro, *Five Republics,* 245; Dana Munro, *A Student in Central America, 1914–1916,* ed. J. S. H. Brown and E. W. Andrews V, Middle American Research Institute, pub. no. 51 (New Orleans: Tulane University, 1983), 20.

14. Munro, *Student in Central America,* 22–23, 34.

15. Lester Langley, *The United States and the Caribbean in the Twentieth Century* (Athens: University of Georgia Press, 1980), 116–25, gives a brief but accurate account of these events. For more detail, see J. O. Baylen, "American Intervention in Nicaragua, 1909–33: An Appraisal of Objectives and Results," *Southwestern Social Science Quarterly* 35

(1954):128–54; Henry L. Stimson, *American Policy in Nicaragua* (New York: Scribner's, 1927); I. J. Cox, *Nicaragua and the United States, 1909–1927* (Boston: World Peace Foundation, 1927); William Kamman, *A Search for Stability, United States Diplomacy Toward Nicaragua, 1925–1933* (Notre Dame, Ind.: University of Notre Dame Press, 1968); and Dana Munro, *The United States and the Caribbean Republics, 1921–1933* (Princeton: Princeton University Press, 1974).

16. See Richard Millett, *Guardians of the Dynasty* (Maryknoll, N.Y.: Orbis, 1977); on Sandino, see Neill Macaulay, *The Sandino Affair* (Chicago: Quadrangle, 1967).

17. Millett's *Guardians* is one of the most informative works on the Somoza years, but there are a number of other useful volumes representing several points of view, including Bernard Diederich, *Somoza and the Legacy of U.S. Involvement in Central America* (New York: Dutton, 1981); Anastasio Somoza Debayle and Jack Cox, *Nicaragua Betrayed* (Boston: Western Isles, 1980); John Booth, *The End and the Beginning: The Nicaraguan Revolution* (Boulder, Colo.: Westview, 1982); Belden Bell, *Nicaragua, an Ally under Siege* (Washington: Council on American Affairs, 1978); and T. W. Walker, *Nicaragua, the Land of Sandino* (Boulder, Colo.: Westview, 1981).

18. Richard Millett, "The Sandinista Revolution of 1979: A Promise Fulfilled, A Promise Broken" (Paper presented at the Eleventh General Brown Conference in History, University of Alabama, 27 Oct. 1984).

19. Arturo Cruz Sequeira, "The Origins of Sandinista Foreign Policy," in Robert S. Leiken, ed., *Central America, Anatomy of Conflict* (New York: Pergamon, 1984), 95–101; see also Carlos Fonseca, *Un nicaragüense en Moscú* (Managua: FSLN, 1980).

20. Works on the Nicaraguan Revolution are appearing rapidly. Among the most useful published to date is Shirley Christian, *Nicaragua, Revolution in the Family* (New York: Random House, 1985). For a discussion of the literature, see Ralph L. Woodward, Jr., comp., *Nicaragua* (Oxford: Clio Press, 1983).

CHAPTER 9: THE UNITED STATES, COSTA RICA, AND NICARAGUA, 1980–1984, BY THOMAS M. LEONARD

1. Franklin D. Parker, *The Central American Republics* (London: Oxford University Press, 1964); Mario Rodríguez, *Central America* (Englewood Cliffs, N.J.: Prentice-Hall, 1965); Ralph Lee Woodward, *Central America: A Nation Divided* (New York: Oxford University Press, 1985); Thomas L. Karnes, *The Failure of Union: Central America, 1824–1975*

(Tempe: Arizona State University Press, 1976); John and Mavis Biesanz, *Costa Rican Life* (New York: Columbia University Press, 1944); Howard Blutstein, et al., *Area Handbook for Costa Rica* (Washington: U.S. Government Printing Office, 1970); Chester L. Jones, *Costa Rica and Civilization in the Caribbean* (New York: Russell & Russell, 1967); and John A. Booth, "Representative Constitutional Democracy in Costa Rica: Adaptation to Crisis in the Turbulent 1980s," in Steve C. Ropp and James A. Morris, eds., *Central America: Crisis and Adaptation* (Albuquerque: University of New Mexico Press, 1984).

2. Memorandum, Secretary of State Dean Acheson to President Harry S. Truman, Jan. 6, 1949, p. 3, Confidential File, box 35, State Department folder 15, Harry S. Truman Papers, Harry S. Truman Presidential Library, Independence, Mo.; U.S. Congress, Senate Committee on Foreign Relations, "Perspectives on Latin America: Report of a Study Mission to Costa Rica, Panama, Peru and Venezuela," 95th Cong., 2d sess., 1978, pp. 1–13, and U.S. Congress, House Subcommittee on Inter-American Affairs, "Central America at the Crossroads," 96th Cong., 1st sess., 1979, 1–20.

3. "Costa Rica Finding the Fiesta Is Over," *New York Times,* Dec. 15, 1980, p. 11.

4. Inter-American Development Bank, *Economic and Social Progress in Latin America, Reports 1970–1982* (Washington: U.S. Government Printing Office, 1970–82); "Costa Rica Finding the Fiesta Is Over," *New York Times,* Dec. 15, 1980, p. 11; "Costa Rica: 'Switzerland' of the Americas Turns Sour," *Christian Science Monitor,* Sept. 16, 1982, p. 2; and "Tough Year for Costa Rican 'Welfare State,'" *Christian Science Monitor,* Dec. 7, 1982, p. 4.

5. "Loans Sought by Costa Rica," *New York Times,* Sept. 19, 1981, p. 30; "Costa Rica Pressing Talks with Banks on Financial Snarl," *New York Times,* Dec. 9, 1981, sec. 4, p. 19; "Latin American Inflation Shakes Welfare States," *Wall Street Journal,* Feb. 2, 1981, p. 49; "Costa Rica Suspending Payment of $70 Million Owed to Import Firms," *Wall Street Journal,* Oct. 5, 1981, p. 17; "Riches to Rags: Lacking Money for Oil, Welfare and Luxuries," *Wall Street Journal,* Oct. 29, 1981, p. 47; "Danger of Leaning Too Hard on Costa Rica," *Business Week,* Sept. 28, 1981, p. 30; and "Raiding Grandma's Cabinet," *Time,* Sept. 28, 1981, p. 42.

6. U.S. Congress, House Ways and Means Committee, "Report on the Committee Delegation Visit to the Caribbean Basin," 98th Cong., 1st sess., 1983, pp. 72–74; U.S. Congress, House Committee on Foreign Affairs, "Report on a Congressional Study Mission to Honduras, Costa Rica, Nicaragua and El Salvador, August 27–September 8, 1984," 98th

Cong., 2d sess., 9–11; "Costa Ricans Vote for a President," *New York Times,* Feb. 8, 1982, p. 9; "Troubled Costa Rica Gets New President," *New York Times,* May 9, 1982, p. 3; "Costa Rica Tightens Belt," *New York Times,* June 29, 1982, sec. 4, p. 1; "Costa Rica Reaches an Accord with Banks on Restructuring Debt," *Wall Street Journal,* Dec. 12, 1982, p. 33; "IMF Approves Loans to Costa Rica, Burma," *Wall Street Journal,* Dec. 22, 1982, p. 41; "Creditors of Costa Rica Agree to Reschedule About $100 Million of Country's Official Debt," *Wall Street Journal,* Jan. 13, 1983, p. 27; "IMF: $19.5 Million for Costa Rica," *Wall Street Journal,* Sept. 9, 1984, p. 30; "The Economic Hurricane Shaking Costa Rica," *Business Week,* Feb. 2, 1982, p. 54; "Careworn Costa Rica," *New Republic,* Dec. 6, 1982, pp. 17–18; and "Central America's Forgotten Democracy," *Commonweal,* May 20, 1983, pp. 301–3.

7. "Costa Rica, Latin Haven, Worries about the Price," *New York Times,* July 30, 1983, p. 18; "Poverty, Conflict Mark Most Central American Nations," *Los Angeles Times,* Jan. 12, 1984, p. 9; "Why Democratic Costa Rica Is Going Down the Tubes," *Christian Science Monitor,* June 21, 1984, p. 4; "Costa Rica's Democracy Stands up to Internal Strife," *Washington Post,* Aug. 26, 1984, p. A19; and "Class War in the Latin Switzerland," *Nation,* Jan. 28, 1984, pp. 94–95.

8. "Costa Rica's Dilemma," *New York Times,* Dec. 27, 1981, sec. 4, p. 15; "Increasing Terrorism in Costa Rica Is Now Causing Concern in U.S.," *New York Times,* Mar. 23, 1982, p. 12; "Costa Rica Bolsters Patrols on Border with Nicaragua," *New York Times,* Mar. 30, 1983, p. 17; "Refugees Strain Costa Rica's Economy," *Miami Herald,* Feb. 19, 1984, p. 14; and "Nicaraguan Businessmen Leave," *Christian Science Monitor,* Apr. 21, 1982, p. 2.

9. U.S. Congress, House Committee on Foreign Affairs and Senate Committee on Foreign Relations, "Country Reports for Human Rights Practices for 1983," 98th Cong., 2d sess., 518–23; U.S. Congress, House Committee on Foreign Affairs, "Report on a Congressional Study Mission to Honduras, Costa Rica, Nicaragua and El Salvador," 9–11; Department of State and Department of Defense, *Background Paper: Central America* (Washington: U.S. Government Printing Office, 1983); "Costa Rica to Tighten Immigration Policy," *New York Times,* June 6, 1982, p. 12; "40 Nicaraguan Exiles Are Being Deported by Costa Rica," *New York Times,* June 20, 1982, p. 11; "Costa Rica Seizes Nicaraguan Rightists," *New York Times,* Aug. 11, 1982, p. 5; "Costa Rica Being Visited by Violence," *New York Times,* Oct. 31, 1983, p. 5; "Threatened U.S. Executives Are Said to Leave Costa Rica," *New York Times,* June 21,

1984, p. 4; "Careworn Costa Rica," *New Republic*, Dec. 6, 1982, pp. 17–18; and "What Could Start the Guns Blazing in Costa Rica," *Business Week*, Apr. 18, 1983, p. 56.

10. "Costa Rica, Long Tranquil, Is Singed in Political Flames of Central America," *New York Times*, Mar. 31, 1981, p. 14; "Costa Rica in Shift Starts to Move against its Foreign Political Exiles," *New York Times*, Apr. 12, 1981, p. 21; "Class War in Latin Switzerland," *Nation*, Jan. 28, 1984, 94–95; "Costa Rica, Isle of Tranquility in an Angry Sea," *U.S. News and World Report*, Sept. 17, 1984, 40.

11. "Salvador and Its Neighbors Form New Alliance," *New York Times*, Feb. 4, 1982, p. 12; "Sandinista Pressing Costa Rica on Rebels," *New York Times*, Apr. 5, 1983, p. 5; "Nicaraguan Reports a Battle with Pastora's Rebel Units," *New York Times*, May 11, 1983, p. 17; "Latin Team Will Inspect Costa Rican Border," *New York Times*, May 14, 1983, p. 11; "Costa Rica Cools to Nicaraguan Rebels," *New York Times*, Sept. 20, 1983, p. 5; "Costa Ricans Being Visited by Violence," *New York Times*, Oct. 31, 1983, p. 9; "Costa Rica Declares Policy of Neutrality in Region," *New York Times*, Nov. 18, 1983, p. 5; "Costa Rica Asks Proof on Bribes," *New York Times*, Apr. 24, 1984, p. 21; "Costa Rica: Base Camp for 1,000 Sandinistas," *Christian Science Monitor*, June 3, 1982, p. 1; "Central American Tug of War: Costa Rica, Nicaragua Agree to Tighten Border Security," *Christian Science Monitor*, Apr. 8, 1983, p. 4; "Costa Rican Forces Keep Weary Eye Along Border," *Los Angeles Times*, May 11, 1983, p. 5; "Frontier Area No Longer Neglected," *Los Angeles Times*, May 23, 1983, p. 3; "Costa Rica Worries Washington with Move to Declare Neutrality," *Miami Herald*, Sept. 13, 1983, p. 6; "Will Costa Rica Go Militaristic?" *Miami Herald*, Sept. 19, 1983, p. 9; "Refugees Strain Costa Rica's Hospitality," *Miami Herald*, Feb. 19, 1984, p. 14.

12. U.S. Congress, House Subcommittee on Inter-American Affairs, "Central America at the Crossroads," 96th Cong., 1st sess., 1979, pp. 1–20; U.S. Congress, Senate Committee on Foreign Relations, "Perspectives on Latin America: Report of a Study Mission to Costa Rica, Panama, Peru and Venezuela," 96th Cong., 2d sess., 1978, pp. 1–13; Thomas L. Karnes, "The Central American Republics," in Harold Eugene Davis and Larmon C. Wilson, eds., *Latin American Foreign Policies: An Analysis* (Baltimore: Johns Hopkins University Press, 1975); and J. Lloyd Mecham, *The United States and Inter-American Security 1885–1960* (Austin: University of Texas Press, 1963), 192–95, 402–6.

13. "Costa Rica Rebuts Mrs. Kirkpatrick," *New York Times*, Aug. 19, 1981, p. 2; "Costa Rica's Dilemma," *New York Times*, Dec. 27, 1981, sec. 4, p. 5.

14. U.S. Congress, House Committee on Foreign Affairs, "Status of U.S. Bilateral Relations with Countries of Latin America," 97th Cong., 1st sess., 1981, pp. 21–230; for a discussion of Reagan's Central American policies, see Thomas M. Leonard, *Central America and United States Policies, 1820s–1980s* (Claremont, Calif.: Regina Books, 1984).

15. "Costa Rica Rebuts Mrs. Kirkpatrick," *New York Times,* Aug. 19, 1981, p. 2; "Salvador and Neighbors Form Alliance," *New York Times,* Feb. 4, 1982, p. 12; and "New Leader in Costa Rica," *New York Times,* Feb. 9, 1982, p. 7.

16. *Public Papers of the Presidents of the United States: Ronald Reagan, 1982* (Washington: U.S. Government Printing Office, 1983), 1:802–3; "Troubled Costa Rica Gets New President," *New York Times,* May 9, 1982, p. 3; "Reagan Promises Aid for Costa Rica," *New York Times,* June 23, 1982, p. 14; "Reagan Goodwill Trip Puts Latin America on His Map," *Christian Science Monitor,* Dec. 6, 1982, p. 3; and "Tough Year for Costa Rican 'Welfare State,'" *Christian Science Monitor,* Dec. 7, 1982, p. 4.

17. U.S. Congress, House Ways and Means Committee, "Designating Eleven Caribbean Basin Countries as Beneficiaries," 98th Cong., 2d sess., 1984; "Background on the Caribbean Basin Initiative," *U.S. Department of State Bulletin* 82 (Apr. 1982):7–32; "The Reagan Caribbean Basin Initiative," *Congressional Digest* 62 (Mar. 1983):69–96; "Strategic Goals Often Appear to Loom behind Assistance for Latin Region," *New York Times,* Jan. 12, 1984, p. 14; and "11 Picked for Caribbean Plan," *Washington Post,* Dec. 2, 1983, p. 1.

18. *Report of the National Bipartisan Commission on Central America* (Washington: U.S. Government Printing Office, 1984), 100; Department of State and Department of Defense, *Background Paper: Central America* (Washington: U.S. Government Printing Office, 1983); and Department of State and Department of Defense, *Background Paper: Nicaragua's Military Buildup and Support for Central American Subversion* (Washington: U.S. Government Printing Office, 1984).

19. Institute for Policy Studies, "Background Information on U.S. Military Personnel and U.S. Assistance to Central America," update no. 7, Nov. 1982, and update no. 8, Mar. 1983; "Costa Rica's Pro-U.S. Policies Begin Paying Off," *New York Times,* Nov. 21, 1982, p. 9; "Proper Washington Support for Costa Rican Democracy," *New York Times,* Feb. 21, 1983, p. 16; "U.S. Trains Costa Ricans," *New York Times,* May 31, 1983, p. 6; "U.S. Offers Road Plan to Costa Rica," *New York Times,* Sept. 25, 1983, p. 11; "Army-less Costa Rica Builds 10,000 Man Civil Force," *Christian Science Monitor,* Jan. 26, 1983, p. 4; "Costa Rica Struggles to

Remain Neutral," *Los Angeles Times,* May 27, 1984, p. 7; "U.S. Set to Send Engineers to Costa Rica, Official Says," *Miami Herald,* Nov. 14, 1983, p. 13; and "Costa Rican Leaders Irked by 'Lip Mistakes' of U.S. Ambassador," *Washington Post,* Feb. 2, 1984, p. 1.

20. "U.S. Is Speeding Up Its Aid to Costa Rica," *New York Times,* May 5, 1984, p. 6; "U.S. Said to Seek Costa Rica Shift," *New York Times,* May 11, 1984, p. 30; "Costa Rican Denies U.S. Pressed Him over Neutrality," *New York Times,* May 12, 1984, p. 12; "Costa Rica to Get about $7 Million in U.S. Military Aid," *Los Angeles Times,* Aug. 24, 1984, p. 11; "Border Clusters Prompt Request for More Arms," *Miami Herald,* June 17, 1984, p. 1; and "Secret Report Says Costa Rica Asks More Aid," *Washington Post,* May 10, 1984, p. 6.

21. "Salvador and Neighbors Form New Alliance," *New York Times,* Feb. 4, 1982, p. 5; "Troubled Costa Rica Gets New President," *New York Times,* May 9, 1982, p. 7; "Costa Rica Wants World to Recognize Its Neutral Stance," *Los Angeles Times,* Sept. 11, 1983, p. 3; "5 Nations Okay Peace Treaty Effort," *Los Angeles Times,* Nov. 11, 1983, p. 9; "Careworn in Costa Rica," *New Republic,* Dec. 6, 1982, pp. 17–18; and "Conflicting Signals on Regional Role," *Central American Report,* Nov. 25, 1983, pp. 361–63.

22. Inter-American Development Bank, *Economic and Social Progress in Latin America, 1982* (Washington: U.S. Government Printing Office, 1983), 227.

Part 4: Nuclear War and Deterrence

CHAPTER 10: PROSPECTS FOR BALLISTIC MISSILE DEFENSE TOWARD THE YEAR 2000, BY DONALD M. SNOW

1. Ronald Reagan, "Remarks on Strategic Defense," Mar. 23, 1983, reprinted in *Weekly Compilation of Presidential Documents* 19, no. 12 (Mar. 29, 1983):447–48.

2. I have discussed this problem extensively in *The Nuclear Future: Toward a Strategy of Uncertainty* (University: University of Alabama Press, 1983), chap. 3.

3. Michael Mandelbaum, "The Future of Nuclear Weapons," *Naval War College Review* 23, no. 5 (Sept./Oct. 1982):66.

4. Harold Brown, *Department of Defense Annual Report, Fiscal Year 1982* (Washington: U.S. Government Printing Office, Jan. 19, 1981), 116.

5. This evolution is described in some detail in Gary L. Guertner and

Donald M. Snow, *The Last Frontier: An Analysis of the Strategic Defense Initiative* (Lexington, Mass.: Lexington Books, 1986).

6. Reagan, "Remarks," 447.

7. Caspar W. Weinberger, *Annual Report to the Congress, Fiscal Year 1983* (Washington: U.S. Government Printing Office, Feb. 8, 1982), p. III–65.

8. Caspar W. Weinberger, *Annual Report to the Congress, Fiscal Year 1984* (Washington: U.S. Government Printing Office, Jan. 31, 1983), 227.

9. This entire issue area has been extensively covered by Clarence A. Robinson, Jr., since about 1977 in *Aviation Week and Space Technology*.

10. Reagan, "Remarks," 447.

11. Guertner and Snow, *Last Frontier*, 125–27.

12. Keith Payne and Colin S. Gray, "Nuclear Policy and the Defensive Transition," *Foreign Affairs* 62, no. 4 (Spring 1984):821.

13. Caspar W. Weinberger, *Annual Report to the Congress, Fiscal Year 1985* (Washington: U.S. Government Printing Office, Feb. 1, 1984), 58.

14. Ibid., 193.

15. Daniel O. Graham and Gregory A. Fossedal, *A Defense That Defends: Blocking Nuclear Attack* (Old Greenwich, Conn.: Devin-Adair, 1983), 44.

16. This approach is discussed in some detail in Snow, *Nuclear Future*, chap. 3.

17. This point is made strongly by the late Herman Kahn in his posthumously released sequel, *Thinking about the Unthinkable in the 1980s* (New York: Simon & Schuster, 1984), 37.

18. Payne and Gray, "Nuclear Policy," 824.

19. Graham and Fossedal, *A Defense That Defends*, 45.

20. Weinberger, *Annual Report, Fiscal Year 1985*, 58.

21. Graham and Fossedal, *A Defense That Defends*, 113.

22. Payne and Gray, "Nuclear Policy," 820.

23. Barry J. Smernoff, "The Strategic Value of Space-Based Laser Weapons," *Air University Review* 33, no. 5 (Mar./Apr. 1982):14.

24. Carl Sagan, "Nuclear War and the Climatic Catastrophe," *Foreign Affairs* 62, no. 2 (Winter 1983/1984):257–92.

25. Payne and Gray, "Nuclear Policy," 840.

26. The term "hostage effect" was coined by Thomas C. Schelling in *The Strategy of Conflict* (Cambridge, Mass.: Harvard University Press, 1960).

27. This issue is discussed in Donald M. Snow, "Ballistic Missile Defense and the Strategic Future," *Parameters, Journal of the U.S. Army War College* 13, no. 2 (June 1983):11–22. Colin S. Gray has also raised the problem in a number of his works.

28. Graham and Fossedal, *A Defense That Defends,* 120.

29. Ibid., 49.

30. Ibid., 55.

31. Steven E. Cady, "Beam Weapons in Space: A Reality We Must Confront," *Air University Review* 33, no. 4 (May/June 1982):37.

32. William E. Burrows, "Ballistic Missile Defense: The Illusion of Security," *Foreign Affairs* 62, no. 4 (Spring 1984):843.

33. Alvin W. Weinberg and Jack N. Barkenbus, "Stabilizing Star Wars," *Foreign Policy,* no. 54 (Spring 1984):164.

34. Alton Frye, "Strategic Build-Down: A Context for Restraint," *Foreign Affairs* 62, no. 4 (Winter 1983/1984):300.

35. Weinberg and Barkenbus, "Stabilizing Star Wars," 168.

36. See, for instance, *Star Wars: Delusions and Dangers* (Moscow: Military Publishing House, 1985), for a complete statement of Soviet-stated objections.

37. Payne and Gray, "Nuclear Policy," 826.

CHAPTER 11:
AMERICAN NUCLEAR WEAPONS PROGRAMS AND STRATEGIES
DURING THE 1980s: COMPARATIVE UNITED STATES AND SOVIET
PERSPECTIVES, BY DANIEL S. PAPP

1. Kenneth E. Boulding, "National Images and International Systems," in William D. Coplin and Charles W. Kegley, Jr., eds., *Analyzing International Relations* (New York: Praeger, 1975), 347–60; Robert Jervis, *The Logic of Images in International Relations* (Princeton: Princeton University Press, 1970); John Stoessinger, *Nations in Darkness: China, Russia, America* (New York: Random House, 1974).

2. Considerable work has been done that analyzes U.S. or Soviet perceptions of nuclear matters by themselves; little has been done on a comparative basis.

3. See Daniel S. Papp, *Contemporary International Relations: Frameworks for Understanding* (New York: Macmillan, 1984), 145–215.

4. V. V. Potashov, "Arms Race in the USA—A Threat to Peace," *SShA: Ekonomika, Politika, Ideologiya,* no. 6 (June 1981):27–40; G. A. Gornostaev, "The American Military Missile Industry," *SShA: Ekonomika, Politika, Ideologiya,* no. 4 (Apr. 1982):77–87.

5. Several of these rationales are mentioned in the Scowcroft Commission Report, *Report of the President's Commission on Strategic Forces* (Washington: U.S. Department of Defense, Apr. 1983), 12–20.

6. For one of many examples, see *Whence the Threat to Peace* (Moscow: Military Publishing House, 1982), 37–38.

7. Ibid.

8. The Soviets have deployed 1,398 ICBMs (*The Military Balance 1984–1985* [London: International Institute for Strategic Studies, 1984], 17).

9. This assumes that by 1981 all 308 SS-18s had been refitted as Mod 2s, with eight warheads apiece; by 1982, at least some SS-18s had been refitted as Mod 4s, with ten warheads apiece (ibid., 133).

10. This observation holds true both to U.S. and Soviet views of the U.S.S.R.'s nuclear weapons program and strategies.

11. For a brief discussion of perceived utilities of the B-1, see Caspar W. Weinberger, *Report to the Congress on the FY 1985 Budget, FY 1986 Authorization Request, and FY 1988–89 Defense Programs* (Washington: U.S. Government Printing Office, 1984), 189–90 (hereafter cited as *1985 DOD Annual Report on the Budget*).

12. B-52Gs began to enter the inventory in 1959, and B-52Hs in 1962 (*The Military Balance 1983–1984*, 120). The average age for B-52 pilots is thirty-one (*Atlanta Journal-Constitution*, Oct. 14, 1984).

13. *1985 DOD Annual Report on the Budget*, 189–90.

14. Ibid.

15. See especially *Krasnaya Zvezda*, Jan. 6, 1982.

16. *Whence the Threat to Peace*, 39.

17. Strategic cruise missiles are here defined as air-launched and sea-launched cruise missiles. Ground-launched cruise missiles are examined in the following section on NATO's intermediate-range nuclear forces.

18. For a discussion of NATO's INF, see Gregory F. Treverton, "Managing NATO's Nuclear Dilemma," *International Security*, Spring 1983.

19. Alexander R. Vershbow, "The Cruise Missile: The End of Arms Control?" *Foreign Affairs* 55, no. 1 (Oct. 1976):133–46.

20. *Krasnaya Zvezda*, Apr. 21, 1977, and *Sovetskaya Rossiya*, June 1, 1977.

21. See, for example, *Pravda*, July 31, 1984.

22. S. Ch. Aitmatov, "Dangers and Problems of the 'Trident' Program," *SShA: Ekonomika, Politika, Ideologiya*, no. 12 (Dec. 1981): 65–67; see also Vladimir Bogachev, "Trident: A Threat to Stability," TASS release, Jan. 18, 1982, as reported in *FBIS* (Soviet Union), Jan. 19, 1982, pp. AA1–AA2; and *Krasnaya Zvezda*, Sept. 3, 1981.

23. Strong Soviet support for a "Zone of Peace" in the Indian Ocean must be viewed with this in mind, even though the Kremlin more often than not points to the U.S. Rapid Deployment Force as the subject of its concern. See *Izvestiya*, Aug. 29, 1981, for example.

24. Treverton, "Managing NATO's Nuclear Dilemma." See also

Harold Brown, *Department of Defense Annual Report FY 1982* (Washington: U.S. Government Printing Office, 1981), 125–29.

25. *Whence the Threat to Peace*, 41–42.

26. See interview with Soviet Minister of Defense Dimitri Ustinov in *Pravda*, May 21, 1984.

27. *Izvestiya*, Dec. 4, 1983; and *Pravda*, Dec. 8, 1983, among others.

28. Yuri Andropov implied this in his Nov. 23, 1983, statement on INF in Europe. See also *Pravda*, Dec. 8, 1983.

29. Richard Pipes, "Why the Soviet Union Thinks It Could Fight and Win a Nuclear War," *Commentary*, July 1977, pp. 1–14.

30. For a discussion of the need for nuclear command and control modernization, see Organization of the Joint Chiefs of Staff, *United States Military Posture for FY 1985*, 29–30. See also *1985 DOD Annual Report on the Budget*, 195–98.

31. *Krasnaya Zvezda*, Oct. 11, 1981.

32. *Soviet Military Power*, 3d ed. (Washington: U.S. Department of Defense, 1984), 40–41.

33. *Krasnaya Zvezda*, Oct. 11, 1984.

34. U.S. ballistic missile defense expenditures for the 1980s are as follows, in millions of dollars: Actual, FY 1982: 462.1; Planned, FY 1983: 519.0; Proposed, FY 1984: 709.3; Proposed, FY 1985: 1,564.0 (U.S. Congress, Senate, *Department of Defense Authorization for Appropriations for FY 1984, Hearings before the Committee on Armed Services*, 98th Cong., 1st sess. [Washington: U.S. Government Printing Office, 1984], 337).

35. *Pravda*, May 3, 1984.

36. Ibid., Mar. 23, 1984.

37. For the Reagan administration's view of Soviet space capabilities, see *Soviet Military Power*, 2d ed. (Washington: U.S. Department of Defense, Mar. 1983), 65–70.

38. For Soviet sources that hint at the following line of reasoning, see *Krasnaya Zvezda*, Sept. 18 and Oct. 11, 1981.

39. See, for example, *Pravda*, Aug. 16, 17, and 18, 1984.

40. This is computed on the basis of one hundred deployed MXs and 240 deployed D-5s, each with ten MIRVs, and 1,398 deployed Soviet ICBMs (*The Military Balance 1983–1984*, 4, 14).

41. David Alan Rosenberg, "A Smoking Radiating Ruin at the End of Two Hours: Documents on American Plans for Nuclear War with the Soviet Union 1954–55," *International Security* 6, no. 3 (Winter 1981–82):3–38.

Contributors

ROBERT F. BURK is the author of numerous articles and books on twentieth-century American politics and race relations, including *The Eisenhower Administration and Black Civil Rights* and *Dwight D. Eisenhower: Hero and Politician.* He is assistant professor of history at Muskingum College in New Concord, Ohio.

CAPTAIN MARK CLODFELTER is pursuing a Ph.D. degree at the University of North Carolina at Chapel Hill prior to duty with the Air Force Academy's Department of History. His dissertation will analyze the efficacy of American strategic bombing in Korea and Vietnam. His article "Culmination: Dresden, 1945" appeared in the October 1979 issue of *Aerospace Historian.*

CHARLES DEBENEDETTI joined the history department of the University of Toledo in 1968, where he taught courses in the history of U.S. foreign relations and peace movements in American history. He has published *The Origins of the Modern American Peace Movement, 1915–1929* and *The Peace Reform in American History,* as well as several articles on the relationship between the peace activism of U.S. citizens and American foreign policy. Most recently, he edited a volume of contributed essays, *Peace Heroes in Twentieth-century America.*

ROBERT H. FERRELL has taught at Indiana University for many years and is the author of such books as *American Diplomacy: A History* and *Woodrow Wilson and World War I.* He is the editor of *Off the Record: The Private Papers of Harry S. Truman* and *The Eisenhower Diaries.*

GEORGE C. HERRING is professor of history at the University of Kentucky. A specialist in the history of United States foreign relations, he is the author of *Aid to Russia, 1941–1946: Strategy, Diplomacy, the Origins of the Cold War; America's Longest War: The United States and Vietnam, 1950–1975;* and, with Kenneth Coleman, *The Central American Crisis.*

HOWARD JONES is professor of American diplomatic history at the University of Alabama and has written *To the Webster-Ashburton Treaty: A*

Study in Anglo-American Relations, 1783–1843; The Course of American Diplomacy: From the Revolution to the Present; and *Mutiny on the Amistad: The Saga of a Slave Revolt and Its Impact on American Abolition, Law, and Diplomacy.* He is completing a study of the Truman Doctrine in Greece, after which he will begin work on a book concerning John F. Kennedy and Vietnam.

THOMAS M. LEONARD is professor of history at the University of North Florida and has been a visiting professor at the Institute for Advanced Studies in Guadalajara, Mexico, and a Fulbright Lecturer at the Instituto Juan XIII in Bahia Blanca, Argentina. He is the author of *United States and Central America, 1944–1949: Perceptions of Political Dynamics; Central America and United States Policies, 1820s–1980s;* and *U.S. Policy and Arms Limitation in Central America: The Washington Conference of 1923.* He is currently working on an analytical history of relations between the United States and Central America, which will be part of a multivolume series on the relations between the United States and Latin America edited by Lester D. Langley and published by the University of Georgia Press.

DANIEL S. PAPP is professor of international affairs and director of the School of Social Sciences at the Georgia Institute of Technology in Atlanta, Georgia. He has been research professor at the Strategic Studies Institute of the U.S. Army War College and senior research associate at the Center for Aerospace Doctrine, Research, and Education at the U.S. Air University. He is the author of *Vietnam: The View from Moscow, Peking, Washington; Contemporary International Relations; Soviet Perceptions of the Developing World during the 1980s: The Ideological Basis;* and *Soviet Policies toward the Developing World during the 1980s: The Dilemmas of Power and Presence.* He has also co-edited *Communist Nations' Military Assistance; The Political Economy of International Technology Transfer;* and *International Space Policy.*

JAMES C. SCHNEIDER is associate professor of history at the University of Texas in San Antonio. A specialist in modern American history and American foreign relations, his published works include essays on American internationalists and aspects of the New Deal. He has completed a book-length manuscript on the foreign-policy debate prior to Pearl Harbor and is now at work on two projects: a study of the Model Cities program and of Lyndon B. Johnson's relations with Congress.

DONALD M. SNOW is professor of political science and director of international studies at the University of Alabama. During 1985–86 he was Secretary of the Navy Senior Research Fellow at the Naval War College, and he has been professor of National Security Affairs at the Air Command and Staff College. His books include *The Last Frontier: An Analysis of the Strategic Defense Initiative* and *National Security: Enduring Problems of U.S. Defense Policy.* Forthcoming books include an edited collection of essays, *Fencers: Soviet-American Relations Face the 1990s,* and *The Necessary Peace: Nuclear Weapons and Superpower Relations,* both to be published by Lexington Books, Lexington, Mass., and, with Dennis M. Drew, *The Eagle's Talons,* to be published by the Air University Press, Montgomery, Ala.

COLONEL HARRY G. SUMMERS, JR., now senior military correspondent for *U.S. News and World Report,* formerly held the General Douglas MacArthur Chair of Military Research at the Army War College. He is the author of *On Strategy* and the *Vietnam War Almanac.* His articles and reviews have appeared in *Air University Review, Military Review,* and *Naval War College Review,* as well as in *American Heritage, Harpers, New Republic,* the *Los Angeles Times,* the *New York Times,* the *Wall Street Journal,* and the *Washington Post.*

RALPH LEE WOODWARD, JR., is chairman of the history department at Tulane University, where he has been professor of Latin American history since 1970. He is the author of *Central America, a Nation Divided,* nine other books on Latin American affairs, and more than sixty articles. He is an associate editor of *The Research Guide to Central America and the Caribbean* and serves on the editorial boards of the *Latin American Research Review; Revista del Pensamiento Centroamericano;* and *Mesoamérica.*

Index